The Quality of Live Subtitling

ŁÓDŹ STUDIES IN LANGUAGE

Edited by Barbara Lewandowska-Tomaszczyk and Łukasz Bogucki

Volume 75

Łukasz Dutka

The Quality of Live Subtitling

Technology, User Expectations and Quality Metrics

PETER LANG

Berlin - Lausanne - Bruxelles - Chennai - New York - Oxford

Bibliographic Information published by the Deutsche Nationalbibliothek
The Deutsche Nationalbibliothek lists this publication in the Deutsche
Nationalbibliografie; detailed bibliographic data is
available online at http://dnb.d-nb.de.

Library of Congress Cataloging-in-Publication Data
A CIP catalog record for this book has been applied for
at the Library of Congress.

This book has been supported by a grant from the
Faculty of Applied Linguists at the University of Warsaw, Poland.

The cover image courtesy of Benjamin Ben Chaim.

ISSN 1437-5281
ISBN 978-3-631-91728-2 (Print)
E-ISBN 978-3-631-92094-7 (E-PDF)
E-ISBN 978-3-631-92095-4 (E-PUB)
DOI 10.3726/b21949

© 2024 Peter Lang Group AG, Lausanne
Published by Peter Lang GmbH, Berlin, Deutschland

info@peterlang.com - www.peterlang.com

Table of Contents

8

Acknowledgements

I owe an immeasurable intellectual and personal debt to Professor Agnieszka Szarkowska, who initiated my interest in audiovisual translation back in 2010 as I was setting sail on my academic voyage in her BA seminar. It is only thanks to her unwavering support and eternal patience that this research is finally seeing light. It is a light at the end of what was a very long tunnel but hopefully is just a beginning of our journey.

I would also like to thank Prof. Małgorzata Tryuk for her support as my first doctoral supervisor and all the intellectual guidance and inspiration I benefitted from as a participant of her PhD seminar.

My journey into media accessibility in general and live subtitling in particular would have been impossible without many years of great collaboration with Monika Szczygielska, who gave me an opportunity to get trained as one of the first Polish respeakers in 2013 and offered me support and inspiration ever since in many accessibility projects we embarked upon together.

My deep appreciation goes to my intellectual Muses: Prof. Pablo Romero Fresco, whose many works have served as milestones on my path and have heavily influenced my thinking (but also led me to spend many rather tedious hours on performing the NER assessment); Dr Gian Maria Greco, for our discussions on quality and accessibility that allowed me to gain new perspectives on many of the issues I discuss in this book; and Dr Breno Silva for his many attempts at making me appreciate the beauty of inferential statistics and for his invaluable help in analysing the results of this research.

I would also like to thank Joanna Pietrulewicz and Maria Łogińska, who helped initiate me in television subtitling back in 2011; Katarzyna Lalik, with whom I had the pleasure to take my first steps as a respeaker; my wonderful team of colleagues from Dostępni.eu, whom I had the great privilege to train and collaborate with and who helped me fulfil my personal dream of working again as a live news subtitler; live subtitlers and my dear colleagues who assisted me in recording, evaluating and re-thinking the quality of TV shows: Karolina Szeląg, Aleksandra Dobrowolska, Aleksandra Urban, Tomas Senda and Agnieszka Grabska; my colleagues from the Global Alliance of Speech-to-Text Captioning: Chris Ales, Jen Shuck and Kimberly Shea; as well as Zoe Moores and Natalie Fresno, for sharing their experience and expertise; my academic role models Dr Wojciech Figiel, Dr David Orrego Carmona and Dr Agnieszka Walczak, who guided me inside and outside of the academia; and Dorota Mierzejewska, for always sharpening my institutional intelligence and helping me navigate the meanders of administrative procedures.

My special thanks go again to Karolina Szeląg and Aleksandra Urban as well as to Eduardo Medina and Jazmín Granell. Without their help and assistance in juggling other projects, finishing this book would have been impossible.

Last but not least, I wish to thank my family, my partner Tomek, my mom Mirka and especially my dad Heniek, who did not live to see this finalized and whom I greatly miss. Thanks to them and to all my friends for putting up with me while I was working on this book.

Needless to say, I am solely responsible for any errors or inaccuracies.

Introduction

Let me remind you of a quote from "Alice in Wonderland":
Anything is possible. You just have to know the ways.

(Live subtitling at the inauguration of the academic year
at the Adam Mickiewicz University in Poznań, Poland.
October 2021. Speech by the Rector, Prof. Bogumiła
Kaniewska.)

We live in the age of information and access to the media is an important prerequisite for full participation in social life (Greco, 2018; Jankowska, 2020; Neves, 2005). For many years there have been numerous efforts to make the mass media more accessible to disadvantaged groups either by the use of audio description, which helps blind people enjoy audiovisual materials, or by the use of subtitles, which allow the Deaf and the hard of hearing to have improved access to audiovisual programs. Subtitling for the Deaf and the hard of hearing (SDH) now plays an important role in the education and entertainment of people with hearing loss (Greco & Jankowska, 2020; Neves, 2005; Zarate, 2021).

In many countries, the quantity of SDH available on TV has increased dramatically over the years, both for pre-recorded and live TV content; however, the quality of subtitling is not always satisfactory (Romero Fresco, 2021). For example, in Poland, the EU and the national legislation and regulations have led to a relatively large rise in the quantity of pre-recorded audiovisual content that is subtitled on Polish television. And while the Deaf and the hard of hearing viewers now enjoy a far greater access to the media, the users have long been advocating for more access to live TV content, especially news and current affairs programmes (Sacha & Kasperkowiak, 2012; Szarkowska, 2010; Szczygielska, 2019).

The provision of subtitling for live TV content has been hindered by a long-held belief among practitioners and broadcasters that live subtitling in Polish is impossible due to technical and organizational challenges involved (Künstler, 2008; Szczygielska, 2019), the belief that was even echoed by the Polish media regulator, the National Broadcasting Council (KRRiT, 2016). In this context, let us remember a scene from a Disney adaptation of "Alice in Wonderland" from 1951. In the film, Alice encounters a small door and shouts in exasperation, "I simply must get through!", to which Doorknob responds, "Sorry, you're much too big. Simply impassable". "You mean *impossible*," Alice asks. "No, impassable. Nothing's impossible."

When I first embarked on this research journey, my main goal was to show that live subtitling in Polish is not impossible; indeed, this door is very much "passable" with the right technology, methods and workflows. In the spirit of action research (Cravo & Neves, 2007), my objective was to prove that live subtitling in Polish can and should be applied in broadcasting settings to increase the accessibility of TV for the hearing impaired audiences. My plan was to review the different methods used to create live subtitling in an effort of identifying the ones that could be used in Polish and then testing them to find the best ones, i.e. the ones that can produce the best quality and the most value for the end user. However, in the early stages of working on this book, a twist of fate took me from attempting live subtitling in the lab and training respeakers in the classroom to doing the same in broadcasting studios as I participated in implementing live subtitling for one of the Polish broadcasters.

As of 2020, when I began this research, all the three main broadcasters in Poland (TVP, Polsat and TVN) had already introduced live subtitling for some of its programming. And due to legal requirements, they will need to keep subtitling more and more shows in the coming years. While there is still a way to go in terms of quantity, I believe it is finally time to look into the quality of live subtitling.

Now that we have passed through the first door, a new "impassable" challenge arises: that of guaranteeing reasonable, fit-for-purpose quality which would mean that subtitles not only serve to fulfil legal obligations but also fulfil the needs of the viewers and allow hearing impaired audiences to have effective access to live TV content. This led to a turn in my research as I switched the main focus to examining the quality of live subtitles.

In view of the above, the present work aims to address the challenge of ensuring quality in live subtitling by examining the available technology, methods and workflows, as well as studying user needs, reviewing and perfecting quality assessment metrics and monitoring the current quality of live subtitles. While the book primarily draws examples from Polish news television channels, the quality issues and metrics it discusses are relevant for viewers, broadcasters and researchers worldwide. The focus on live subtitling quality is essential for enhancing standards in areas and among broadcasters where quality currently falls short. Equally, it ensures that those who have achieved acceptable levels of quality, particularly as they shift towards more automated subtitling methods involving AI, continue to meet these standards. Therefore, establishing clear quality standards, rigorously testing metrics, and consistently monitoring quality are essential steps for advancing live subtitling practices.

To provide the necessary context for understanding the complexities of live subtitling quality, the first chapter begins with a definition of live subtitling as differentiated from semi-live subtitling and pre-recorded subtitling. Following this, it situates the concept of live subtitling within the theoretical framework of Translation Studies – particularly in the realm of audiovisual translation – and Accessibility Studies.

In the second chapter, I discuss the history of live subtitling. I look at the roots of subtitling and the innovations that brought about live subtitling and then led to the invention of respeaking as one of the main methods of creating live subtitles. As this book concerns live subtitling in Polish, I pay particular attention to the beginnings of SDH in Poland, and the development of live subtitling in Polish in various settings: at live events, in online streaming and on TV. As progress in accessibility in general and live subtitling in particular is inextricably linked with legislation and regulatory efforts, I present the legal context of accessibility in Poland within a wider context of accessibility regulations in the EU and the US. Finally, I discuss the current state of live subtitling in Poland and the challenges for the future.

The focus then switches to technology that allows for the creation of live subtitling. The third chapter introduces all the major methods of producing live subtitles, which are then critically examined to identify their potential as well as limitations. Special emphasis is placed on finding out which of these methods can be applied to create live subtitles in a wider array of languages, including Polish. Once speech recognition (SR) in general and respeaking in particular are established as most promising in terms of producing live subtitling, the technology behind SR is discussed in detail to explain what it can and cannot do and why. Again, special emphasis is given to the performance of SR in Polish, the comparisons of systems available for this language and the potential of future development. Finally, this chapter discussed the new generation of SR systems that was made possible by leveraging large language models.

The fourth chapter switches the focus from technology to people and discusses the users of subtitling, their needs and expectations, as well as their role as one of various stakeholders in live subtitling. As all users agree in expecting quality subtitling, in the fifth chapter I discuss what quality means, and how it can be conceptualized as well as measured. After identifying and analysing various dimensions of live subtitling quality, both linguistic and technical ones, the focus moves to describing existing metrics of live subtitling quality such as accuracy, latency, subtitle speed and reduction rate. Then a new metric is proposed to measure text segmentation quality. This is followed by a discussion of the differences between subjective perceptions and objective measurements. The chapter closes by summarising the current knowledge on the impact of different live subtitling workflows on the quality of live subtitles.

The sixth chapter presents the details of the study on the quality dimensions of live and semi-live subtitling on three Polish news channels: TVP Info, Polsat News and TVN24. After discussing the method, the materials and the procedure, I present and critically examine the results on various quality dimensions; most notably: accuracy, latency, subtitle speed, reduction rate and segmentation score. In the case of each of these metrics, the chapter then discusses the statistical methods which were used to examine the data and confirm the statistical significance of the results. The chapter closes by discussing major differences between live subtitles provided by the three Polish news broadcasters, as well as the interaction between various quality dimensions.

The conclusions drawn from the analysed data hold significant implications for the study of live subtitling and respeaking. They also offer practical and conceptual insights for broadcasters, live subtitlers and media regulators. The book concludes with recommendations for broadcasters and media regulators, aimed at enhancing the quality and effectiveness of live subtitling practices.

Chapter 1: Live subtitling at the crossroads of Audiovisual Translation and Accessibility Studies

The below chapter attempts to situate live subtitling within its traditional home discipline of Audiovisual Translation (AVT) and a recently emerging field of Accessibility Studies. First, I define what live subtitling is. This is followed by a discussion of how AVT emerged within the field of Translation Studies and how the concept of accessibility reshaped AVT. Finally, I attempt to outline the new field of Accessibility Studies and how it overlaps with AVT.

1.1. Live subtitling as a mode of Audiovisual Translation

Live subtitling is traditionally defined as a type of audiovisual translation (AVT), a field within Translation Studies (Díaz Cintas & Remael, 2007). AVT is "concerned with the transfer of multimodal and multimedia speech (dialogue, monologue, comments, etc.) into another language/culture" (Gambier, 2012, p. 45) and live subtitling is one of a number of AVT *modes* or *modalities*, such as subtitling, dubbing, voice-over (Remael, 2010). At the same time, live subtitling is an example of an *access service* that enables persons with disabilities to consume audiovisual content (Díaz Cintas, 2005, pp. 3–5).

Subtitling in general is a "translation practice that consists of presenting a written text, generally on the lower part of the screen, that endeavours to recount the original dialogue of the speakers" but also the information in the soundtrack (for instance, songs) or text that appears in the image (e.g. inscriptions) (Díaz Cintas & Remael, 2007, p. 8). Live subtitling in turn is also a text representation of utterances and might also include descriptions of other pertinent sounds. The difference lies in how it is made. In contrast to pre-recorded subtitling, which is fully prepared in advance, live subtitles are created in real time and usually appear with some delay related to the time it takes to prepare them.

Most subtitling is pre-recorded (also known as offline or postproduction subtitling), meaning that the subtitles are prepared beforehand with precise time codes, that is, in-cues (or in-times), which signal when the title should paper on the screen, and out-cues (or out-times), which determine when the subtitle should disappear (Díaz Cintas & Remael, 2007). The cueing will follow various technical rules. For instance, the subtitler will try to avoid crossing shot changes.

Subtitling is a painstaking and time-consuming process, and preparing SDH can take between 7 and 10 minutes of work per each minute of content.

Live subtitling can be done fully live or can be pre-prepared to the same extent; in which case it is referred to as semi-live (Romero Fresco, 2011). Semi-live subtitling is used for live programmes which include pre-edited segments (i.e. parts of the show were recorded before) or are heavily scripted. For instance, in a news bulletin, even though it is broadcast live, all the news segments can be pre-recorded and while the news presenter is speaking live, he or she might actually be reading from the teleprompter the text that was drafted beforehand.

This means that the subtitler can work with the text before the broadcast, editing it and diving it into chunks which will be displayed as subtitles. In this way, the subtitles can be prepared in advance and only released in real time Such a list of subtitles does not include timecodes. Instead, during the broadcast, the subtitler will cue the subtitles manually. This means that subtitlers will be watching the live show and whenever they start hearing a particular line of text, they will press a key to release the subtitle. It usually takes a fraction of a second for the operator to notice the utterance and press the key, which will create a slight delay (known as subtitle latency). Otherwise, semi-live subtitles will have no delay.

Most live TV shows actually feature a mix of live spontaneous segments with pre-recorded or scripted segments (Lambourne, 2006; Romero Fresco, 2011), and thus live and semi-live subtitling can sometimes be combined for various parts of the same show. Indeed, from the perspective of the users, semi-live subtitles are essentially the same as live subtitles; the viewers might not be aware of the technical differences in how the subtitles were created.

Live subtitling is mostly done intralingually, that is the source audio and the final product (the subtitles) are in the same language. However, live subtitling can also be interlingual (Pöchhacker & Remael, 2018; Romero Fresco & Pöchhacker, 2018; Saerens et al., 2020). In the UK, live programmes in Welsh are sometimes subtitled in English. In Denmark, Belgium and the Netherlands live political speeches, debates or award ceremonies are often subtitled from English into Danish and Dutch respectively (Romero Fresco, 2011).

While live subtitling is the dominant term in Europe, it is also known as "real-time captioning" or "live captioning" in the United States (Downey, 2008; Robson, 2004; Romero Fresco & Pöchhacker, 2018) and some scholars prefer to talk of "live-titling" as "subtitle" and "surtitle" suggest a particular positioning on the screen (Pöchhacker & Remael, 2018). Live subtitles are used on TV and during live events in social, cultural or political settings such as talks, parliamentary debates, conferences or Q&A sessions, whenever the subtitles cannot be fully pre-prepared in advance (Romero-Fresco, 2011).

Over time, scholars viewed live subtitling from a number of lenses. Gambier (2003) called it a "challenging" type of AVT in contrast to the "dominant" (well-established) types such as dubbing or voice-over. Pérez González classified it among "new forms of intersemiotic assistive mediation" (Pérez González, 2014, p. 24), an *assistive modality* (Pérez-González et al., 2019). The evolution of how live subtitling was perceived within AVT followed the evolution of AVT itself and its relationship with Translation Studies, which we will explore in the following section.

1.2. Audiovisual Translation and Translation Studies

The first interest in live subtitling starts in Audiovisual Translation, an academic area of research within the field of Translation Studies. AVT is "interdisciplinary by nature" (Remael, 2010, p. 16) and the field of Translation Studies was itself an interdiscipline (Snell-Hornby et al., 1994) or a "poly-discipline" (Gambier, 2018, p. 61), born at the crossroads of linguistics and other disciplines.

For quite some time translation was "the Cinderella of linguistic and literary studies" (Delabastita, 1989, p. 193). It was only in the late 1950s that Translation Studies became independent from linguistics and comparative literature. Half a century later, a number of researches set out to show what makes AVT distinct from other forms of translation and why it "deserved to have a separate room, as it were, in the Translation Studies building" (Romero Fresco, 2018a, p. 188) as AVT texts had long been perceived as different from other forms of translation due to their particular features and the complexity of its multimodal source text (Robert & Remael, 2016).

Audiovisual Translation was known previously by numerous names such as film translation, language transfer, versioning, screen translation, translation for the media or multimedia translation. While audiovisual translation is now the most commonly used term (Gambier, 2012, p. 46), the terminological diversity can still be seen in the name of an organization of AVT researchers, European Association for Studies in Screen Translation (ESIST), founded in 1995[1] or the special issue of the journal the Translator titled Screen Translation (Yves Gambier, 2003).

Routledge Encyclopedia of Translation Studies, first published in 1998, included separate entries on dubbing and subtitling. Starting from its 2nd edition

---

1 ESIST Constitution, available at: https://www.esist.org/wp-content/uploads/2016/06/ESISTConstitution_Amended-2011..pdf (accessed on February 29, 2024)

in 2009, the encyclopaedia includes an entry to "audiovisual translation" defining this area of research "as a branch of translation studies concerned with the transfer of multimodal and multimedial texts into another language and/or culture" (Pérez-González, 2009, p. 13). Among the modalities of audiovisual translation, it also lists subtitling for the Deaf and the hard of hearing (as a type of intralingual subtitling) and audio description (as a type of intralingual narration) although neither necessarily has to involve translation into another language. Even more traditional modalities such as dubbing or voice-over, which do involve language transfer, are differentiated from more established types of translation due to their constraints.

Initial research publications on AVT date from the mid-fifties and sixties (Chaume, 2018, p. 41), but a true research and publication boom did not occur until the early 1990s (Remael, 2010). In 1971, Katharina Reiss paved the way for AVT research when trying to establish standard terminology for Translation Studies. She classified texts into four types. The first three types were informative, expressive and operative texts. Attempting to find a way for fringe types of translation that did not fit elsewhere, Reiss proposed a fourth term, *audio-medial texts*. She defined them as "written texts that are »accompanied« by »texts« in the »language« of music or of pictures" (1989, p. 111).

However, "translation studies of all disciplines have been rather reluctant to include film translation among their subjects of study" (Delabastita, 1989, p. 214) as some scholars did not see it as translation proper and preferred to call it an adaptation because of all the spatial and temporal constraints (Díaz Cintas & Remael, 2007, p. 9). Catford (1978, p. 53) went as far as to say that "translation between media is impossible (i.e. one cannot 'translate' from the spoken to the written form of a text or vice-versa)".

It is on this backdrop that Gambier put forward the term *transadaptation*, with the hope of going "beyond the usual dichotomy" (Yves Gambier, 2003, p. 178). Other scholars referred to Jakobson's (1959) classification of translation into three types: interlingual, intralingual and intersemiotic, arguing that even if access services do not involve interlingual translation (i.e. between two languages), they still involve either intralingual translation (between the sub-codes of one language) or intersemiotic translation (between different semiotic codes). For instance, live subtitling when done in the same language as the language of the soundtrack involves intralingual translation, understood as "an interpretation of verbal signs by means of other signs of the same language" (Jakobson, 1959, p. 233). And when descriptions of pertinent sounds are added, this constitutes intersemiotic translation from non-verbal signs (sounds) to verbal ones (words).

This battle over the status of AVT lasted a few decades but has now been won as "translation is perceived by most scholars as a more flexible and inclusive term, capable of accommodating new realities" (Díaz Cintas & Remael, 2007, p. 11). As a result of this prolonged debate, however, AVT is a relative newcomer within the field of Translation Studies (Remael, 2010), gaining formal academic recognition with the inclusion of this field of professional practice and scholarly inquiry in translator training curricula in the mid-1990s (Pérez-González, 2014). It has then quickly moved "from the field's periphery to its centre" (Remael, 2010, p. 12).

Chaume (2018) sums up the evolution of AVT research in the form of four turns (the descriptive, the cultural, the sociological and the cognitive) with the focus of AVT research shifting from the source text to the target text (the descriptive turn), then away from the actual text to other phenomena such as the cultural concepts (the cultural turn), then to the translators themselves as well as other agents involved in translation (the sociological turn), with the current focus on reception studies and empirical research (the cognitive turn).

Research first focused on the source text and differences between AVT and other types of translation, as scholars tried to identify distinctive features of audiovisual texts. Delabastita defined a film as "an organized whole or 'text', the various component signs of which enter into complex sets of relations" (1989, p. 201) and noted that it is a multi-channel and multi-code type of communication. Unlike in literary translation, where a typical unillustrated novel includes just one semiotic channel (the visual channel) and one type of signs (written verbal signs), "in AVT sense is produced neither in a linear sequence nor with a single system of signs" (Gambier, 2012, p. 55). Instead, an audiovisual product consists of a number of "signifying codes that operate simultaneously in the production of meaning" (Gambier, 2012, p. 47) and the meaning of the film as a whole is more than a simple sum of all the elements.

Gottlieb (1994) pointed out that in the case of a subtitled film, communication takes place through three synchronous semiotic channels: image, dialogue and subtitling itself, whereas Delabastita (1989, p. 196) distinguished two channels: the visual and the acoustic. He also listed four categories of signs:

- verbal signs presented visually;
- verbal signs presented acoustically;
- non-verbal signs presented visually;
- non-verbal signs presented acoustically.

The verbal signs transmitted through the visual channel include road signs, advertisements, letters, newspapers or any other text which is part of the world portrayed in a scene as well as on-screen text which is added to the image such as credits or indeed subtitles (Delabastita, 1989, p. 198). The verbal signs presented through the acoustic channel include dialogue and song lyrics. The acoustic channel also includes non-verbal signs such as music and sound effects. Finally, a film is first and foremost a visual medium and plenty of information is communicated through the visual channel in the form of non-verbal signs.

Both verbal and non-verbal signs come from a diverse range of codes (or systems of signs) that are involved in audiovisual communication. Aside from the most obvious verbal code (with its many linguistic and paralinguistic subcodes such as geographical and historical variation, style, register, dialects), Delabastita (1989) mentions a number of other codes such as the literary code (conventions of plots constructions and narrative strategies), proxemic code (distance between the characters) or the cinematic code (conventions of the cinema), to give just a few examples.

Gambier (2012, p. 48) introduces a number of relationships between signs. For instance, one sign can add something to the previous sign (complementarity), two signs can express the very same information (redundancy) or can oppose each other (contradiction). Tomaszkiewicz (2006, pp. 58–63) adds more types of relationships: equivalence (e.g. an image of something and a verbal description of it), parallelism (e.g. a photo of a politician whose words are quoted) and interpretation (i.e. visual sign helps to understand the verbal sign or vice versa; for instance, an image of a person and a subtitle with the name and the function).

The relationship of redundancy is of particular importance as if often allows AVT translators to save space by omitting or condensing verbal information that is redundant (i.e. it is also expressed in another way, for instance, through other non-verbal signs). Gottlieb (1998, p. 247) distinguishes two types of redundancy:

- intersemiotic redundancy (the occurrence of the same information in two channels; for instance, a newspaper title is shown on-screen and also read out, i.e. both the visual and the acoustic channel contain the same information);
- intrasemiotic redundancy (information is repeated within one channel; examples include elements of dialogues as repetitions, self-corrections, paraphrases or phatic language aimed at maintaining the conversation).

Tomaszkiewicz (2006) introduces a yet another type of redundancy. She points out that redundancy does not lie only in the film itself, but can arise from the viewer's interaction with the film. In other words, some verbal signs can be redundant not because the information they express is repeated by other signs but because the viewer already knows this information from another source (such as general knowledge). Predictable conversation structures (the so-called adjacency pairs) are one example of verbal redundancy related to viewer's cognitive knowledge. For instance, when one person says "Hello", the other is likely to respond with a greeting as well. The meaning of such exchanges can easily be predicted and might require no translation. (It might also be reinforced by visual cues such characters shaking each other's hands.)

The above categorization of channels and codes leads to an important realization on the nature of audiovisual translation modes. For instance, dubbing is a *covert* type of translation (as it substitutes the verbal sings in the acoustical channels with new signs, leaving no trace of the source text) and subtitling is an *overt* type of translation as it accompanies the original version, making it easy for viewers to compare and criticize (Gottlieb, 1994), indeed, for this reason, subtitling is known as *vulnerable* translation.

Gottlieb (1994) pointed out that both written translation and interpreting (as well as dubbing) are *horizontal* in a sense that they carry messages from one language to another without the change in the semiotic channel (translation turns writing into writing and interpreting turns speech into speech). However, intralingual subtitling is *vertical* as it turns speech into writing and interlingual subtitling is *diagonal* as it turns speech in one language into writing in another language. Live subtitling, if done intralingually, is an example of Gottlieb's vertical translation.

As subtitles provide the viewers "with a bird's eye view" of the dialogues (Gottlieb, 1994, p. 101), what happens is that verbal signs from the acoustic channels (spoken words) are turned into verbal signs in the visual channel (written words in the form of subtitles). This is a challenge due to the asymmetry of spoken and written language with features such as intonation, dialects or defective speech that are difficult (or impossible) to reflect in the written form (Delabastita, 1989, p. 204).

This shift from spoken to written communication brings with itself an important constraint of reading speed. Although written communication (reading a printed text) in general tends to be faster than spoken communication (listening to a spoken text), the pace of the film dialogues is often too fast for subtitles to keep up and present a verbatim rendition of the dialogues. First of all, that is because subtitling is a dynamic text type that presents itself in real time (Gottlieb, 1994). In contrast to the literary translation, the reception time is not up to the reader. It is pre-defined by the subtitler and depends on the temporal constraints of the medium. Secondly, subtitling is not a text that is consumed in isolation. Rather, it is an addition to a complex "text" of the film. As such, it is constrained by conventions related to how much space (number of lines and characters) and time (presentation time) subtitling can take. All these conventions are based on the assumption that watching a film is not meant to be an exercise in reading and viewers need to have time to look at the image as well. Gottlieb (1994, p. 114) was the first to recommend "that the time left for non-verbal viewing should match the time spent reading".

All the above means that the text in the subtitles has to be compressed (Delabastita, 1989, p. 203). Fortunately, thanks to a polysemiotic nature of audiovisual media, the original image and soundtrack act as aids and the reduction of dialogue can be obtained without major information loss, i.e. the same information can be communicated with fewer words (Gottlieb, 1994). This is more or less the case, depending on the text type as some films mainly serve to communicate information and others serve to entertain (Delabastita, 1989, p. 209). In this context, Gottlieb (1994) argues that subtitling is better suited for expressive genres (TV fiction) rather than informative genres (documentaries, news).

Due to the constraints described above, Titford (1982) referred to subtitling as *constrained translation*. And indeed, all audiovisual translation is "governed by a number of constraints related to the conditions of its material transmission" (Delabastita, 1989, p. 198). While all types of translation constrain the translator, the constraints involved in the audiovisual context are different and greater (Gottlieb, 1994).

Once scholars had identified the basic concepts of AVT research such as the characteristics of the multimodal audiovisual texts and the constraints inherent in AVT modes, new system theories brought about the descriptive turn. Díaz Cintas (2004) analysed two system theories that originated in the Translation Studies: the polysystem theory and the descriptive translation studies (DTS) framework and noted that while these methodologies were designed in the world of literary translation, they can act as useful tools in AVT.

The polysystem theory was developed by Even-Zohar (2012). He proposed *polysystem* as a new term to refer to a system that includes other systems within itself. Various systems within a polysystem are far from separate; they can intersect and overlap. Even-Zohar put forward the idea that translated literature operates as a part of the system of the target language literature (i.e. translated works of literature both influence and are influenced by the target literary system). The hierarchy of the systems is dynamic and translated literature can occupy a primary or secondary position depending on the status of the literary system as central or peripheral, strong or weak. Importantly, the position of the translated literature in the polysystem impacts the translation strategy (e.g. whether translators follow or break source conventions).

Polysystem theory fed into developments in descriptive translation studies, a field that was first proposed by Holmes in his attempt at mapping the area for

Translation Studies (Munday, 2016). Holmes saw DTS as the empirical branch of the discipline (the other branch being translation theory). Toury developed the field, formulating the objectives and putting forward a systematic methodology for DTS.

For Toury, translations are "facts of target cultures" (Toury, 1978/2012, p. 23) and the first step for the DTS research is to situate the text within the target culture system (what is the status of the text, i.e. how significant it is in the target culture), then perform a textual analysis of the corresponding segments in the source text and the target text to identify translation shifts. The final goal is to attempt generalizations about the translation process (i.e. identify the patterns that occur regularly). These are conceptualized as *norms* and *laws of translation.*

The idea of norms is one of the central concepts within DTS. Toury defined norms as "the translation of general values or ideas shared by a community – as to what is right or wrong, adequate or inadequate – into performance instructions appropriate for and applicable to particular situations" (Toury, 1978/2012, p. 63). Norms influence the strategy that translators choose and the particular translation solutions they adopt (see Figs. 1 and 2). Researchers can study those solutions to identify the strategies and the norms that drive decision-making in translation.

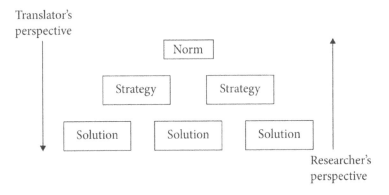

Fig. 1: *Translation norms, strategies and solutions (Pedersen, 2011, p. 38)*

It should be emphasized that within DTS norms are understood in a non-prescriptive way. Rather than recommending how translations should be done, Toury's norms describe how they are done and try to provide an explanation why they are done this way. Based on a number of norms, one can then formulate laws of translation (understood as probabilistic explanations that are true for most translations but allow some exceptions).

Fig. 2: *Norms as constraints on translation that are weaker than rules (e.g. legislation) but stronger than conventions (which are more informal than norms) (Munday, 2016, p. 177)*

In relation to the concept of norms, Toury introduced a distinction between adequacy and acceptability in translation. If the translators subject themselves to the norms of the source culture/language, they will produce an adequate translation. If the norms of the target culture/language prevail, the result will be an acceptable translation. This mirrors to some degree the distinctions put forward by Scheiermacher (foreignizing vs. domesticating approach), Nida (formal vs. dynamic equivalence), House (overt vs. covert translation) or Venuti (resistant vs. fluent translation) (Pym, 2017, p. 96).

Toury (1978/2012) went on to apply his methodology in a number of case studies, and he identified two laws of translation: the law of growing standardization (i.e. translations tend to include linguistic options that are more common in the target language and have less variation in style) and the law of interference (some linguistic features of the source text are copied into the target text).

Following the work of Toury, Chesterman (2016) proposed a set of norms that he divided into product norms and professional norms. Product norms are also called expectancy norms, as they refer to expectations on the part of the readers of translated texts as well as other norm authorities such as publishers, literary critics or teachers of translation. Product norms determine three professional norms: the accountability norm (i.e. an ethical obligation towards the commissioner and the reader), the communication norm (to ensure maximum communication) and relation norm (i.e. equivalence between the source and the target text, understood in a wide sense).

We have seen above how the new theories brought the descriptive turn away from the source text to the target text and away from recommending how translations should be done to describing how are they done and why. The DTS methodology is now well established in AVT and was applied, for instance, to study interlingual subtitling (Pedersen, 2011) or SDH (Mliczak, 2019; Neves, 2005).

Let us now come back to the map of Translation Studies, proposed by Holmes and updated by Munday (2016, p. 17). The map (see Fig. 3) positions descriptive translation studies as a part of the "pure" (i.e. not applied) translation studies, divided into three sub-areas that are oriented towards either product, process or function. The current research is descriptive, product-oriented (live subtitles) and synchronic. It is medium-restricted (i.e. television), area-restricted (i.e. current language and culture), and text-type restricted (i.e. specific genre news subtitling) and time-restricted.

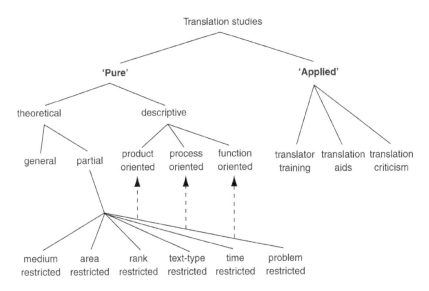

Fig. 3: *Holmes's map of translation studies (Munday, 2016, p. 17)*

Toury also pointed out that "translation activities should rather be regarded as having cultural significance" (Toury, 1978, p. 198). And attention to such concepts as ideology, otherness, post-colonialism or censorship resulted in the cultural turn. The inspiration from sociology, and especially the works of Bourdieu, led many researchers to study the role of the translator. Finally, the advances of technology opened avenues for more sophisticated experimental research methods with the use of eye-tracking or biometric sensors as researchers are trying to investigate what happens in the AVT audience'-s (or translator'-s) brains (Chaume, 2018, p. 41). Running parallel to these trends, inspirations from linguistics continue to feed into AVT, for instance the Relevance Theory is used to investigate translation as a form of secondary communication (Bogucki, 2020).

AVT has "now developed its very own theoretical and methodological approaches, allowing it to claim the status of a scholarly area of research in its own right" (Díaz Cintas, 2009, p. 7). Over the past two decades, AVT has moved from Translation Studies periphery to its centre as "very dramatic developments in translation studies have occurred in the field of audiovisual translation, most notably subtitling" (Munday, 2016, p. 275). Indeed, subtitling is "one of the most thriving areas within the wider discipline of Translation Studies" (Díaz Cintas & Remael, 2007, p. 8).

It is interesting to note the pace of AVT development. In 1989, Delabastita described the field as a "virgin area of research" (1989, p. 202). In 2009, Pérez González remarked that AVT "has outgrown its core domain of enquiry and annexed neighbouring fields under an all-inclusive research agenda" (2009, p. 13). And in 2010, Remael predicted that the 21st century may well see the advent of the "audiovisual turn" in Translation Studies (Remael, 2010, p. 15).

As Audiovisual Translation is coming to the forefront of Translation Studies, the idea of accessibility is becoming a central issue within AVT. The audiovisual turn within Translation Studies seems to be mirrored by the accessibility turn within AVT. In the next section, we will look at the idea of access, which will be followed by a discussion on how accessibility found its place within AVT.

1.3. The rise of Media Accessibility in AVT

The idea of access comes from the respect of the human dignity and is based on the idea of human rights (Greco, 2018, p. 208), which came to the forefront in the interwar period after WWI. To guarantee human dignity, all people need to have a certain minimum standard of quality of life. To this end, every person needs access to some material and immaterial goods such as food, work, education or cultural life. It is not enough to just make sure that these goods exist; all people need to have access to them.

And having access does not just mean owning something but refers to "being able to use, interact with, and enjoy that good" (Greco, 2018, p. 208). While access is most commonly associated with physical barriers, it refers to many areas of life (Jankowska, 2020). Indeed, the advent of information and communication technologies led to a situation where access to the media became an important prerequisite for full participation in the social life, giving rise to access services such as subtitling for the Deaf and the hard of hearing (SDH), audio description (AD) or sign language interpreting (SLI).

At first, the practice of those new access services was not followed by much research. Indeed, very little research had been carried out in the area of media accessibility in general and "virtually no studies had been conducted in these topics from a translational perspective, the first rigorous works not appearing until the mid-2000s" (Bogucki & Díaz-Cintas, 2020, pp. 23–24). Since then, AVT scholars have embraced accessibility, seeing some access services as new modes of translation (Jankowska, 2020). Such access services as SDH and AD have become a new, if at first marginal, area of research within AVT, where they were seen as new AVT modalities.

Thanks to the pioneering work of some scholars (Yves Gambier, 2003; Orero, 2004; Díaz Cintas, 2005) Media Accessibility became recognized as an area of research within AVT. In a map of AVT, put together by Di Giovanni and Gambier, accessibility is one of the four areas with the other three being language policy, descriptive studies and applied research[2] (Di Giovanni & Gambier, 2018, p. viii). Díaz Cintas defines media accessibility as "making audiovisual programmes available to people that otherwise could not have access to them, irrespective of whether the barriers are sensory or linguistic" (Bogucki & Díaz Cintas, 2020, p. 24).

Initially, MA was positioned as a field concerning exclusively "subtitling for the Deaf and the hard of hearing (SDH) and audio description (AD) for the blind and the visually impaired" (Orero, 2004, p. VIII). Over time, however, the list of particular modalities got "longer and longer" (Greco & Jankowska, 2020, p. 63). And Media Accessibility started attracting scholars from various fields "from engineering, psychology, through filmmaking, computer science, until performing arts" (Greco, 2018, p. 216). Jankowska classified current research in MA into four research avenues: MA history; accessibility legislation and provision; textual and multimodal analysis; and experimental studies (Jankowska, 2020).

Accessibility quickly gained ground within AVT to such an extent that some researchers now define AVT as a form of Media Accessibility (Díaz Cintas et al., 2007), "stretching the concept of »translation« to include »translation« from sounds or images into words" (Remael, 2010, p. 14). Accessibility has now become a "major, booming topic of interest" both in translation teaching and research (Bogucki & Díaz-Cintas, 2020, p. 24).

This happened as a result of profound changes that accessibility brought about in AVT. In the next sections, we will examine how the concept of accessibility changed over time and how it affected many research areas, including AVT, in what Greco (2019, p. 17) calls "the revolution of accessibility".

---

2 However, such a conceptualization is problematic as both descriptive studies and applied research have a place within accessibility. Indeed, both kinds of research have been carried out in the field.

1.4. The revolution of accessibility and the three shifts in AVT

We now live in "the age of access" (Greco, 2018, p. 209) and over the past few decades how we view accessibility and how we talk about it has changed. One of the reasons was the shift from the traditional *medical model* of disability to the *social model*. The medical model sees disability as a physical or mental defect that a person has. In this approach, a person with a disability needs to be fixed. The social model, in turn, sees disability as created by the environment (in other words, the way the society is organized). It is the environment that needs to be fixed, not the person. For instance, the medical model sees a Deaf person as disabled and can offer him or her a fix in the form of an implant or a hearing aid. The social model sees a Deaf person as abled as long as the environment is accessible. This model can offer services such as subtitling, sign language interpreting or forms of written communication (Jankowska, 2020). As long as such services are available, a Deaf person's ability to communicate is on par with anybody else.

This traditional view of access services has been evolving as well over the recent years as accessibility is now seen as "an ever more key issue within a process that is reshaping the very fabric of society" (Greco, 2018, p. 205). Accessibility is at the core of multiple European policies and programmes from EU's New Framework Strategy for Multilingualism, through European Accessibility Act to Digital Single Market Strategy and "has been producing a paradigm shift in research, giving way to new research methods and models" (Greco, 2018, p. 209).

In the context of AVT, the idea of accessibility has been producing three major shifts: from a maker-centred to a user-centred approach, from reactive to proactive approaches and from particularist account to a universalist account of accessibility (Greco, 2018, p. 206). Let us examine these shifts one by one.

The first paradigm shift that was brought by accessibility is one that places users at the centre. Traditionally, more prominence used to be assigned in AVT to the views of policymakers, professionals and researches (Bogucki & Díaz-Cintas, 2020). However, accessibility challenges such maker-centred approach as there can be "no accessibility without participation" (Greco, 2018, p. 213). With accessibility came the realization that users possess valuable knowledge that should be taken into account when investigating accessibility, and that users should have active involvement in the design of accessibility services.

This was a novelty in AVT, which used to have translation products at it centre. Researchers would look at audiovisual texts to evaluate and compare them. Now it is users who are at the centre with their need to have access to content (Greco, 2018). The new goal of bridging the maker-user-gap reshaped AVT and resulted in a shift towards experimental and reception studies (Jankowska, 2020).

Another shift has to do with the reactive versus proactive approaches. Scholars and practitioners alike have been complaining for years that AVT is usually "an afterthought in the filmmaking process" (Pérez-González et al., 2019). The localization of audiovisual products is "relegated to the distribution stage" (Romero Fresco, 2019) and it starts once production is already over. Accessibility provides a bigger picture for this phenomenon as we now realize that this problem exists with accessibility processes in many areas of life as "accessibility has been relegated to the ex-post stage for decades" (Greco, 2018, p. 214).

Such a reactive approach is not without consequences. Taking accessibility into account at the very end of the design and production process, makes it more expensive, more difficult to make and less effective to users (Greco, 2018). In AVT, it often means that "translators have to translate films in very limited time [...] and with no access to the team behind creative filmmaking decisions" (Romero Fresco, 2019).

Such a reactive approach is dominant in live subtitling as well. For instance, news shows are made accessible as an ex-post solution, after the realization of their inaccessibility. Newscasters write lengthy texts and then tend to speak very fast to read all of it in the little time they have, making it harder for all viewers to process information. This then requires the subtitles to be edited down (otherwise viewers will not have time to read them). Incidentally, it also raises the need for access services such as slow audio so that users can slow down the news narration. The graphical elements of the news channels are designed in such a way and news materials are shot and edited in such a way that there is usually no place available for subtitles, and they might cover speaker's mouth or infographics.

While non-English viewers (many of which rely on subtitling) are now a majority of consumers of American television series, many series are still edited in such a way that the opening credits appear at the very bottom of the screen, in the area where subtitles are usually placed. This means that subtitles need to be repositioned, usually to the top of the image, where they often end up covering an actor's face. This is makes it more difficult for users to read these subtitles and makes the scene less enjoyable to watch.

This is all not just impractical but perhaps also surprising on a business level, once we look at the big picture. Romer Fresco (2019, p. 499) notes that almost 60% of the revenue obtained by the top-grossing Hollywood films "comes from the translated (subtitled or dubbed) or accessible (with subtitles for the Deaf or AD for the blind) versions of those films, and yet only between 0.1% and 1% of their budgets is usually devoted to translation and accessibility".

Greco (2018) calls for a shift from reactive to proactive approaches, where users and their needs are placed at the heart of the design process and are considered from its very beginning. While this shift is only beginning to happen, the evidence for it is growing. One example is the approach of accessible filmmaking, which aims to "integrate AVT and accessibility as part of the filmmaking process through collaboration between filmmakers and translators" (Romero Fresco, 2019, p. 499). For instance, it introduces the role of the director of accessibility so that accessibility issues are considered from the start of the film production process.

The third shift has to do with the target audience of access services. Up until recently, access was believed "to concern *exclusively* or *mainly* specific groups of people" (Greco, 2018, p. 211). This is evident in the very name of SDH, subtitling for *the Deaf* and *the hard of hearing*. Similarly, audio description is often referred to as "audio description for the blind" (Orero, 2004).

Such an approach turned out to be too simplistic. For instance, polls from the Flemish public television VRT show that over 70% of the people using SDH hear normally (Waes et al., 2013). The research by the UK Office of Communications (Ofcom) brought similar results: of the 7.5 million people who actively used the intralingual subtitles, "6 million did not have a hearing impairment" (Ofcom, 2006).

To account for that, scholars proposed the idea of *primary* and *secondary* audiences (Jankowska, 2020). While the SDH is first and foremost aimed at the Deaf and the Hard-of Hearing (its primary audience), it is also of benefit to secondary audiences such as non-native speakers and language learners, including migrants, and all those without hearing loss who do not wish to or cannot listen to the original soundtrack as they watch in noisy environment such as bars or public transport, or parents who do not want to wake their kids.

Such views represent a *particularist* account of accessibility, as referring only to specific groups of people, as opposed to a *universal* account in which access is "understood to concern *all* human beings" (Greco, 2018, p. 211). I discuss this distinction in more details in the following section, where we will look at how these three shifts brought about by accessibility reshaped the very concept of AVT.

1.5. The three accounts of Media Accessibility

As the concept of accessibility has brought profound changes to AVT itself, the way this area of research is conceptualized within AVT has been changing as well. Greco (2018) classified varying perceptions of Media Accessibility into three accounts (see Fig. 4), the first two of which are *particularist* accounts and the third is a *universalist* account.

The Three Accounts of Media Accessibility

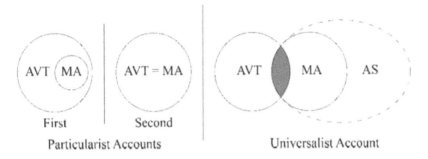

First   Second

Particularist Accounts   Universalist Account

Fig. 4: *Three accounts of media accessibility (Greco, 2019, p. 19)*

The first particularist account restricts Media Accessibility both in terms of modalities (i.e. only AD and SDH) and audience (only persons with sensory disabilities) (Greco & Jankowska, 2020, p. 63), and considers it as one of many research areas in AVT. This is the oldest account, originated at a time when first AVT researchers looked to accessibility with SDH and AD as their main interests.

Over time, interest in media accessibility grew and the list of accessibility services became longer as some scholars went as far as to argue that accessibility is a human right. Others pointed out that such claim confuses "the means with the end" (Greco & Jankowska, 2020, p. 64) and that accessibility is a tool needed to ensure true access to such human rights as information, education or cultural life. In other words, people need accessibility to truly enjoy some of their human rights but accessibility is not a human right in itself.

Still, this reflection brought a change of thinking to AVT. Human rights are not specific to only one group of people, they are for all humans. As the principle of universal design (or Design for All) has been gaining ground (Preiser & Smith, 2011), it started to be problematic for access services to be aimed *only* at persons with sensory impairments. This led some researchers to conclude that MA can no longer be restricted to persons with sensory barriers; linguistic barriers need to be taken into account as well.

Indeed, following a lengthy debate on whether such accessibility services as SDH or AD can even be called translation (Bogucki & Díaz-Cintas, 2020), a pendulum went the other way as some scholars started wondering if perhaps all translation practices are forms of accessibility. Díaz Cintas and Remael point out that "to lip-sync, to subtitle or to voiceover a programme shares as much the idea of accessibility as SDH or AD. Only the intended audiences are different" (Díaz Cintas & Remael, 2007, p. 13).

While the first account views MA as one of many areas of AVT, the second account "makes it overlap with AVT itself" (Greco & Jankowska, 2020, p. 63). Critics see this as a power struggle on the part of AVT scholars who "want to maintain the control stock in the hands of translation studies by allocating a dominant role to translation practices" (Greco, 2018, p. 218).

Such approach has a number of shortcomings. Firstly, it still restricts MA to linguistic and sensory access only. Secondly, it leaves no room for media accessibility services that do not involve translation. Thirdly, it extends MA to such a degree that it coincides with AVT, bringing more confusion than clarity.

But the principle of Universal Design offers an inspiration for the third, universalist account of Media Accessibility, that does away with any particular target groups. Access services are aimed at everyone who wishes to use them. This approach also extends the field beyond translation and includes non-translation-based services such as audio introductions, audio subtitles, clean audio or tactile reproductions (Greco & Jankowska, 2020, p. 71). By making translation not the only one but one of many driving forces behind Media Accessibility, the universal account allows for "the inclusion of other groups and access services, favours the convergence of the different conceptions of accessibility services developed in other fields, and encourages the design of solutions that are more inclusive" (Greco, 2018, p. 218).

To sum up, originally scholars thought that media accessibility concerns sensory barriers only. Over time, this was widened to include both sensory and linguistic barriers. Finally, a shift is now taking place to the universalist account that sees media accessibility as concerning "access to media products, services, and environment for all persons who cannot, or cannot completely, access them in their original form" (Greco, 2018, p. 211).

Greco cautions, however, that the shifts described above are not linear in time as the versions of the two particularist accounts still co-exist today. In 2014, in his seminal work, *Audiovisual translation: Theories, methods and issues*, Pérez González does not acknowledge the existence of Media Accessibility as sub-domain of AVT and uses the term accessibility once only, when talking about how "AD (…) has become equally important in ensuring the accessibility of audiovisual products to the visually impaired" (Pérez González, 2014, p. 25). In later years, he goes on to recognize access services as a small area of assistive

AVT modalities (Pérez-González et al., 2019), this way affirming the first particularist account.

Díaz Cintas, in turn, continues championing the second particularist account, in his belief that language and sensory barriers are alike and the ultimate aim of all AVT practices is "to facilitate access to an otherwise hermetic source of information and entertainment" and accessibility is "a common denominator that underpins these practices" (Bogucki & Díaz-Cintas, 2020, p. 24).

Many university translation programmes are still firmly embedded in the first account. Accessibility-related content is restricted to few services and compartmentalized into separate courses, kept at a safe distance from "traditional" translation practises. For instance, Universidad Autonoma de Barcelona has a single module titled "Audio Description and Subtitling for the Deaf and Hard of Hearing"; the University of Roehampton offers a course called "Media Access: Audiodescription, Subtitling for the Deaf and Respeaking" (Greco & Jankowska, 2020, p. 73) and the University of Warsaw offers separate courses in AD, SDH, respeaking, Deaf awareness and live events accesibility, all under the umbrella of accessibility, with students able to choose just one of these five courses.

Even Jankowska who herself champions the universal view of media accessibility (Greco & Jankowska, 2020), still continues to refer to primary and secondary audiences (Jankowska, 2020), a distinction the universal account aims to abolish. And those sceptical of the universalist account might argue that creating services that meet everybody's needs is much harder than tailoring them for a specific audience, if at all possible. Can we not end up with services that attempt to please everyone and satisfy no one? The shift to the third account seems to still be in the making.

As we have seen, the concept of accessibility has been reshaping AVT through a series of three shifts. From the perspective of Translation Studies, audiovisual media accessibility is still seen as part of AVT (Jankowska, 2020) but "the boundaries between AVT and MA are somewhat blurred, and it may be problematic to consider the latter as a sub-area of the former" (Romero Fresco, 2018a, p. 189). We have seen how AVT "has outgrown its core domain of enquiry and annexed neighbouring fields" (Pérez-González, 2009, p. 13) and now this story repeats itself with Media Accessibiliy, which has outgrown AVT. Guided by advocates of the need for it "to move beyond translation studies" (Greco & Jankowska, 2020, p. 75) and find a "bigger room" than AVT can provide (Romero Fresco, 2018a, p. 188), Media Accessibility is now overflowing the boundaries of Audiovisual Translation and chartering a territory for a new discipline.

1.6. Towards Accessibility Studies

The idea of accessibility brought profound changes not only to AVT but to many disciplines and has created numerous new research areas (Greco, 2019, p. 18). Over time, these "have been detaching from their original fields and moving towards one another, intertwining and cross-contaminating, producing a wealth of new methods and models" (Greco & Jankowska, 2020, p. 75). This process should sound familiar to Translation Studies scholars as it mirrors the birth of Translation Studies themselves, as separate areas of research within linguistics and comparative literature, among many others, came together to from this new interdiscipline.

Similarly, as new areas of accessibility research come together, a new inter-discipline of Accessibility Studies is emerging, defined as "the field concerned with the investigation of accessibility processes and phenomena, and the design, implementation and evaluation of accessibility-based and accessibility-oriented methodologies" (Greco, 2018, p. 205) with Media Accessibility seen as one of its most vibrant and developed areas.

Accessibility Studies as a new discipline comes with a number of opportunities. Access services require collaboration of experts from various fields as "approaching audiovisual media accessibility from just one field of expertise [...] is not enough to carry out quality research and provide quality access services" (Jankowska, 2020) and media accessibility has already been enriched by insights from sociology, Deaf studies or philosophy, to just name a few.

However, researchers from different fields pursue parallel tracks and rarely communicate with one another (Jankowska, 2020). Bringing them all under a common umbrella of Accessibility Studies should help overcome the lack of collaboration between different scientific disciplines. Even those who still see Media Accessibility as contained within the boundaries of AVT agree that the way forward "has to be found in its interdisciplinarity and potential synergies with other branches of knowledge, especially within the humanities" (Bogucki & Díaz-Cintas, 2020, p. 27) and Accessibility Studies provides this "bigger room" that scholars have been advocating for.

Accessibility Studies can also provide the conceptual framework needed for a "complete curriculum overhaul in education and training courses" (Greco & Jankowska, 2020, p. 73) to bring academic programmes in line with the up-to-date universal view of media accessibility, which will also help in mainstreaming access services (Jankowska, 2020).

Clearly not all accessibility problems are translation problems and not all translation problems are accessibility problems. Recognizing Media Accessibility position at the crossroads of Translation Studies and Accessibility Studies will help researchers integrate insights from both without being unnecessarily restricted by the boundaries of either. As Greco and Jankowska point out: "it is not a matter of which one is the subfield of the other, but how they can fruitfully interact and help humanity progress" (Greco & Jankowska, 2020, p. 74).

In the sections above we have seen how Translation Studies, an interdiscipline on its own gave birth to AVT and how AVT moved from the margins to the centre of Translation Studies. A similar path was then followed by Media Accessibility, a research area born on the fringes of AVT, that over the years helped reshape the field of AVT and now takes a centre stage as at the crossroads of Audiovisual Translation and Accessibility Studies. It is from this vantage point that we look at live subtitling in this book. In the following chapter, we will adopt the perspectives of both Translation Studies and Accessibility Studies to examine the past and present of live subtitling as an AVT modality and as an access service.

Chapter 2: Live subtitling: Past and present

In this chapter, I discuss the history of live subtitling,. We will look at the roots of subtitling and the innovations that brought about live subtitling and then led to the invention of respeaking as one of the main methods of creating live subtitles. As this book concerns live subtitling in Polish, I will pay particular attention to the beginnings of SDH in Poland, the legal framework of accessibility that brought about the increase in the provision of SDH, the beginnings of live subtitling in Polish and its development over the years in various settings: at live events, in online streaming and on TV. Finally, I will discuss the current state of live subtitling in Poland and the challenges for the future.

2.1. The history of live subtitling

While today live subtitling can be interlingual (see Section 1.1), it originated as a form of intralingual subtitling aimed at the Deaf and the hard of hearing. Thus, to examine the history of live subtitling, we will first look at the roots of intralingual subtitling in general.

2.1.1. Beginnings of intralingual subtitling

Although subtitles as such were already used in the 1930s, the first subtitles were interlingual (Lambourne, 2006). In 1970s, in the US, experiments were done with intralingual subtitles to respond to the needs of Deaf viewers who did not understand TV broadcasts. In 1971 *The French Chef* on PBS was the first TV programme to be subtitled. The first news programme was aired with subtitles by PBS in 1973. These were "open subtitles" (known as "open captions" in the US), which means that they were burned on the images and visible to all the viewers; there was no way to turn them off (Romero Fresco, 2011).

The invention of closed subtitles (or "closed captions") made it possible to include subtitles that are activated by a decoder and are not visible on screen unless the viewer decides to turn them on (Neves, 2005). These were first introduced in 1980 using a decoding unit called Telecaption Adaptor (Downey, 2008) and since then most intralingual subtitles are available as closed, so much so that intralingual subtitles came to be identified with closed subtitles (Pérez-González, 2009). Indeed, the term "closed captions" is used, especially in the USA and Canada, as an equivalent of SDH.

In Europe, the beginnings of SDH are linked with the invention of teletext, a technology that allowed coding additional information in a television signal

(Romero Fresco, 2011). The first programmes with SDH were broadcast in 1979 by BBC and France 2. Followed by German public broadcasters ARD and ZDF in 1980, Belgian VRT in 1983 and Italian RAI in 1986. Catalan public TV introduced SDH as the first broadcaster in Spain in the 1990s. Polish public broadcaster TVP started airing programmes with SDH in 1994 (Künstler, 2008) and Portuguese public broadcaster RTP did that in 1999. Interestingly, there are still places in Europe where there is no SDH on TV. For instance, as of 2022, the Lithuanian public broadcaster LRT still does not offer SDH and hearing impaired audiences can only rely on interlingual subtitling.[3]

2.1.2. Live subtitling is born

The first programmes with live subtitles were broadcast in 1982 independently in the US and Europe using different methods and technologies (Romero Fresco, 2011). In the US, the National Captioning Institute employed court reporters who had experience in using steno machines to transcribe court hearings (Downey, 2008; Robson, 2004). In Europe, Belgian VRT used a team of two people. One person would dictate the text and another would type the subtitles as fast as possible using a standard QWERTY keyboard. Also in 1982, the British channel ITV experimented with a similar method, the difference being that they used a single typist (Lambourne, 2006). As this method was not fast enough, in 1987 they started to use Velotype with one operator and then, to speed it up further, two operators working in tandem. BBC set up its own live subtitling unit in 1990, first using keyboards and then switching to steno machines. For other broadcasters it took much longer. The regional TV3 channel in Catalonia was the first Spanish broadcaster to provide subtitles for live programmes in 1990 but these were actually semi-live subtitles. The live subtitles were introduced by Catalan TV3 in 2000, with Italian RAI following suit in the same year.

2.1.3. The rise of respeaking

Romero Fresco (2011) notes that the origins of respeaking in the US may be traced back to court reporters in 1940s. They would usually take shorthand notes of the courts proceedings and then dictate their notes for transcription, which required around two hours of dictation for an hour spent in court. Using microphones in the courtroom was problematic because of the noise and the overlapping speech. Horace Webb proposed a method called *voice writing*, where reporters would repeat every word into a microphone using a stenomask to

---

3   Personal communication with Dr Jurgita Astrauskienė from the Vilnius University.

cancel the noise. The transcription could then be done based on the recording, thus saving time. Romero Fresco (2011) concludes that although there was no SR technology at the time, the basic principle of respeaking is the same.

However, US court reporters started using speech recognition to transcribe court sessions only from 1999, and so it was in Europe where respeaking was first developed. It was proposed as a method to produce live subtitles as early as 1975 by Damper and colleagues who suggested using SR to transcribe speech and keyboards to change the colour and position of live subtitles (Lambourne et al., 2004). As the SR technology was not yet developed enough, the first experiments were carried out much later, in 1997, by Synapsys Ltd. and University of Hertfordshire. Respeaking was first implemented in Flemish-language Belgian public broadcaster VRT and the BBC in the UK in 2011. BBC tested respeaking in 2001 with the World Snooker Championship, followed by Wimbledon. Other sports events and then parliament sessions and news bulletins followed suit. In 2003 respeaking was first used to produce live subtitles on US television. Spanish TVE started testing respeaking in 2004, French TF1 in 2007 and Italian Rai 3 in 2008 (Romero Fresco, 2011).

2.2. The legal context of accessibility in the US and the EU

Remael (2007, p. 25) points out that developments in SDH and live subtitling usually go hand in hand with either "new legislation or other forms of agreement brokered between governments and, for instance, public broadcasting channels, following constant pressure from the Deaf and hard of hearing organisations". Thus, in this section, I will summarize the most important legislation that refers to live subtitling. As some of the provisions of the EU legislation on accessibility seem to have been inspired by the US laws on accessibility, I will start with the American legislation. Then I will discuss the EU directives on media accessibility and their implementations as well as other relevant laws in various member states. In the following section, we will look at how the implementation of EU directives influenced the development of live subtitling on the example of Poland.

The first legal attempts at ensuring the provision of SDH on TV were made in the US. The Television Decoder Circuitry Act in 1990 required all television receivers with screen 13 inches or lager to be capable of displaying closed subtitles (Downey, 2008). However, a substantial increase in captioning did not occur. In 1996, through the Telecommunications Act, the US Congress ordered the Federal Communications Commission (FCC) to develop a timetable for phasing in mandatory subtitling (Romero Fresco, 2011). Starting from 2006, as a principle, all television programming in both English and Spanish must be captioned (but small broadcaster can apply for exemptions). Crucially, the FCC requires that all the content that was subtitled when broadcast on TV also has to be subtitled when shown online (for instance, on the broadcaster's website, on a VOD platform or on YouTube).

While the US legislation was very effective in ensuring the quantity of subtitling on TV, it was less successful in ensuring quality. FCC is now believed to purse a soft, complaint-driven approach and does not actively monitor subtitle quality (Romero Fresco, 2021). This can be contrasted with the approach of the UK regulator, Ofcom, or the Canadian CRTC, which rely on quality audits. While Fresno (2019) found that the quality of live subtitles for a presidential debate was quite acceptable on most national channels, some local state-level broadcasters have switched to automatic live subtitling, raising concerns that the quality of live subtitling is decreasing.[4] See Fig. 5 for an example of such automatic subtitles.

Fig. 5: *Live subtitling for the Super Bowl 2022 on Arizona 12 News (source: Kimberly Shea/Global Alliance of Speech to Text Captioning)*

Note. The subtitle includes the transcription of the US anthem with various misrecognized words.

---

4   Personal communication with Kimberly Shea from the Global Alliance of Speech-to-Text Captioning.

Interestingly, the US legislation does not only mandate the provision of sub-titling on television but also in education and at public events. The American with Disabilities Act from 1990 gives the Deaf and the hard of hearing the right to request access to real-time transcription in classrooms and public events by viewing text on a screen (Robson, 2004).

In the EU, the first major legislation on media accessibility was Television Without Frontiers from 1989 (updated in 1997). In 2008, The European Parliament in 2008 called on the Commission to put forward "a legislative proposal requiring public-service television broadcasters in the EU to subtitle all of their programmes" (Romero Fresco, 2011, p. 9). And European Union Audiovisual Media Services directive (2007/65/CE[5]) urged all member states to introduce accessibility regulations requiring broadcasters to provide some of their programs with subtitling, audio description and sign language interpreting (the details on the specific quotas were left for each member state to decide). The motif 46 of the preamble to the directive stated that:

> "The right of persons with a disability and of the elderly to participate and be integrated in the social and cultural life of the Union is inextricably linked to the provision of accessible audiovisual media services. The means to achieve accessibility should include, but need not be limited to, sign language, subtitling, audio-description and easily under-standable menu navigation."

It should be pointed out that some member states took steps to ensure the provision of SDH much earlier. For instance, an agreement between VRT (the Flemish-speaking public broadcaster in Belgium) and Flemish government from 2006 stated that VRT should provide SDH for 95% of all Flemish programmes by 2010. That required live subtitling as some of the programmes were live. In 2009 Flemish parliament obliged private broadcasters with a market share of 2% or more to provide subtitling. The obligation was phased in with the SDH required for the main newscast in the first year and subtitling of all news broadcasts and 90% of all news and current affairs programmes within 3 years of the law coming into effect (Romero Fresco, 2011, p. 10).

France first obliged its broadcasters to provide SDH in 2000 and the quota introduced was 7% of the annual broadcasting from 2002. In 2005, large broad-casters (with minimum audience share of 2.5%) were required to make 100% of their programming accessible by 2010. The obligation could be fulfilled by providing either subtitling or sign language interpreting.

---

5   Audiovisual media services without frontiers directive 2007/65/EC, Brussels 29.03.2007
     COM(2007) 170 final 2005/0260 (COD)

In Italy, the Stanca law from 2004 required national broadcasters to increase volume of subtitles programmes (Romero Fresco, 2011). Additionally, the government signed an agreement with RAI, the main public broadcaster in Italy, which determined the SDH quota. The 2006 agreement required RAI to subtitle 60% of its programmes by the end of 2009. In Spain, SDH quotas on TV were first set by law from 2009 which stipulated that the public broadcaster RTVE should subtitle 90% of their programmes by 2013. Other national broadcasters had a quota of 75%.

2.3. The beginnings of live subtitling in Poland: Live events, television, online streaming

This section describes the beginnings of live subtitling in Poland in various settings (at live events, in online streaming and on TV) at the backdrop of the development of subtitling in general and SDH in particular as well as a summary of the legal context of accessibility in Poland. This will be followed by a discussion on the current state of live subtitling in Poland and the challenges for the future.

2.3.1. SDH before the advent of regulation

Poland is known as a voice-over country (Bogucki, 2010; Gottlieb, 1998; Szarkowska, 2009) and indeed voice-over has been the default mode for localizing foreign audiovisual productions for decades, at least on TV. The television audiences are so used to voice-over that a poll commissioned by the Polish public broadcaster TVP found in 2007 that only 4% favoured subtitling (Szarkowska, 2008).

As a result of voice-over domination, Polish viewers with hearing impairments were more disadvantaged than their counterparts in countries where subtitling was the preferred method of audiovisual translation. Until the 1990s, subtitling in Poland was mostly present in cinemas and it was interlingual.

Polish public broadcaster TVP was the first television in the country to introduce SDH subtitles in 1994 through teletext (Künstler, 2008). Interestingly, the first programme to receive SDH was subtitled interlingually (*Rio Grande*[6]). Initially, TVP subtitled only pre-recorded content including feature films, soap

---

6   While technically the SDH for the film was interlingual, the subtitles were probably based on the voice-over translation of the film. As viewers were watching the subtitles together with the Polish voice-over version, it could be argued that in a way the subtitles were intralingual.

operas, documentaries and pre-taped quiz shows. In 2003, *Teleexpress* became the first news bulletin to be subtitled. The show was broadcast live but was completely scripted as the news presenter only read what was displayed on the prompter and there were no conversations with correspondents. As a result, it lent itself well to semi-live subtitling. The script was edited and divided into chunks of text that were then manually cued in live during the broadcast.

More subtitling became available with the advent of DVDs, mostly inter-lingual, although TVP also published some of its own feature films and series on DVD with intralingual SDH subtitles. TVP's flagship news broadcast, *Wiadomości*, was first subtitled in 2007 (Künstler, 2008). As the show occasion-ally included live conversations with correspondents, some short segments were subtitled live with a subtitler attempting to provide a summary of the utterance by typing on a QWERTY keyboard.

Back in 2009, the head of the TVP subtitling unit, Izabela Künstler, stated that it was technically impossible in Poland to subtitle shows for which the text cannot be prepared in advance. "So far speech-to-text software has not been developed for Polish and typing longer passages of text live does not produce satisfactory results" (Künstler, 2008, p. 116). At the same time, she estimated that between 8% and 10% of all programmes on TVP1 and TVP2 channels were broadcast with SDH.

In 2010, the public broadcaster suffered financial problems and attempted to slash costs. Subtitling for some of its programmes, including the news show *Teleexpress*, was discontinued. In the same year, a pay TV channel Canal+ became the first private channel to introduce SDH in its broadcasts (Sacha & Kasperkowiak, 2012).

2.3.2. First legal requirements for TV subtitling

On 1 July 2011 SDH provision became obligatory as a result of Poland imple-menting EU Media Services directive (Szczygielska, 2019). Under the new law[7], all TV stations broadcasting in Poland were obliged to offer access services such as SDH, audio description or sign interpreting for at least 10% of their quarterly broadcasting time with the exception of commercials. The broadcasters had a choice of which access service(s) they are going to provide and most opted for SDH, as it is cheaper than the two other services: audio description and sign language interpreting. As a result SDH appeared for the first time on numerous

---

7   Dz. U. [Journal of Laws] of 2011, no. 85, item 459

privately-owned TV channels. At the same time many smaller channels seemed to ignore the requirement, waiting for the National Broadcasting Council (KRRiT) to lower the required quota, which it did in June 2013, requiring some smaller channels to provide access services for only 5% or 1% of its broadcasting time, depending on the turnover of the broadcaster and the number of viewers it had.

Over time, meeting this requirement became easier for TV stations because they could repeat the shows they subtitled in the past, as re-runs also count towards the compulsory quota. In fact, the public broadcaster quickly surpassed the required quota. In the first quarter of 2013, according to a TVP press release, 31.8% of its main channel TVP1 programming was broadcast with SDH.[8] The numbers for other state-owned terrestrial channels varied from 16% to 19.7%. TVP's satellite channels broadcasting re-runs and archive programming TVP HD and TVP Seriale had subtitles for around 55% of their content. Main private channels Polsat and TVN achieved 16% and 15% respectively.

The Polish regulator, KRRiT, did not monitor access services quality and focused on checking their quantity instead, relying on self-reporting done by broadcasters, and thus promoting self-regulation. In June 2013, KRRiT pub-lished the content of an agreement reached by all digital terrestrial broadcasters regarding the implementation of the 2011 law[9]. The document provides a defi-nition of AD, sign language interpreting, SDH and live subtitling. Crucially, in this agreement the broadcasters pledged to provide 11 hours of AD quarterly for programmes on channels with the biggest audience share (TVP1, TVP2, Polsat, TVN) and 6 hours of AD for other terrestrial channels (TVP Polonia, TVP Kultura, TVP Historia, TVN7, TV4, TV6, Puls, Puls2, ATM Rozrywka, TTV). Regional public TV channels and sport channels were exempted from providing AD due to "broadcasting characteristics", but pledged to provide 10 hours of sign language interpreting quarterly. The agreement did not set a number of hours for SDH. Instead, it stated that SDH should complement AD and sign language interpreting in order to fulfil the 10% quota of broadcasting time with the excep-tion of commercials and telesales.

In the agreement, the broadcasters also pledged to provide information on programmes with SDH, AD and sign language interpreting, which should

---

8   http://www.tvp.pl/o-tvp/centrum-prasowe/komunikaty-prasowe/tvp-liderem-w-niwe lowaniu-barier/11348322 (in Polish, accessed on March 11, 2020)

9   http://www.krrit.gov.pl/Data/Files/_public/Portals/0/Nadawcy/aktualnosci/porozu mienie_nadawcow.pdf (in Polish, accessed on February 29, 2024)

include the type of access service available for a given broadcast, its time and duration. Such information should be presented in all advertisements of the programmes, on the broadcasters' web pages, in Electronic Programming Guides (EPGs), in teletext (if a given channel has it) and, if possible, in paper-based TV guides. The agreement came into effect on July 1, 2013. A the end of 2013, only the public television included the information on broadcasts with SDH on its website. As of April 2020, the survey of terrestrial TV channels[10] showed that most of them include this information on their websites (the exceptions being WP HD and ZOOM TV).

However, the self-regulation was only partially successful at promoting good practices. Let us take the example of making information on programmes with SDH available online. All cable and satellite channels broadcast by Polsat and Canal+ broadcasting groups now include this information in their online programming guides, even though they are not party to the self-regulatory agreement signed by the terrestrial channels, meaning that they are not legally required to do so. Still some other satellite or cable TV channels[11], for instance, the news channels TVN24 and the entertainment channel 4FunTV, do not publish such information on their websites. This is particularly concerning as *Making TV Accessible* report (ITU, 2011, p. 11) warns that if such information is not available, "access services are to all intents and purposes hidden from their potential users". The channels in question do show an on-screen graphical sign at the beginning of a subtitled broadcast so that viewers know they can turn on subtitles (as this became a legal requirement from 2018) but viewers have no way of checking in advance which shows are subtitled.

2.3.3. The first cases of live subtitling in Poland

Quite uniquely, the origins of live subtitling in Poland are not linked to television as in countries such as the UK, Belgium or Spain or to the courts and education as in the US (Romero Fresco, 2011). Live subtitling in Polsat started at live events and was led by NGOs with some help from public institutions.

---

10   Only terrestrial channels available in the whole territory of Poland were analysed. For instance, 4FunTV is a satellite channel that also airs terrestrially in a few regions.
11   It should be noted that while POLO TV in theory does publish information on accessibility services in its online programming guide, in the period from April 6 to April 12, 2020, as per its website, it did not air any shows with subtitles.

Live subtitling in Polish (without the use of pre-prepared text) was first used on June 7, 2013, at a conference on the accessibility of the public sector organized by the Widzialni Foundation in Sejm, the Polish parliament (Szczygielska & Dutka, 2019). The organizers, together with the Parliament's IT centre, carried out a test with two versions of live subtitling: one produced by trained typists working on QWERTY keyboards (these were members of the parliament staff, experienced in producing the minutes of the proceedings based on recordings), the other version was produced through respeaking.

As at that time there were no trained respeakers who could work in Polish, two acting school graduates were hired for the test as the organizers believed that voice skills would be crucial for respeaking. They worked in a separate insulated room, where they could follow the conference on a screen and heard the audio through headphones. The event was also the first case of live subtitles being streamed online, on the parliament's website. However, the IT centre deemed the use of respeaking too risky and decided to stream online the live subtitles produced by typists only.

Szczygielska and Dutka (2019) note that at that time accessibility professionals in the country as well as the organizations representing the Deaf and the hard of hearing believed that providing live subtitles in Polish is impossible as the speech recognition in Polish is not advanced enough. The first respeakers used the speech recognition software Magic Scribe, developed by a Polish company Unikkon Integral (rebranded as Radcomp Integral, as of 2020). The software was far from perfect and even in the marketing materials the company promised an accuracy of 90% for general topics (meaning that out of 100 words 10 would be misrecognized). Indeed, Magic Scribe was unable to recognize most proper names such as institution names or surnames. On the one hand, it often omitted one-letter or two-letter words; on the other hand, it had a tendency to interpret background noise as short words.

In the venue of the conference, the participants could follow two versions of live subtitles on two large screens. The text on both screens looked similar (see Fig. 6): it appeared phrase by phrase and was displayed in high contrast (yellow on a black background), in all caps sans-serif font, with no punctuation.[12] The participants did not know which screen shows which version of subtitles

---

12   The actors who worked as respeakers at the event had no previous training in respeaking. Crucially, they were not trained in dictating punctuation commands (possibly because early versions of MagicScribe struggled to recognize punctuation commands).

(as the typists did not use punctuation either and their text was also presented in all caps).

At the end of the event, 16 participants filled in a questionnaire, evaluating the two versions. They were also asked to indicate which version was produced by typing and which by respeaking. Most participants preferred subtitles produced by respeakers and they indicated that these were more accurate and appeared with less delay. At the same time, most participants mistakenly believed that these better subtitles were produced by typists. The subtitles were generally evaluated as helpful, although participants suggested areas for improvement: adding punctuation, ensuring that the text is more verbatim and appears at a more even pace and placing screens in such a way that room lights are not reflected in the screens.

Fig. 6: *First tests of live subtitling in Polish in 2013 at a conference at the Polish Parliament (source: Dostępni.eu/M. Pawluczuk)*

An attempt at making these improvements was made later that year at a conference celebrating the anniversary of Poland adopting the UN Convention on the rights of persons with disabilities. The event was hosted at the Polish President's Palace. This time the subtitles were produced through respeaking with parallel correction. The text was spelled with regular capitalization (as opposed to all caps) and included punctuation. It was displayed phrase by phrase but this time the newest phrase was displayed in yellow, whereas the rest of the text was displayed in white (all on a black background). The intent was to make it easier for users to notice that a new text appeared (and avoid re-reading previous text). The screen with subtitles was positioned next to another screen with the presentation (to make it more comfortable for users to switch their visual attention between the two). A sign language interpreter was standing next to both screens (see Fig. 6 above).

Interestingly, as the connection over the internal network in the building failed, the respeakers had to rely on the wireless network (set-up at the last minute) and they needed to move from an underground sound-insulated room to a catering room next to the main conference room, which meant they were working among the noise of waiters setting out plates and cutlery. This highlighted the need for setting standards of live subtitling provision and minimum requirements for the service.

Another milestone happened on 27 April 27 2014, which was the first case of interlingual live subtitling as well as the first case of respeakers working remotely. Live subtitles were provided in Polish, English, Italian and Spanish for the canonization mass of Pope John Paul II in Rome. The subtitles were produced remotely by a team of more than 50 people from Poland, Italy, Spain and the US. The Polish subtitles were produced by Dostepni.eu in a studio in Warsaw. The video and the audio of the event was provided through the Internet by the Vatican Television Centre. The respeakers saw a live signal that was then streamed online with a 30 second delay. Subtitles were available on a webpage, below the video player. The Polish team included a Polish-Italian interpreter, a respeaker and a corrector.

A similar workflow with an interpreter, a respeaker and a corrector was also used in September 2014 at a conference "Telewizja dostępna dla wszystkich" [Television accessible to all] organized at the Polish parliament with speakers from the Czech Republic and the UK and in May 2015 at a conference on the European Digital Market, organized in Warsaw with English-speaking representatives of the European Commission. At both events live subtitles were provided as a form of translation so Polish participants could choose to either use headphones and listen to the interpreter or read the subtitles. Szczygielska and Dutka (2019) provide a more detailed discussion on these and other early cases of events with live subtitling.

Following on the success of these first attempts, live subtitling continued to develop in the context of live events. Dostepni.eu established contacts with Red Bee Media, a leading British provider of access services for television, and VerbaVoice, a German provider of live subtitling and sign language interpreting for parliamentary proceedings. This coincided with a research project on respeaking lead by Agnieszka Szarkowska at the University of Warsaw. Within the scope of the project, in 2015, a series of training workshops in respeaking were organised with leading international trainers: Carlo Eugeni from

International Association of Respeakers, Pablo Romero Fresco from University of Roehampton and Juan Martinez Perez from Swiss TXT, a live subtitling provider from Switzerland. This effort helped train new respeakers and ultimately lead to creating the first academic course in respeaking in Poland at the Institute of Applied Linguistics, which was first offered in 2017.

The ILSA project, led by a consortium of five European universities (including the University of Warsaw) from 2017 to 2020, produced an open e-learning course that went live in 2020[13] and includes training materials on a number of skills related to live subtitling, including pre-recorded subtitling, interpreting, intralingual respeaking and interlingual respeaking. It also includes a specific module on respeaking at live events as well as practise materials in Polish. Finally, the project produced three sets of guidelines on implementing live subtitling: at live events, in education and on TV. The guidelines are available online in Polish, English, Spanish, German and Dutch.[14]

2.3.4. The (slow) beginnings of live subtitling on Polish TV

Although live subtitling was provided for a parliamentary conference on the accessibility of television in 2014, it took a few more years for live subtitles to make an actual appearance on TV as the development of live subtitling in Polish had been hampered by two main issues: regulatory framework and technology (Szczygielska & Dutka, 2019).

Importantly, in 2013, the self-regulatory agreement signed by terrestrial TV channels introduced the definitions of subtitling and live subtitling with the latter defined as "a service that enables persons with hearing impairment to access audio content that accompanies the images in almost real time (that is, with a slight delay), used for news shows and chat shows".[15]

However, the TV channels did not need to explore live subtitling as they were able to fulfil the required quota by subtitling pre-recorded content only. In 2014, 14.2% of all programming on TV channels subject to the legislation had an access service, mostly subtitling, with the percentage slowly increasing over the following years (Szczygielska, 2019). Broadcasters also believed that creating live subtitling in Polish is impossible or extremely difficult, a notion echoed by the regulator itself in a position paper on the access services (KRRiT, 2016)

---

13 The ILSA course: https://mooc.campusdomar.es/courses/course-v1:ILSA+001+2019/about (Accessed on February 20, 2021)

14 http://ka2-ilsa.webs.uvigo.es/guidelines/ (Accessed on February 29, 2024)

15 All the quotes are translated by the author unless indicated otherwise.

where KRRiT stated that: "[for live shows] SDH have been provided to a limited degree because of technical and organizational difficulties involved in producing subtitles in real time".

Thus, although the Deaf and the hard of hearing viewers had been demanding more subtitles for live shows for quite some time (Sacha & Kasperkowiak, 2012), TV stations were slow to respond. The breakthrough came in 2017 and was forced by the users themselves. When Polsat, the biggest commercial broadcaster in Poland, started airing a new season of the Polish edition of *Dancing with the stars* that featured Iwona Cichosz, a Deaf contestant, some Deaf viewers were outraged that they cannot watch the show. (Although Ms Cichosz had a sign language interpreter on set, neither sign language interpreting nor live subtitling was provided for the show's viewers during the first episode.) In social media, Deaf activists started a petition to the broadcaster demanding live subtitling or sign language interpreting[16]. The petition was widely covered by the specialized media industry websites[17]. It argued that "the estimated cost of providing live subtitling for the entire season is not significantly greater than [the cost of] 1 minute of commercials aired during the show"[18]. And it made an appeal to the broadcaster:

"Polsat is helping us, the Deaf, to break down one of these barriers by inviting our colleague to perform and showing that a person with a hearing impairment can be successful. We ask [the broadcaster] to break down another barrier and allow us to watch the show with subtitles."

Just three days before the airing of the second episode, Polsat decided to provide live subtitling for the show in partnership with Unikkon Integral, a speech recognition provider, and Dostępni.eu (as we saw in the previous section, the two companies already had experience in providing live subtitling at live events). Unikkon Integral integrated its speech recognitions software, Magic Scribe, with a live subtitling software, FAB Subtitler Live, making it possible to produce live subtitling through respeaking with parallel correction with a respeaker dictating the text and a live corrector editing it on one workstation. To minimize delay, the subtitles were not produced at the Polsat's broadcasting centre, but instead at

---

16   The full text of the petition is available on Facebook https://www.facebook.com/krwa wykrzysztof/posts/1354234291301920 (in Polish, accessed on February 29, 2024)

17   http://www.portalmedialny.pl/art/58697/dancing-with-the-stars-taniec-z-gwiazd ami-z-iwona-cichosz-srodowisko-guchych-pisze-petycje-do-polsatu.html (in Polish, accessed on February 29, 2024)

18   This and the following quote as translated by the author.

the ATM Studio, at the outskirts of Warsaw, where the show was being recorded, so that respeakers could rely on direct audio from the show (as opposed to the broadcast signal). The subtitlers experimented with various conventions through the first few episodes and ultimately settled for displaying subtitles at the top of the screen (so as not to cover dancers' legs as well as graphics with numbers that viewers used to vote on their preferred contestants). Some speakers (the jury members) were identified through the use of colours with other speakers identified through name tags when needed (similarly to the established convention for pre-recorded SDH).

The show proved that the pressure from the viewers can have an effect on the broadcasters and that technology is no longer a blocker when it comes to live TV subtitling in Polish. Although Polsat did not decide to provide live subtitling for any other shows that year, in 2018 TVP provided live subtitling for its coverage of the elections, which seemed to be the first case when the state broadcaster produced live subtitling through respeaking[19]. TVP partnered with VoiceLab (a company based in Gdańsk, Poland) that integrated its speech recognition technology with TVP's proprietary subtitling software[20]. Later on that year TVP started to provide subtitling for some political talks, including *Gość Wiadomości*, a series featuring interviews with politicians aired after the main news bulletin.

2.3.5. The increase of the subtitling quota on TV

In March 2018, in its yearly report, KRRiT included the results of the audit of TV accessibility in 2017. In the sample of 103 TV channels supervised by the Polish media regulator[21] (KRRiT, 2018, p. 31), 19.5% of their programming was broadcast

---

19 Szczygielska (2019, p. 208) suspects that TVP could have used live subtitling through respeaking for its coverage of World Youth Days in Kraków in July 2016, including the mass with the Pope Francis. However, this was probably a case of semi-live subtitling with the use of scripts available beforehand.

20 Personal communication with Jacek Kawalec, VoiceLab's founder and Zbigniew Kunecki, accessibility manager at the TVP SA. TVP refuses to disclose information on its accessibility practises and its subtitlers claim to have signed non-disclosure agreements that forbid them from sharing information about their work.

21 Some Polish-language TV channels are registered abroad and as such are supervised by regulatory bodies of their countries of origin. For instance, Ofcom for channels registered in the UK or Commissariaat voor de Media for channels registered in the Netherlands. (Polish-language TV channels which are not registered in Poland tend to be registered in either the UK or the Netherlands for various legal and tax reasons.) Both regulators set different subtitling quotas for foreign TV channels (lower than the ones they set for domestic channels).

with an access service, either subtitling (13.6%), audio description (3.2%) or sign language interpreting (2.7%). That is almost all of the channels fulfilled the required quota of 10%. The main public channel TVP1 had subtitles for 47% of its programming. TVP Seriale and Super Polsat, channels mostly airing re-runs of soap operas, both had subtitles for more than 80% of its shows. Among commercial TV channels airing new content, Canal+ had the most SDH (29%). TVP Sport was the only channel that did not comply with the required quota.

Around the same time a major amendment of the Broadcasting Law[22] was introduced, raising the quota of TV programming with access services to 15% in 2019, 25% starting from 2020, 35% from 2022 and 50% from 2024. The goal for 2019 did not seem particularly ambitious given that already in 2018 the TV channels had subtitles for 15.2% of their programming (KRRiT, 2019, p. 53).

The new law granted the National Broadcasting Council the right to fine-tune these requirements, by specifying which access services should be provided for which types of programming and enforcing more specific quotas (Szczygielska, 2019). As with the previous law, KRRiT had the power to lower the quota for some broadcasters or even grant exemptions.

In November 2018, KRRiT issued a regulation on access services,[23] which included the first legal definition of each access service as well as numerous specific requirements for TV broadcasters. The document differentiated three types of subtitles: SDH, regular (interlingual) subtitling without SDH features, and live subtitling. For the reporting purposes, KRRiT required the broadcasters to report each minute of SDH subtitling or live subtitling as 1, and each minute of regular subtitling as 0.7. This is meant to reflect the fact that regular interlingual subtitling does not offer the same value as an access service as SDH because it lacks sound descriptions and speaker identification, which are important to the Deaf and the hard of hearing viewers.

For the first time, KRRiT determined the make-up of the overall quota, stipulating that in 2024, out of the quota of 50% or programming, at least 40% should have subtitling, 7% audio description and 3% sign language interpreting. The regulator also fine-tuned the requirements, taking into account different types of content. As many as 44% of news shows and chat shows should be subtitled by 2024, with only 10% of children's shows having this requirement. Finally, the shows which are aired between 3 a.m. and 5 a.m. no longer count towards the

---

22   Ustawa z dnia 22 marca 2018 r. o zmianie ustawy o radiofonii i telewizji oraz niektórych innych ustaw [Law of 22 March 2018 amending the Broadcasting Law and certain other acts, Dz.U. 2018, item 459].

23   Dz.U. [Journal of Laws] of 2018, item 2261.

quota (which was an attempt to curb cases where broadcasters subtitled or audio described a limited number of shows and aired their re-runs again and again at a time of lowest viewership).

As the quota goes up to 50% in the following years, many more channels are likely to provide live subtitling, as it will be difficult to meet the requirement with subtitling pre-recorded content only. This is especially true for news channels (that will have to subtitle 44% of its programming), social-religious channels (42%) and sports channels (40%). It should be noted that these are also the channels which tend to include more live programming than others ranging from news bulletins, political talks, through masses and other religious celebrations to broadcasts of sports competitions. This will finally offer more variety to the viewer who for many years have been complaining that SDH is mostly provided for soap operas and feature films (Sacha & Kasperkowiak, 2012).

The first results of the new regulatory framework became evident in 2020 with an increase in the mandatory subtitling quota from 10% to 22% for news and current affairs programmes. For news channels that air mostly live shows (the main being TVP Info, Polsat News and TVN24), this made it more difficult to fulfil the legal obligation subtitling pre-recorded shows only. As TVP Info already had live subtitles for some news programming in the evening, it did not need to do more to meet the quota. However, potentially in an effort to show that as a public broadcaster it is doing more than commercial broadcasters, from March 2020, it started providing live subtitling for some afternoon news shows aired between noon and 3 pm.[24]

---

24 The increase of live subtitling on TVP Info coincided with the electoral campaign before the Polish presidential elections and might have also been motivated politically. In the present work TVP is described as a "public broadcaster" for the sake of clarity. However, in the years 2015–2023 most of its funding came directly from the government or state-owned companies (as opposed to the license fee). In that period, TVP was seen by many as a state-owned broadcaster and propaganda mouthpiece. At the same time, for the Deaf and the hard of hearing viewers who relied on terrestrial television for their news, TVP Info as well as other TVP channels were the only source of subtitled news programmes during the electoral campaign of 2020 (as out of the other two news channels, TVN24 was only available via the satellite or cable TV, and Polsat News was only available terrestrially in some areas of few largest cities). In December 2023, TVP went into a restructuring process as a new government announced plans to make the broadcaster more independent from political pressures. As part of the restructuring, the flagship news broadcast Wiadomości was replaced with a new one, titled 19.30, and created by a new team of journalists. The broadcaster justified the rebranding as an effort to regain credibility and restore viewers' trust.

Polsat News responded to the change in the mandatory quota by starting to provide live subtitles from 15 February 2020 for some of its prime time programming, including the main news bulletin, *Wydarzenia*, aired at 6:50 pm, its main evening political interview, *Gość Wydarzeń*, aired after the news bulletin, a current affairs programme at 9 pm and the evening news at 9:50 pm. The subtitles were then edited and re-used for the re-runs of these shows aired after midnight and early in the morning.

Initially, TVN24 adopted a different approach. Instead of subtitling the evening news shows live, it produced pre-recorded subtitling for the re-runs of these shows, which were aired after midnight. It is not clear, however, if that was enough to meet the mandatory quota. There were also cases reported by users on social media where some morning and evening news programming was identified by the broadcaster as subtitled (with a graphic being shown briefly at the beginning of the show) and yet these shows had no subtitles when broadcast live, and the subtitles were available only for late night re-runs. From the fourth quarter of 2020, TVN24 finally changed its approach and started to provide live subtitles for its evening shows (and not only for re-runs).

2.3.6. Live subtitling in online streaming

While live subtitling is traditionally associated with broadcasting settings, it can also be used online. Live events can be streamed online with the view of allowing more people to participate. As this practice becomes more common, a need arises for streaming live subtitles. This turned out to be a challenge as the existing live subtitling solutions for live events were not designed with streaming in mind. In live events, the aim was to display the text as fast as possible. The text did not have timecodes and it appeared to the users immediately once it was corrected. In live streaming, the video was delayed due to technical reasons, which meant that the text might actually appear before the corresponding utterance is spoken in the video. Thus, to sync the text with the live stream timecodes were necessary. Television subtitling software did produce timecodes but streaming providers had no experience with live subtitling formats used on TV and were unable to use them.

The first cases of live streaming with live subtitles in Polish are linked with the Polish parliament (Sejm) and were streamed on its website at www.sejm.gov.pl. The subtitles did not appear on the video but instead were presented in an area below the video player (this way the subtitles did not cover the video). These were closed subtitles as it was also possible to switch them on or off. The parliament's video player was designed in an accessible way, meaning that the blind or partially-sighted users could read subtitles through screen readers (software that can read out the text through speech synthesis).

The Magic Scribe developers found a way to encode timecodes with each phrase that was recognized by the software in such a way that the Sejm's video player could re-sync the text, minimizing the subtitle latency in a live stream and eliminating it in a recording. The text appeared phrase by phrase as three lines of scrolling text, up to 40 characters per line. The text segmentation could not be controlled as there was no way to introduce a line break.

When other events where streamed by commercial streaming providers, live subtitles were usually displayed as open subtitles (that is, they were overlaid on the image as pixels) and did not have timecodes. This was due to streaming providers using generic video players that did not have an option for receiving and showing subtitles as text. Szczygielska & Dutka (2019) point out that while such a solution serves its purpose for the Deaf and the hard of hearing users, it is imperfect as the subtitles cover part of the image, they cannot be switched off and screen reading software does not recognize such subtitles as text.

2.3.7. Live subtitling during the COVID-19 pandemic

The coronavirus pandemic highlighted the importance of access to information as people relied on the audiovisual media more so than usual. For instance, many crucial health-related information or regulations were announced by the Polish government during press conferences. Although the information was relevant for all citizens, the Deaf and the hard of hearing citizens often did not have access to it. While some conferences had sign language interpreting provided by the organizers (mostly the press conferences organized by the Prime Minister's Office or the Ministry of Health), no conferences had live subtitling available. And even if organizers provided sign language interpreting, the camera operators from television stations often did not include interpreters in some shots, meaning that sign language users could not follow the interpretation when broadcast by a news channel.

Some press conferences could be watched with live subtitling on TVP Info, public broadcaster's news channel. This depended on the timing of the conferences. From March 2020, TVP Info provided live subtitling for news shows between noon and 3 pm and then from 5 pm to 8 pm[25]. If a press conference was organized during these two time windows and was aired live on TVP Info,

---

25 https://www.tvp.pl/dostepnosc/napisy-dla-nieslyszacych (Polish, accessed on February 29, 2024)

it tended to have live subtitles. Press conferences organized before noon had no live subtitling when aired by the public broadcaster.

Regarding live events, in March 2020, the restrictions introduced due to SARS-COV-2 virus pandemic caused most live events to be cancelled or moved online. With this came a challenge of how to provide accessibility for events that are organized online. In the venue, subtitlers were often connected to screens through HDMI cables or wireless receivers. Although live streaming was practiced in the past, it usually meant that the subtitlers and the live streaming provider were sitting in the same room and they were connected locally. Even if subtitling was done remotely, it meant that it was done away from the event venue, but the whole team responsible for subtitling was still working together from the same place. As a result, the previous live subtitling workflows did not work in the time of the pandemic when social distancing rules meant that ideally all people should be working from different locations, without having physical contact with each other.

Some events took a hybrid approach. PARP, The Polish Agency for Enterprise Development, organized a series of 20 online webinars with live subtitling in May 2020. Although all the audience was online, all the people working for the event, including the live subtitlers, were based in a studio in Warsaw. Other events moved fully online with all speakers and the technical staff working remotely.

At the beginning, this meant that live subtitles could only be streamed as open subtitles (an imaged added to the video). Most videoconferencing tools were not ready for live subtitling as a closed service. For instance, although Google Meet and Microsoft Teams do provide automatic subtitling (only in English, though, and with no ability to correct the input), they do not allow live subtitlers to feed their output in the videoconferencing tool and display the subtitles to event participants. Out of major videoconferencing tools used, only ZOOM and Cisco Webex have features allowing human-made live subtitling to be displayed.

Cisco Webex allows a live subtitler to participate in the meeting and input text that is then displayed to participants. The text is not shown on top of the video, it is displayed in a separate, smaller window (see Fig. 7). No parallel correction is possible. Webex also allows the meeting host to share a link to a video or a webpage that will be opened as a small window within Cisco Webex interface. Live subtitles can be shared this way if they are displayed as a webpage.

ALICE SANDREL:
Good morning, all! We
have a full agenda today.
There are also a few
housekeeping things to

∨ Closed Captions   ×

This is an example of a text.

Fig. 7: *Subtitles displayed in Cisco Webex as a separate window within the Webex interface as a website (top) or within Webex's Closed Captions window (bottom)*

ZOOM offers more options with two possible input methods for live subtitling and two display modes. Regarding the input, the tool allows live subtitlers to participate in the meeting and type or dictate text directly within the ZOOM app. As with Cisco Webex, in this first method no parallel correction is possible and once the text is sent it cannot be changed or withdrawn. However, ZOOM also allows the meeting host to generate a special link (called "token") that can be used by external applications to send subtitles to ZOOM. A number of companies have developed their proprietary tools to work with ZOOM and there are now also paid services such as StreamText or OnceCapApp that allow live subtitlers to connect with ZOOM. This way, parallel correction is possible as the text can be dictated by one person and edited by another before it is displayed to meeting participants.

Regarding display methods, similarly to Webex, ZOOM can display subtitles in a separate window. Once a live subtitler sends the first subtitle to ZOOM, a new "Closed Captioning" icon appears to the participants of a meeting or a webinar. The users can choose the option "View Transcript" or "View Subtitles". When they choose the first option, rather than one-line or two-line subtitles,

ZOOM displays blocks of many lines of text and adds a timestamp at some intervals. The user can scroll back to see earlier text, search through the text for specific words and save all the text as a .TXT file.

The second display method is more akin to television subtitling as ZOOM shows one, two or three lines of text with a maximum of 50 characters per line (see Fig. 8). If more text is sent at once and it cannot fit within the three lines, the rest of the text will be truncated and will not be displayed this way (although it will still be displayed in the Transcript window once the user opens it). The subtitles can also be displayed word by word if the text is sent this way.

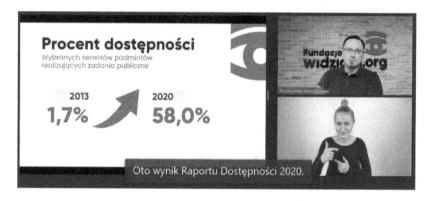

Fig. 8: *A closed subtitle displayed in ZOOM on top of the video*

Depending on the version of the ZOOM app and the device used, a number of customization options might be available. Users can click on a subtitle and move it around the screen, this way changing the position of subtitles (for instance, to uncover speakers' mouth or an important graphic in a presentation). In the "Subtitle options", the user can also make subtitles bigger or smaller.

ZOOM displays open subtitles, which means they will not be saved to the meeting recording as part of the video. They might instead by saved as a separate .VTT files with timecodes. This file can then be edited if needed and used to display subtitles when the recording of the meeting is shared. The fact that ZOOM uses open subtitles also offers an advantage for users of screen readers as subtitles can be read out by synthetic voices. Indeed, blind users can navigate all of ZOOM interface with keyboard and a screen reader and ZOOM offers customization options so that for instance, during the meeting, only the subtitles will be read out by the scree nreader (as opposed to the chat messages, for instance).

In Poland, Dostepni.eu collaborated with Bartosz Marganiec, a Deaf programmer, to develop a tool that would be able to send subtitles to ZOOM, would allow for parallel correction and would enable respeakers and live correctors to work remotely. The first event with Polish live subtitles in ZOOM was a meeting by a Warsaw-based NGO Kulawa Warszawa on May 19, 2020.

Other teams of live subtitlers started to appear too. Polska Bez Barier [Poland Without Barriers], an NGO, partnered with a group of live subtitlers working for TVP, and started offering subtitling for some of its online webinars with first events in September 2020. The subtitles were displayed as text in a Google Docs document (see Fig. 9) that event participants can open as a separate window next to the live video stream. Each speaker was identified with first and last name. An utterance of each new speaker was displayed as a new paragraph. The was dictated by a respeaker was immediately shown to the users who were also able to see the corrections made afterwards. The cursor position of the respeaker and the live correctors were graphically identified by the Google document interface, which could be distracting to users but also brought users' attention to places where the edits were being made.

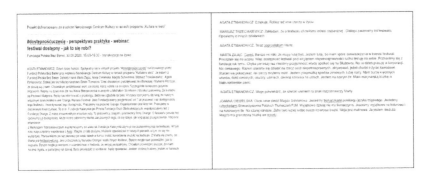

Fig. 9: *Live transcription for an event organized by Polska Bez Barier Foundation (the text is displayed in the form of a Google document)*

Following a near-ban on abortion, mass protests erupted across Poland in October 2020 with social media and live streams being an important communication tools for protesters. The Deaf and hard of hearing who participated in the protests or followed them took to the social media to ask for sign language interpreting or subtitles.

Providing accessibility for protests and social media messaging around is a challenge, especially when protests are organized by informal structures and have no or little funding. Demonstrations at least are usually called some time in advance, whereas live streams can be entirely spontaneous as people react to events unfolding. This lead to what we could call activist accessibility with sign language interpreters, for instance, volunteering to provide interpretation for speeches during demonstrations. Katarzyna Bierzanowska, a disability rights activist herself and a live subtitler at TVP, organized an online fundraiser (see Fig. 10) where she collected money for "accessible reactions", including audio description of social media posts related to the protest, sign language interpreting and what she called "live transcription".

Fig. 10: *Screenshot from an online fundraiser page which aimed to collect money for making the audiovisual reactions to the protest accessible (source: private archive of the author)*

Indeed, with her colleagues she provided live transcription, for instance, for a press conference of the Ogólnopolski Strajk Kobiet [All-Poland Women's Strike], an umbrella organization coordinating the protests. The transcription was again available as a Google document (see Fig. 11) and, interestingly, journalists could use it to quote declarations from the press conference that they would normally need to transcribe themselves.

However, this event showed a limitation of this method. As too many users tried to access live transcription during the press conference, the document displayed an error message of "overload"[26] and, users no longer saw changes made to the document. In other words, new text no longer appeared as if the transcription stopped. Reloading the document allowed a user to see new text but it had to be repeated every few seconds.

Fig. 11: *A screenshot of a Facebook post (left) announcing a press conference organized by Ogólnopolski Strajk Kobiet [All-Poland Women's Strike] and the document with the live transcription of the event (source: private archive of the author)*

Note. The post contains a link to a live stream on Instagram followed by information that the sign language interpretation is available as a separate live stream. The post also includes the link the document where the live transcription of the event is available.

Such accessibility activism seems an interesting solution to provide access to demonstrations and spontaneous live streams when traditional business model of providing accessibility is impossible or too slow to use.

2.3.8. The beginnings of automatic live subtitling in Polish

A new Polish law[27] enacted on 4 April 2019 as an implementation of The Web Accessibility Directive, an EU-wide attempt to make public sector websites more

---

26 As per Google Docs documentation the maximum number of users that can access a Google document simultaneously and see the changes being made there is up to 100. Source: https://support.google.com/drive/answer/2494822 (accessed: February 17, 2021)

27 Ustawa z dnia 4 kwietnia 2019 r. o dostępności cyfrowej stron internetowych i aplik-acji mobilnych podmiotów publicznych [Act of April 4, 2019 on digital accessibility of websites and mobile applications of public entities], Dz.U. [Journal of Laws] of 2019, item 848 https://isap.sejm.gov.pl/isap.nsf/DocDetails.xsp?id=WDU20190000848

accessible, required all public bodies to provide subtitles for all the video materials they publish on their websites or their official profiles on YouTube or social
media. This new requirement affects all videos published after 23 September
2020 and all public organizations, from big national agencies to small local organizations. The legislation makes an exception for live streams and only requires
pre-recorded subtitling, allowing institutions 14 days to prepare them. Still, for
small organizations it is a challenge as it often means they now try to provide
subtitling for the first time, something they might have never done before and
have no experience with.

In the second half of 2020, this lead a number of companies to start offering
the service of providing subtitling for videos: either in a fully automatic way or
with some post-editing. Providers usually rely on commercially available cloud
speech recognition from Google, Microsoft or Amazon; a few use their own proprietary speech recognition technologies. Some also started offering such service
for live streams.

For instance, Voice Lab[28] (based in Gdańsk, Poland) and Newton
Technologies[29] (based in Prague, the Czech Republic; under the brand BeeY)
offer automatic subtitling in Polish based on their own speech recognition technology. A user uploads a video and receives an automatic transcription that can
then be post-edited by the user and exported as an .SRT subtitle file. VoiceLab
also offers to do post-editing as a separate service. Both companies claim their
solution can be used for live streams as well. However, both have a significant
processing delay. In other words, the tool analyses a longer portion of the video
(or a live stream) in advance before starting to produce transcription. In the case
of BeeY, the processing delay is up to 30 seconds[30], which makes it difficult to
apply in TV settings.

Stream360, a streaming provider based in Szczecin, Poland, offers automatic
subtitles for live streams. The service is fully automatic with no post-editing.
The text does not include any punctuation and words seem to be capitalized at
random. The way the text is divided into subtitles and how these are segmented
does not seem to follow any particular rules (see Fig. 12). Crucially, when some
words are misrecognized, the text becomes unintelligible. The company uses a
player that allows to display open subtitles.

---

28   https://napisy.voicelab.pl/
29   https://www.beey.io/pl/#features
30   Personal communication with Krzysztof Struk, company representative in Poland;
      December 2020.

Fig. 12: *Automatic subtitling provided by stream360.pl (screenshots from an example video the company provides on its website[31])*

Another provider, Posiedzenia.pl, aims it services at the local government councils and it provides hardware and software for live streaming, recording and archiving of the proceedings of local government's bodies. It offers automatic subtitling for recordings but also for live streams. In the examples of automatic subtitling provided by the company on their website, the subtitles include punctuation and sentences start with capital letters (it is not clear if this is done automatically or in post-editing).Subtitle segmentation seems to be done at random. As the punctuation is not taken into account when the text is divided into subtitles, the subtitles often start or end mid-sentence (see Fig. 13). The company uses YouTube as its video player (which allows for open subtitling) but they display closed subtitling.

Fig. 13: *Examples of automatic subtitling from Posiedzenia.pl (source: private archive of the author)*

Note. Subtitle segmentation ignores punctuation with subtitles starting and ending mid-sentence (as indicated by the red arrows).

---

31   https://stream360.pl/index.php/streaming-info/165-napisy-otwarte-w-transmisjach-na-zywo (Accessed on February 29, 2024)

LiveAffect, a brand operated by Expertlab, based in Warsaw, offers live subtitling as one of a number of services related to live streaming. They use their own proprietary video player and can display subtitles or sign language interpreting as open services (allowing the user to switch them on or off). The player can also pause the video to automatically, allowing extra space for audio description. However, the company does not provide examples of events where live subtitling would be provided this way and I was unable to identify any such events.

2.3.9. The current state of live subtitling in Poland

The past few years saw a growth in how much live subtitling is available in Polish across television, live events and online streaming. In the television market, the first results of the 2018 regulation were felt at the beginning of 2020, where the increased quota came into effect. In February, Polsat News started providing live subtitling for some of its prime time shows. And in March 2020, after 10-year break, TVP re-started live subtitling for the news show *Teleexpress,* now aired both on TVP1 and the news channel TVP Info. It also added live subtitling for afternoon broadcasts on TVP Info between noon and 3 pm. TVN24 first started subtitling the after-midnight re-runs of its flagship news bulletin *Fakty* and the political chat show *Kropka nad i.* From October 2020, it started providing live subtitling for some of its prime time news programming.

The major news channels in Poland (in the order of audience share, as per Nielsen Audience Measurement, February 2020[32]) are TVN24, TVP Info, Polsat News, TVP3 and TVN24 BiS. TVP Info and TVP3[33] are broadcast terrestrially in the whole country, while Polsat News can be received terrestrially in some regions only. All three channels are also available on satellite and on cable TV. TVN24 and TVN24 BiS are only available on cable and on satellite. While the terrestrial channels are freely available to all the viewers, cable and satellite channels tend to require additional equipment or are included in paid TV packages. In the case of cable TV providers, subtitling might or might not be available depending on the signal provider.

As of February 2020, on weekdays the public broadcaster news channel TVP Info broadcasts up to 320 minutes of new content with live subtitling (excluding

---

32 https://www.wirtualnemedia.pl/artykul/ogladalnosc-kanalow-informacyjnych-luty-2020-tvn24-rekord-polsat-news (in Polish, accessed on February 29, 2024)

33 It should be noted that TVP3 is technically a network of regional channels which combine joint national and separate regional programming. TVP3 airs regional news shows, each of which is only broadcast in part of the Polish territory.

re-runs of news broadcasts and other pre-recorded content after midnight).[34] Polsat News airs up to 120 minutes of new content with live subtitling.[35] Similarly to TVP Info, Polsat News re-runs the subtitled news shows after midnight, and airs some pre-recorded shows with subtitles. TVN 24 and TVN 24 BiS do not include on their websites information on broadcasts with subtitles. Analysis of prime-time broadcasts between 5 pm and 11 pm done from April 6 to April 10 2020 showed that TVP3 does not have subtitling for news broadcasts.

Major general channels Polsat and TVN do not broadcast live subtitling. In the case of Polsat, the flagship news show *Wydarzenia* does not have subtitles on the main channel but it is subtitled on Polsat News where it airs simultaneously. The situation is similar with TVN and its news show Fakty. Main public channels TVP1 and TVP2 have live subtitling for their news bulletins (*Teleexpress, Panorama, Wiadomości*), all of which are simultaneously aired with subtitles on TVP Info.

As SDH becomes more available on terrestrial television, it is important to point out that more and more people view television via the Internet on their smartphones, tablets, laptops or TV sets. As early as 2012, the Deaf and the hard of hearing users organizations demanded that if a show is broadcast with subtitles on TV, these subtitles should also be made available when the show appears on the broadcaster's VOD platform (Sacha & Kasperkowiak, 2012). However, neither the law of 2011 nor its subsequent amendments covered the accessibility of online audiovisual content such as live streaming or VOD.

As of February 2021, the survey of four streaming services that allow Polish viewers to watch terrestrial TV channels online (Horizon Go by UPC, Orange TV Go, WP Pilot, TVN24 GO, Canal+) showed that SDH subtitles are not available in online streaming even if they are provided when the channels are broadcast terrestrially. In fact, some video players used by these services do not even display an option to turn on subtitles (the only exceptions being Orange TV GO and Canal+).

The three major Polish TV broadcasters (TVP, Polsat, TVN) allow viewers to watch some or all of its broadcasts streamed live on its VOD platforms (TVP

---

34 Calculated based on the broadcaster's website, for the period from April 6 to April 10: https://www.tvp.pl/dostepnosc/napisy-dla-nieslyszacych

35 Calculated based on the broadcaster's website, for the period from April 6 to April 10: https://www.polsatnews.pl/program-tv/ (The show durations that the broadcaster provides include commercials. Commercials were excluded from the calculation, taking into account that there's on average 12 minutes of commercials per hour).

VOD, Ipla.pl by Polsat and Player.pl by TVN/Discovery). Online streaming is free for TVP channels and it is a paid subscription in the case of Polsat and TVN. None of the broadcasters make subtitling available in their online streams.

Currently, international streaming platforms are not regulated by Polish or EU law. If they provide SDH in Polish, they do it as a good practice. For instance, as of February 2021, Netflix provides Polish SDH for most of Polish productions and a few English productions which touch on the lives of the Deaf (for instance, *The Deaf U* or *Audible*). Otherwise English shows tend to have SDH only in English with non-English shows having SDH available in their main language and in English. As of 2022, some new English-speaking content also has SDH available in several other languages but not in Polish.

To sum up, subtitling is rarely available online for most TV content even if the content has been subtitled when broadcast terrestrially. Only public institutions are required to subtitle its online audiovisual content, as stipulated in the law on the accessibility of public web pages (Szczygielska, 2019). However, the requirement refers only to pre-recorded content. SDH is not legally required in cinemas, on DVDs/Blu-ray Discs or in VOD. It should be noted, however that from 2016, the Polish Film Institute requires that all feature films which receive its financial support need to have SDH and audio description, which have to be made available to cinemas.

2.3.10. Challenges for the future

As 108 Polish TV channels regulated by National Broadcasting Council increase their provision of subtitles, with the overall mandatory quota for access services set to rise to 50% by 2024, many channels will have to start providing live subtitles and continue doing so at scale, sustaining and improving quality so as to make sure that this service addresses the needs of the viewers. This will be an organizational challenge for TV stations that will need to set up in-house live subtitling units or find external providers. Either way, this will require the development of new workflows and practices. It will also be a challenge for training live subtitlers as many more professionals will be needed. Parallel to that, as television broadcasting moves to the Internet, the regulations will need to catch up to avoid the paradox of more and more access services being available for terrestrial TV, watched by fewer and fewer viewers.

Taking into account the paths of other countries, once the provision of subtitling reaches a high level, the regulator should probably (and the Deaf and the hard of hearing viewers will certainly) focus more on monitoring the quality of subtitling.

Chapter 3: Technology: Methods and tools for creating live subtitling

3.1. Methods of creating live subtitles

Although live subtitling is seen by some as synonymous with respeaking (Pérez-González, 2014, p. 25), there are, in fact, various different methods of producing live subtitling. Although the present work is mainly concerned with respeaking, it is important to consider other methods, not least to determine how they compare to respeaking. This section aims to provide an overview of different methods that are used to produce lives subtitling and determine which of them can be used for live subtitling in Polish.

The methods can divided into keyboard-based and SR-based. The keyboard-based methods involve typing and the most common ones are: stenography, QWERTY keyboard, dual keyboard, and Velotype keyboard (Lambourne, 2006; Romero Fresco, 2011, 2018b). SR-based methods include automatic speech recognition (ASR), ASR with human post-editing, respeaking with self-correction and respeaking with parallel correction.

The main criteria to evaluate the available methods is their speed, the percentage of errors, the ease of finding or training subtitlers skilled in a given method and whether the method is language-dependent or not. Of these criteria, the basic one is speed as it is important to be able to follow live speech, given that speech on TV can be quite fast with news speech rate in English in the UK as fast as 180 words per minute (Lambourne, 2006) and the average speech rate on news shows in Polish found to be 134 words per minute (see Section 6.5).

3.1.1. Stenography and stenotyping

There is some terminological confusion related to stenography and stenotyping as these terms are sometimes used interchangeably (Jankowska, 2020). In fact, stenography refers to the process of writing in shorthand, which does not require any equipment, other than pen and paper. While stenotyping is a system of machine shorthand. In other words, it is a machine-based type of stenography. it always requires the use of a stenotype, also known as a steno machine (Romero Fresco, 2011).

A stenotype is a sort of a chorded keyboard (see Fig. 14). While on a regular keyboard, the typist normally presses a single key to produce one letter, a chorded keyboard allows its operator to press multiple keys (i.e. a chord). Not all the letters are present on the stenotype keyboard and typing is based on the phonetics rather than orthography so the operator has to presses a key or a couple of keys for each sound but not for each letter in a word (Downey, 2008). Pressing a combination of keys with a single hand motion can produce whole words or even phrases, which allows for a much faster typing with experienced operators typing speed ranging from 220 to 300 words per minute (wpm) Lambourne (2006) notes that stenotypists which work for live television (called "stenocaptionists" in the US) can provide subtitles at the speed of 180 to 200 words per minute; as compared to respeakers who can transcribe utterances at the speed ranging from 140 to 160 words (Lambourne, 2006). Indeed, the speed of stenotyping is its biggest advantage. As of now, no other method can match such speeds and skilled stenotypists can work with any audiovisual genres, including fast-paced news or debates.

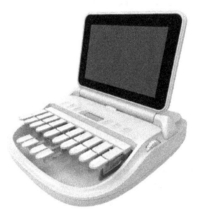

Fig. 14: *A typical steno machine (a model sold by Stenograph, a manufacture of steno machines based in the US) (source: Stenograph press materials)*

However, there are two significant limitations linked with this method. First of all, the stenotyping systems are not universal and have to be developed with a specific language in mind. While in some languages such as English, French or Spanish, stenotype systems has been used for years, for other languages they might be non-existent. Developing a machine-based system involves designing a keyboard layout and set a of rules for pressing combinations of keys that would make it possible to spell out specific words and phrases that are used in a given language

For instance, a number of shorthand systems for the Polish languages were used in the past and some people might still be using them, but a machine-based system was not yet developed (Domagała-Zyśk, 2017), which means that steno-typing cannot be used to produce live subtitling in Polish. Attempting to type in Polish using a steno machine will be pointless, as the software will only be producing English words and phrases.

But even if a stenotyping system is available for a given language, mastering the technique requires from two to four years of training (Romero Fresco, 2011). As skilled stenotypists are not easy to find, they usually receive high remuneration, which makes this method more expensive. And recruiting a large number of stenotypists can be challenging. While stenotyping is widely used in the USA and to some extent in Canada, Australia and the UK (Lambourne, 2006; Romero Fresco, 2011) as well as Italy (Ramondelli, 2006), this method is not available for most languages.

3.1.2. QWERTY keyboard

QWERTY is the standard computer keyboard layout and with some regional variations (such as QWERTZ in some German-speaking countries or AZERTY in French-speaking countries), it is used across the globe. QWERTY keyboards have been used to create live subtilting as far as 1982 by ITV in the UK to subtitle headlines of a visit of the Pope and the football World Cap (Romero Fresco, 2011).

The main advantage of this method is simplicity and ease of use as QWERTY keyboards are ubiquitous and finding skilled typists is much easier than in the case of stenotyping. The main disadvantage of this method is that it is very slow. An average professional typists reaches a speed of 50–70 wpm with the average speech rate of TV presenters around 180 wpm in English (Lambourne, 2006). For comparison, when 134 Polish students taking part in the respeaking course at the University of Warsaw in the years 2017–2020 were tested, their average typing speed in Polish was just 34.7 wpm. Interestingly, their typed faster in English (reaching on average 48 wpm). Sustaining even such speeds over long run might be difficult and misspellings become more common as typists get tired. Therefore, this method allows to present only a summary of what is being said.

3.1.3. Dual keyboard

A method known as dual keyboard, aims to overcome the speed limitation of typing on a QWERTY keyboard through a set-up involving two operators working in tandem and transcribing alternate utterances. Lambourne (2006) reports that the dual keyboard method can produce high-quality subtitles at up to 150 wpm with training taking 6 months. In theory, the speed can be improved further by adding more operators. Catalan broadcaster TV3 is known to have modified this method even further by allowing up to five subtitlers transcribing utterances simultaneously (Romero Fresco, 2011). The method does require software that would coordinate the work of two or more typists. So far, it has never been used in Polish (Domagała-Zyśk, 2017) as no broadcaster has developed such software. After doing a survey of live subtitling software currently available on the market, I did not find any software that would support the dual keyboard method.

3.1.4. Velotype keyboard

Another alternative method is Velotype, which similarly to stenotyping, uses a chorded keyboard, but, unlike stenotyping, Velotype is not based on the principles of stenography. The Velotype was invented in the Netherlands by Nico Berkelmans and Marius den Outer and initially it was called Veyboard (van Noorden, 1988). Up until today this method is most prevalent in the Netherlands (de Korte, 2006).

Fig. 15: *A Velotype keyboard (source: Velotype press materials)*

Unlike stenography, Velotype is not based on pronunciation but follows closely ortography. Typists can press multiple keys (including multiple letter keys) in one stroke. The layout of the Velotype (see Fig. 15) is designed in such a way that the typist can press even two keys with one finger, thus theoretically as many as 10 keys could be pressed with one hand motion. When using a regular QWERTY keyboard, the typists can write letter by letter, with Velotype they can go syllable by syllable or word by word. Advanced users can also start using shortforms, where for most frequent letter combinations or word endings they no longer have to press a key for every letter they want to type, thus saving time.

Users might expect that being able to press so many keys at once should result in a dramatic increase in the typing speed. However, as typing motions are much more complex with Velotype (involving coordinated pressing movements by up 10 fingers rather than just one, two and three as with regular keyboards), typing a combination of keys on a Velotype keyboard takes considerably more time than pressing a combination of keys on a QWERTY keyboard (van Noorden, 1988). For instance, while users of Velotype can spell out a word "good" (4 letters) with just one motion, typists using QWERTY can press keys faster and are able to press two or three letters consecutively in the same time it takes to press fours keys simultaneously on Velotype. Therefore, while Velotype is still faster than QWERTY keyboards, the speed difference is not as dramatic as could be expected.

Thus, Velotype is not as fast as stenography and average sustained speeds for live subtitling achieved by Velotype typists are around 90–120 wpm (Lambourne, 2006). Still, Velotype has a number of advantages. The equipment is cheaper and the training is simpler (no need to master the principles of stenography), shorter (the speeds noted by Lambourne are after 12 months of training). Also, the training is free add-on to the keyboard itself. The manufacturer of Velotype, created a self-learning tool Velotype Academy, and claims it is enough to practise for six months, an hour a day, to master the keyboard.

Velotype (like stenotyping) needs to be adapted for each language (combinations of key presses need to be mapped to syllables and words used in a given language). However, in recent years, the manufacturer created keyboard layouts and adapted its training software for more than 20 languages, including Polish. However, Velotype is still mostly used in the Netherlands, Belgium, the UK and Sweden. As per the information from the company, there were just a few users who attempted to use Velotype in Polish.[36] So far, it has never been used to provide live subtitling (Szczygielska & Dutka, 2019). I attempted to learn typing on a Velotype keyboard. However, after six months of practice, I still typed slower on Velotype than on a QWERTY keyboard. Also, the Polish implementation of Velotype still needs to be improved before this method can be used for live subtitling as occasionally typing some more complex combinations of letters in Polish is not feasible as the positions of fingers required to make the relevant key presses are not anatomically impossible.

---

36 Personal communication with Sander Pasveer and Wim Gerbecks from Velotype VOF.

3.1.5. Automatic Speech Recognition

Automatic Speech Recognition (ASR) can be used to create transcripts without human involvement and has been used for quite some time (Peacocke & Graf, 1990). However, speech recognition tends to produce errors, or misrecognitions (see Section 3.2. for a detailed discussion of speech recognition technology). The number of errors is especially high if the quality of audio is low and there are background noises as well as when speakers use terminology or proper names that the ASR system was not trained for. Also, ASR tends to better recognize the speech if it has been trained on the voice of a specific speaker (or a speaker of similar voice characteristics).

The advantage of ASR is the fact it can produce a verbatim transcript of the speech no matter how fast speakers talk (this could be argued to also be a disadvantage in the case of live subtitling as transcribing all words can translate into very high subtitle speeds). However, the main disadvantage is that ASR can also produce so many misrecognitions that the resulting text is very difficult to understand. So far, ASR has not produced good results for live subtitling in Polish (Szczygielska & Dutka, 2019). While some TV broadcasters do use ASR to create live subtitles, most notably in the US, it is not currently seen as a viable method (Saerens et al., 2020).

ASR can be improved by adding human posteditors that correct the text live. However, in the case of fast speech rates typical for TV programmes, ASR produces a lot of text that editors struggle to correct in time. While previous research found that human correction can significantly improve the quality of the ASR output (Szczygielska & Dutka, 2016), the output was still not good enough to be used for creating live subtitles. While advances in speech recognition technology can make it more realistic in the future to use ASR with human postediting as a method of creating live subtitles, high subtitle speeds might still be a concern.

3.1.6. Respeaking

Respeaking was conceived as a method to produce real-time subtitles for the Deaf and hard of hearing for live programmes (Romero Fresco, 2011). With respeaking the quality of speech recognition output can be improved (as compared to ASR) because the respeaker, trained in the use of speech recognition, acts as a sort of a filter that ensures good audio quality, consistent voice characteristics, volume, intonation and speech rate. Respeaking can involve repeating, re-phrasing or translating from one language to another and respeaker can add punctuation as well as speaker identifiers or sound descriptions.

The terminology used to talk about respeaking varies with many terms used to describe the same practice. Romero Fresco (2011) lists as many as eight different terms just for English. While the term respeaking is now widely used both in the academia and in the industry in Europe (Romero Fresco, 2018b), the alternative term *voice writing* continues to be employed in the US. While some languages have localized the term respeaking (for instance: *rehablado* in Spanish, *rispeaker-aggio* in Italian, *sous-titrage vocal* or *la technique du perroquet* in French), other languages such as Polish or German adopted the calque from English.

Similarly to previous methods, respeaking requires a computer and at least two types of software. Firstly, a speech recognition application that recognizes the respeaker's utterances and can output text. Secondly, a subtitling application that shows the recognized utterances as subtitles on screen (Romero Fresco, 2011). Respeaking can be carried out in different set-ups involving one person to up to three (see Section 3.1.7.).

The main advantages of respeaking as method of creating live subtitles involve the fact that it can be used in many languages (as long as speech recognition technology is available), it does not require such a long training as in the case of stenotyping (Arumí Ribas & Romero Fresco, 2008) and it can still produce text output at very fast speeds, from 140 to 160 words (Lambourne, 2006). A disadvantage of this method is that it tends to take a bit longer to produce text this way (as both the respeaker and the speech recognition software need some time to process the utterances). Depending on the effectiveness of the speech recognition software (which will be discusses in Section 3.2) and the training of the respeaker, respeaking will create more or less errors (misrecognitions) and correcting them also takes time. Thus, respeaking can produce more delay than stenotyping.

It should be noted, however, that the delay caused by the process of respeaking does not have to translate in the latency live subtitles as seen by the TV audience. There is always a slight delay inherent in live broadcasting as the satellite or terrestrial signal takes some time to reach viewers' devices. This means that all television viewers will see the show a second or two after the audience in the studio. If respeakers receive audio and video signal through a direct link from the TV studio before the signal is actually broadcast, they might gain a second or two, which will mean that the subtitles will have less delay. On top of that, the broadcaster might decide to delay the signal, (which is sometimes done, for instance, to censor strong language), which is known as antenna delay (Saerens et al., 2020) might results in subtitles being displayed with no latency or even ahead of the content (Romero Fresco, 2011).

3.1.7. Respeaking with self-correction vs. respeaking with parallel correction

There are three approaches to correction: no correction, self-correction and parallel correction (Romero Fresco, 2011). No correction reduces the latency of subtitles but results in more errors seen by viewers. On the other hand, trying to achieve error-free subtitles might result in high latency so it is a delicate balance that has to be found. If there is a correction stage, it might happen either before the subtitles are sent to the screen or once they are already live. Correction can be done by the respeaker (self-correction) or by another subtitlers (parallel correction). Parallel correction can be carried out by one person (as typical in Belgium and Poland) or even two people (France 2 and TF1 in France). Romero Fresco (2011, p. 16) notes that the French broadcasters achieve this way "error-free subtitles" at the cost of up to 15 second delay between the audio and the subtitles.

In the UK, the most common approach is self-correction carried out after the text has been displayed. That means that once an utterance is recognized, it is automatically sent to be displayed. If the respeaker notices an error (a misrecognition), depending on the company and live subtitling software used, they can either press a button to remove the last utterance from the screen and dictate it again or leave the error on screen and dictate the correct version preceded by a hyphen. The assumption is that viewers will recognize this convention and will know it is a correction. While Romero Fresco (2011) notes that the latter technique is more common, either way the viewers might see the error, even if briefly.

An alternative is not to have the text displayed immediately once it is recognized, but wait till the respeaker decides that the utterance is ready to be displayed and presses a key or dictates a command that sends the text. It is possible to combine such a command with punctuation so that, for instance, dictating a full stop will also send all the text up to this point. If the respeaker spots an error, he or she can decide not to send the text and then go on to correct it either with the use of a keyboard or by selecting the misrecognized word or phrase and dictating it again, overwriting the previous version. Once the error has been corrected, the respeaker sends the text to the screen. The advantage of this approach is that the viewers will only see the final, corrected version. However, they might have to wait a few more seconds to see the text as the correction time will add up to the delay.

Finally, the correction can be done in parallel to respeaking. It can be argued that respeaking is already a challenging task as is and adding the extra burden of self-correction might result in cognitive overload (Chmiel et al., 2017). In the case of parallel correction, the respeaker can fully focus on listening to the speakers and dictating the text, while another subtitler spots and corrects the errors. Romero Fresco (2011) notes that the delay involved in self-correction is always smaller than in parallel correction, but this is not necessarily true. Although in many cases the parallel correction does increases the latency of subtitles, if the recognized utterances are displayed automatically and the correction is done on the already displayed text (which might not always be possible on TV but it is much easier at live events), it will have no impact on the delay, which would be impossible to achieve with self-correction as self-correction will always impact delay. After all, if there is continuous speech, as the respeaker is correcting an error in one utterance, they cannot respeak the next utterance. Indeed, while the respeaker is performing the correction, they might miss the next utterances altogether. And even if they are able to split their attention and follow the next utterances, they might have to omit some of them or summarise them to compensate for the time it took to make the correction. (See Section 5.7 for a more detailed discussion of self-correction and parallel correction as well as their impact on the quality of live subtitles.)

3.1.8. The best method(s) for Polish

As we have seen in the previous sections, there are various methods available for creating live subtitling. However, not all of them are available in Polish. While stenotyping can produce impressive speeds, it is only available for several languages such as English, French, Spanish and Italian (not to mention the issues with finding skilled stenotypists or training them). As of now, steno machines cannot be used to create text in Polish as no Polish system of stenography has been adapted to work on a computer.

While in theory Velotype can be used in Polish, making it work for live subtitling would require improvements in the implementation of the Polish language in the Velotype software as well as training numerous Velotype typists. It is not clear if such efforts would succeed given that currently there are no Polish typists that use Velotype on a regular basis.

Using QWERTY keyboards for live subtitling in Polish is possible but does not produce satisfactory results as the typing speeds achieved on regular keyboards are not fast enough as compared to typical speech rates. While using more than one typists simultaneously (the dual keyboard method) could theoretically solve that, there is no software on the market that would allow such solution to be tested.

Summing up, respeaking with parallel correction seems currently the best method available for creating live subtitling in Polish. It is faster than using keyboards and allows live subtitlers to match typical speech rates found on television. Also, it requires relatively short training period.[37] And attempts at training respeakers in Polish have already been successful, especially in the case of training students who received some previous training in interpreting (Szarkowska et al., 2018). As respeaking relies on speech recognition, in the following sections we will look at the speech recognition technology, which will allow us to gain a better understanding of respeaking, as well as its potential and limitations.

3.2. Speech recognition technology

This section briefly introduces the field of speech and language processing. It attempts to describe the challenges of speech recognition, the process itself and the components of speech recognitions systems. This understanding is crucial to appreciate the specific difficulties in recognizing speech in Polish.

3.2.1. Speech processing

The speech and language technology takes its roots in computer science, linguistics, mathematics, electrical engineering, and psychology (Jurafsky & Martin, 2019). The goal of this field is to get computers to perform useful tasks involving human language, such as enabling human-machine communication, improving human-human communication, or simply doing useful processing of text or speech . Interestingly, language technology can be seen as a form of "assistive" technology that "helps overcome the 'disability' of linguistic diversity and makes language communities more accessible to each other"(Miłkowski, 2012, p. 43). It finds various applications areas such as computer-assisted language learning software, plagiarism detection systems or social media monitoring.

From the very beginnings of the field of speech and language processing, one of the main interests has been to develop conversational agents or dialogue systems, that is systems that converse with humans in natural language. The various components that make up conversational agents include language input (automatic speech recognition and natural language understanding) and language output (dialogue and response planning and speech synthesis) (Jurafsky & Martin, 2009).

While conversational agents still cannot match human abilities in communication, components such as speech recognition (speech-to-text) or speech

---

37   Monika Szczygielska from Dostępni.eu, a Polish accessibility services provider, estimates that it takes three months to train a respeaker.

synthesis (text-to-speech) have been perfected over the years (Benzeghiba et al., 2007; Huang et al., 2014; Miłkowski, 2012) and are now readily available for many languages (Besacier et al., 2014). Speech recognition in particular has now become a part of everyday life. People encounter it when talking to (semi-)automated call centres, controlling their car navigational systems by voice, dictating a text message or searching through online videos (Jurafsky & Martin, 2009).

It should be noted that automatic speech recognition (ASR) is separate from the technology for natural language understanding. This is a crucial distinction to bear in mind from the perspective of respeaking. While ASR allows computers to recognize speech and turn it into text, ASR in itself does not allow machines to understand language as humans do (Huang et al., 2014). What ASR can do is to identify words that are read aloud or spoken into a sound-recording device such as a microphone. While the ultimate purpose of ASR technology is to allow 100% accuracy with all words that are intelligibly spoken by any person regardless of vocabulary size, background noise, or speaker variables (In-Seok Kim, 2006), in practise, the SR systems rarely achieve 100% in real life.

3.2.2. The process of speech recognition

Automatic speech recognition (ASR) converts a speech signal into a textual representation, i.e. sequence of said words by means of an algorithm (Besacier et al., 2014). One of the major challenges of ASR systems is to accurately recognize the words a user utters. This is more difficult, the less restricted is the range of possible user utterances (Miłkowski, 2012). Based on this restriction, several types of natural speech and corresponding ASR systems are identified: spelled speech (with pauses between letters or phonemes), isolated speech (with pauses between words), continuous speech (when a speaker does not make any pauses between words), spontaneous speech (e.g. in a human-to-human dialog), and highly conversational speech (e.g. meetings and discussions of several people) (Besacier et al., 2014). ASR systems tend to struggle more with spontaneous speech and highly conversational speech.

When analysing speech, ASR systems search through a space of phoneme sequences for the correct word. This is difficult as the acoustic input is usually ambiguous, that is "multiple, alternative linguistic structures can be built for it"(- Jurafsky & Martin, 2009, p. 4). The most difficult task in speech recognition is resolving ambiguity. To do it well, state-of-the-art ASR systems generate multiple recognition hypotheses about an input and then evaluate them using various language models to output the best recognition hypothesis (Besacier et al., 2014).

The section below briefly describes the architecture of a typical ASR system and how such a system is created. Then it goes on to discuss in more details the main components of ASR systems.

3.2.3. The architecture of ASR systems

General architecture of a standard ASR system is presented in Fig. 16. It integrates three main components: acoustic (acoustic–phonetic) modelling, lexical modelling (pronunciation lexicon/vocabulary) and language modelling (Besacier et al., 2014).

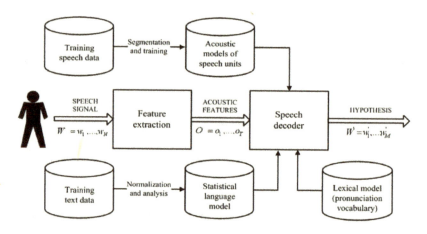

Fig. 16: *The architecture of a state-of-the-art automatic speech recognition system and its components (Besacier et al., 2014, p. 90)*

The task of speech recognition requires knowledge about phonetics and phonology: how words are pronounced in terms of sequences of sounds (Jurafsky & Martin, 2009). Speech and language technology relies on formal models, or representations, of the knowledge of language at the levels of phonology and phonetics, morphology, syntax, semantics, pragmatics and discourse. A number of formal models including state machines, formal rule systems, logic, and probabilistic models are used to capture this knowledge.

Humans acquire language skills in two different ways: learning from examples and learning the underlying language rules. ASR systems "acquire" language capabilities in a similar manner (Miłkowski, 2012). First, ASR needs a lot of examples, that is language input. Recordings of radio broadcasts, parliamentary speeches, or similar sources serve as starting point for corpus creation, and the main challenge is to either edit and transcribe the recordings so that they are useful for ASR processes or to leverage off active or unsupervised training methods (Besacier et al., 2014).

Any state-of-the-art ASR system works in two modes: model training and speech decoding. The purpose of the system training process is to create and improve models for speech acoustics (recordings of a lot of speakers are required for speaker-independent ASR), language (a corpus of training text data or sentence grammar is needed) and recognition lexicon (a list of the recognizable tokens with single or multiple phonetic transcriptions) (Besacier et al., 2014).

The work associated with the process of language resources creation is mostly manual, which is both costly and not very effective, e.g. manual transcription can take several times as long as the recording duration and manual annotation on the phone level takes even tens of times longer. On the other hand, to satisfy the needs of statistical models employed in modern speech-related technologies, a large amount of training data is required (Besacier et al., 2014). It makes corpus creation a very difficult task for researchers who wish to provide such data (Żelasko et al., 2016). The particular types of data needed to build acoustic, pronunciation and language models are further explained in the sections below.

In the process of creating and improving ASR, the system is evaluated again and again and the standard measure of ASR quality is Word Error Rate (WER) (Jurafsky & Martin, 2023). It is "an intuitive and adequate measure for word-oriented analytical languages with quite simple morphology"; however, some languages are morpheme-based while some others are syllable-based (Besacier et al., 2014, p. 94).

WER can be computed by a relatively simple formula: "divide the words substituted for correct words, plus words deleted or inserted incorrectly, by the actual number of correct words in the sentence" (Jurafsky & Martin, 2009 p. 420).

Substitutions + Deletions + Insertions Word Error Rate (%)= No. of words in the correct sentence

In this formula, the lower the percentage, the more accurate the word recognition system. As a rule of thumb when the word error rate exceeds 10 %, a better algorithm needs to be developed (In-Seok Kim, 2006).

WER might not be the most appropriate measure for morphologically-rich languages (Besacier et al., 2014) like Polish. WER treats all errors equally and any change in the word is treated as an error, whereas in morphologically-rich languages, due to the number of word forms, it is quite common for ASR to make many minor mistakes, where only the ending of the word is incorrect. To take this into account, other measures have been developed: Letter/Character Error Rate (LER or CER), Phone Error Rate (PER), Syllable Error Rate (SylER) and Morpheme Error Rate (Besacier et al., 2014, p. 94).

3.2.4. Acoustic models

Acoustical modelling allows for the representation of the audio signals in such a way as to distinguish basic speech units (context-independent such as mono-phones, syllables or context-dependent such as allophones, triphones, pent-aphones), taking into account speech variability with respect to the speakers, channel, and environment (Besacier et al., 2014). State-of-the-art ASR systems typically employ context-dependent Hidden Markov Models (HMM) to model the phonemes of a language (Besacier et al., 2014, p. 92). Put simply, HMM com-putes the probable match between the input it receives and phonemes contained in a database of hundreds of native speaker recordings. In other words, a speech recognizer based on HMM computes how close the phonemes of a spoken input are to a corresponding model, based on probability theory. High likelihood represents good pronunciation; low likelihood represents poor pronunciation (In-Seok Kim, 2006). (The HMM model will be explained in more detail in the following section on language models).

Lexical modelling aims at generating the recognition vocabulary and assign-ing each orthographic token (words or sub-words) of the lexicon with the corre-sponding spoken representation (phonetic transcription). Language modelling is needed to impose the constraints on recognition hypotheses generated during ASR and to model the structure, syntax and semantics of the target language. Statistical language models are based on the empirical fact that a good estima-tion of the probability of a lexical unit can be obtained by observing it on large text data (Besacier et al., 2014).

3.2.5. Language model

Based on the acoustic model, the SR system comes up with a number of hypoth-esis on what has been said. As speech input is usually noisy (with lots of extra-neous acoustic information) and ambiguous (allowing for multiple hypothetical recognitions), the system needs a tool to evaluate each hypothesis so that it can choose the best one (Jurafsky & Martin, 2009).

For an SR system, the best hypothesis is the one that is most likely to occur in natural language. Thus, the system needs to calculate the probability of a word or phrase occurring in the language. Such knowledge is operationalized in the form of a probabilistic model. The key advantage of probabilistic models is their ability to solve the many kinds of ambiguity problems. Almost any speech and language processing problem can be recast as "given N choices for some ambiguous input, choose the most probable one" (Jurafsky & Martin, 2009, p. 31). Models that assign probabilities to sequences of words are called language models.

The probability can be calculated simply by looking at how frequent a given word or phrase is. The system would need a frequency list of all or most words in the language, and then when considering a few possible options, it would always choose the most frequent one. For instance, when working on a speech input that can be interpreted as "meat" or "meet", it would choose "meet" as it is more frequent. This would be the right choice when working on a utterance "Let's meet", but not if the utterance is "Vegetarians don't eat meat". This shows that frequency itself is not enough. The systems needs to know how often a word or phrase is used in a given context. For an SR system to work out "that you said I will be back soonish and not I will be bassoon dish, it helps to know that back soonish is a much more probable sequence than bassoon dish" (Jurafsky & Martin, 2023, p. 32).

Statistical language models provide an estimate of the probability of a word sequence. One of the most efficient statistical language modelling schemes is based on word n-grams (bigrams, trigrams, and more) (Besacier et al., 2014). N-gram language models estimate a probability to each possible next word or to an entire sentence (Jurafsky & Martin, 2023).

The language model is trained using a training corpus (a selection of texts). During the training process, the texts are analysed to establish how often certain words and phrases appear close to each other. The probabilities in n-gram language models are commonly determined by means of maximum likelihood estimation (Besacier et al., 2014). The model is then evaluated on a test corpus (a corpus of new, similar texts). This shows how good the model is at predicting each new word in the test corpus (Jurafsky & Martin, 2023). This makes the probability distribution dependent on the available training data. Thus, to ensure statistical significance, large training data are required in statistical language modelling (Besacier et al., 2014).

Calculating the probability of the next word or phrase is a daunting task and the more text is taken into account, the more computing power is required and the more complex the task becomes. To make it more feasible, SR systems need to limit the scope of the analysis. The most strict limitation is to only consider one previous word. Such an assumption, that the probability of a word depends only on the previous word, is known as Markov assumption (Jurafsky & Martin, 2023).

Markov language models, however, have a serious drawback in speech recognitions as they can only take into account observed events (in this case, words). But different words might be pronounced the same ("meet" vs "meat") or even spelled the same ("Let's meet" vs "Let's have a meet"). These words are different parts of speech. The part-of-speech information is not present in the acoustic data that the SR system analyses so it is not an observable event. As such the part of speech is hidden as it is not observed directly. However, it can be worked out from the sequence of the words (if the language model is taught the syntax of the language). The system does not know the part of speech of a word, it has to infer it from the word sequence. If the SR systems knows which part-of-speech should occur at a given point in a sequence of words, it can better evaluate the hypothesis on which words have really been uttered.

This is made possible thanks to a Hidden Markov Model that lets the SR system take into account both observed events (words) and hidden events (part-of-speech tags) (Jurafsky & Martin, 2023). As a result, the Hidden Markov Model (HMM) has proven to be an effective method of dealing with large units of speech and is one of the most dominant algorithms in speech recognition (In-Seok Kim, 2006).

To sum up, language models offer a way to assign a probability to a sentence or other sequence of words, and to predict a word from preceding words (Jurafsky & Martin, 2023). Most SR systems are based on the Hidden Markov Model and use n-grams with some SR systems now also employing neural networks.

3.2.6. Neural networks

A modern neural network is a network of small computing units, each of which "takes a set of real valued numbers as input, performs some computation on them, and produces an output" (Jurafsky & Martin, 2023, p. 137). Neural networks are a fundamental computational tool for language processing. Speech recognition systems may also use neural language models and these have advantages over n-gram ones. They can handle bigger context and generalize contexts of similar words, offering a higher predictive accuracy. This comes at a prices as neural models take far longer to train than n-gram ones.

The neural networks include single hidden layer neural networks and multiple hidden layers neural networks, the latter also being called deep neural networks because they have many layers (Besacier et al., 2014). These can be used for both language modelling and acoustic modelling. The use of modern neural nets is often referred to as deep learning (Jurafsky & Martin, 2023). Using machine learning techniques, language models can also be generated automatically from speech corpora, i.e., large collections of speech audio files and text transcriptions (Miłkowski, 2012).

3.3. Challenges for developing speech recognitions systems in Polish

SR systems have been available in English for many years. For instance, one of the most popular speech recognition programmes, Dragon NaturallySpeaking, offered by Nuance, a US-based company, appeared on the market as early as in 1990 as Dragon Dictate (Romero Fresco, 2011). In 1997, Dragon NaturallySpeaking was launched; and the latest commercial version is sold under the name Dragon Professional 15.[38] However, SR systems in Polish have taken much longer to appear with no commercially available systems when the Polish public broadcasters first started to look for one in the 2000s (Künstler, 2008).

While most of the progress in the ASR field was done for English language, "ASR systems are below the level of human speech recognition capability, even for English" (Żelasko et al., 2016, p. 586). At the same time, "there is a yawning technological gap between English and Polish, and it is currently getting wider" (Miłkowski, 2012, p. 38).

Polish is the official language of Poland and the most spoken West Slavic language around the world. Miłkowski observes that "with almost 50 million speakers, the Polish language is fairly well positioned compared to many languages" (2012, p. 37). The Polish Wikipedia is among the largest in the world, and with more than 2 million registered domains, the top level domain .pl ("Poland") is one of the world's largest country-specific top level domains. (Miłkowski, 2012). Why then the ASR in Polish has not been as readily available as in some other languages?

Unlike other information technologies, which are relatively easy to transfer to new markets, speech recognition technology requires laborious adaptation. Due to the specificity of each language, it is difficult to transfer technological achievements from one language to another (Brocki et al., 2012). And speech recognition in Slavic languages, including Polish, is in principle more difficult than in English and gives worse results due to the flexible character and great syntactic freedom of Slavic languages (Brocki et al., 2012; Ziółko & Ziółko, 2011).

---

38   https://www.nuance.com/dragon/business-solutions/dragon-professional-individual. html (accessed on February 29, 2024)

Figure 17 shows the result of an analysis of current language resources in speech processing conducted by META-NET, a Network of Excellence funded by the European Commission. The analysis focused on the 23 official EU languages as well as other important national and regional languages in Europe (Miłkowski, 2012).

Excellent support	Good support	Moderate support	Fragmentary support	Weak/no support
	English	Czech	Basque	Croatian
		Dutch	Bulgarian	Icelandic
		Finnish	Catalan	Latvian
		French	Danish	Lithuanian
		German	Estonian	Maltese
		Italian	Galician	Romanian
		Portuguese	Greek	
		Spanish	Hungarian	
			Irish	
			Norwegian	
			Polish	
			Serbian	
			Slovak	
			Slovene	
			Swedish	

Fig. 17: *Speech processing: state of language technology support for 30 European languages (Miłkowski, 2012, p. 66)*

The META-NET concluded that Polish had fragmentary support. In other words, it was thought to be an under-resourced language when it comes to speech processing. It is interesting to note that languages such as Czech, Finnish and Dutch, all used by smaller language communities than Polish, were judged to have moderate support. English was the only language to receive "good support" badge with no language enjoying excellent support.

In 2009, Loof and colleagues pointed out that "published results on large vocabulary speech recognition for the Polish language are scarce. (…) [P]ublications deal either with isolated word, or small vocabulary recognition" (2009, p. 88). Many researchers reckon that these setbacks are due to the fact that, for fifty years now, the methods and algorithms of computational linguistics and language technology application research have first and foremost focused on English (Miłkowski, 2012, p. 38).

In order to develop ASR systems, "a database of tens, even hundreds of hours of recorded speech is required for both training and testing purposes" (Żelasko et al., 2016, p. 586). However, for Polish, similar databases are scarce; there are few corpora of recorded speech, and very few available to be licensed. Lack of corpora of appropriate quality and size is among the main issues blocking development of ASR systems in Polish.

Another factor is that Polish exhibits some specific characteristics, "which contribute to the richness of the language" but are challenging for its computational processing (Miłkowski, 2012, p. 45). For instance, speakers can express ideas in a wide variety of ways as Polish is non-positional; that is, the word order is relatively free in Polish sentences, and it is used to stress the importance of information rather than simply follow from the rules of grammar. This makes it harder for n-gram language models to predict the probability of words being used next to each other in Polish as compared to fixed word-order languages like English where the word order is fixed. Standard statistical language models are not so efficient for languages like Polish because high order n-grams (3-grams and more) have a high perplexity and a low n-gram hit rate, so huge corpora are needed to estimate probabilities for these models (Besacier et al., 2014). And, as has been pointed out above, such corpora were not available until recently.

Polish speech contains very high frequency phonemes (fricatives and plosives) and the language is highly inflected (Żelasko et al., 2016). Polish is so morphologically rich that for roughly 180 thousand base forms of words, there are almost 4 million inflected word forms (Miłkowski, 2012). Other specific characteristics of Polish that make automatic processing of language difficult are the tendency to use comparably long and nested sentences. In addition, the lack of articles makes detection of noun phrases relatively hard, as the only way to detect them is to rely on morphological information (case, number, gender), which is ambiguous (Miłkowski, 2012). On the other hand, it should be noted that Polish is a quite homogenous language. Unlike in English, dialects and regional accents do not pose a significant problem for developing ASR in Polish (Żelasko et al., 2016).

3.4. Current state of speech recognition technology in Polish

Gradually, Polish ceases to be under-resourced language in terms of speech recognition technology (Żelasko et al., 2016, p. 586) as a number of valuable linguistic corpora have been created. For instance, the National Corpus of Polish (*Narodowy Korpus Języka Polskiego*, NKJP) (Przepiórkowski et al., 2012) is a large resource of Polish texts, which consists of literature, journalism, letters,

Internet texts and others. It is also a resource of recorded conversations and media speeches, which unfortunately, are not provided with time aligned annotation that would make it easier to use it in developing SR systems (Żelasko et al., 2016). AGH corpus is one of the largest documented corpora of spoken Polish (over 25 h and 166 speakers), featuring a variety of speech scenarios, including text reading, issuing commands, telephonic speech, phonetically balanced 4.5 h subcorpus recorded in an anechoic chamber and others (Żelasko et al., 2016). Also, a large-vocabulary Polish speech recognizer for telephone dialogs has been developed by Loquendo for use in the European Union project LUNA; (Loof et al., 2009) as part of TC-STAR project, used recording from the European Parliament plenary sessions of original speakers and interpreters, together with preliminary transcriptions (in the original languages) and the final minutes of the meeting (available in most official languages) (Loof et al., 2009).

Polish is covered by some multilingual corpora such as GlobalPhone, SpeechDat-e and the corpus of the recordings from the European Parliament. The most well-known speech corpora for Polish include CORPORA, Jurisdic, LUNA and SARMATA ASR (Żelasko et al., 2016).

Over time, the efforts of developing speech recognition in Polish intensified due to an increase in demand for voice user interfaces (Miłkowski, 2012). In 2012, Miłkowski noted that that the key players in ASR in Poland are PrimeSpeech and Skrybot, which offer voice user interfaces for partially or fully automated telephone services for such domains as banking or telecommunications. Miłkowski predicted that "the usage of spoken language as a user-friendly input modality for smartphones will gain significant importance" and noted observable improvement of speaker independent speech recognition accuracy for cloud speech dictation services that were offered to smartphone users (2012, p. 58). At the similar time, the availability of several open-source and free ASR toolkits, which could be adopted by technology developers to any target language using available training data, lowered the threshold for developing new ASR system. These toolkits included HTK, Julius, Sphinx, RLAT, RASR, KALDI, and YAST (Besacier et al., 2014).

In 2010s a number of desktop ASR systems in Polish appeared, including Skrybot, MagicScribe, Newton Dictate and VoiceLab Dictate (Szczygielska & Dutka, 2019). Google, Apple, Microsoft also made speech recognition in Polish available as part of their cloud services. The most popular desktop speech recognition system in English, Dragon Naturally Speaking, has not been made available in Polish. Since 2011, Nuance has been making Dragon Dictation and Dragon Search applications available in Polish, running on iOS mobile devices connected to the Internet. However, they only allow for voice searching and dictating short text messages and notes and thus cannot be used for respeaking.

So far, MagicScribe and Newton Dictate 5 as well as VoiceLab Dictate (Szczygielska & Dutka, 2019)[39] have been used for respeaking in Polish. It is important to point out that these systems do not understand morphology. Newton does not understand variations of individual words (e.g. recognizing that *doors* is plural), which requires knowledge about morphology, i.e. the way words break down into component parts that carry meanings like *singular* versus *plural*. The system is able to process speech but not to understand it as a human does. It has some understanding of syntax through the language model but no pragmatic, dialogue or discourse knowledge. In other words, SR systems like Newton are heavily based on phonetics and phonology and to some extent on syntax but these SR systems have no knowledge of morphology, semantics, pragmatics or discourse (Jurafsky & Martin, 2009).

3.5. New generation of automatic speech recognition powered by large language models

The advances in deep learning have facilitated the development of increasingly large neural networks, enabling the integration of expansive large language models (LLMs) into ASR systems. A quintessential example of this innovative approach is Whisper, an open-source language model developed by OpenAI and introduced in September 2022[40]. Whisper epitomizes the new generation of ASR systems, benefiting significantly from cutting-edge deep learning methodologies, including unsupervised pre-training techniques. Such methodologies allow the model to learn directly from raw audio data, obviating the necessity for prior comparison with existing transcriptions (Baevski et al., 2020). This advancement has enabled the training of the model on an unprecedented scale of speech corpora. Consequently, there has been a notable enhancement in the model's capability to recognize speech across a wide array of language pairs, with its accuracy and robustness nearing human levels (Radford et al., 2022).

A crucial difference between previous generations of ASR and new models like Whisper is that the latter support multiple languages. Whisper was trained on a diverse dataset encompassing a wide variety of languages and can automatically

---

39   Personal communication with Jacek Kawalec, vice-president of VoiceLab, who stated that public broadcaster TVP uses a custom-made version of VoiceLab Dictate. The broadcaster does not publicly disclose the software it is using.

40   https://openai.com/research/whisper (Accessed on February 29, 2024)

detect the language spoken. From the perspective of live subtitling, this makes it easier to apply ASR in multilingual settings. Respeakers can switch from one language to another without having to switch between separate language-specific ASR systems. Whisper is also better at understanding context, especially when dealing with longer recordings, which increases accuracy for pre-recorded speech. However, with live subtitling, as the audio is live and latency is an issue, the model has to process shorter portions of speech, which limits the context available.

The integration of LLMs into ASR systems has not only improved accuracy but also expanded the potential applications of speech recognition technology across various fields. From accessibility solutions to interactive voice-responsive systems, the wider use of new ASR systems in live subtitling can lead to gains in quality. However, the increased complexity and capabilities of these models have introduced new challenges, such as the phenomenon of "hallucinations," where the system generates text that does not correspond to the input audio, potentially leading to misinformation or misunderstanding (Choi et al., 2024). As multilingual systems perform language detection, they can sometimes detect the language incorrectly (for instance, Spanish speech might be recognized as Italian, or utterances in Polish might be recognized as Russian or Hebrew), which could lead the model to produce inaccurate text in another language.

3.6. The future of speech recognition

Future developments should combine ASR and the technologies for natural language understanding. Miłkowski (2012) believes that the next generation of SR technology will feature software that understands not just sounds but entire words and sentences, and supports users far better because it actually understands their language. As more research is being done on how to apply speech technologies more easily to under-resourced languages (Besacier et al., 2014), over time the ASR should improve in languages like Polish as more speech corpora become available and new modelling techniques are applied.

Improvement in ASR accuracy is also possible if visual information is captured and integrated into speech recognition. Visual speech information from the speaker's mouth region has been successfully shown to improve ASR as it provides complimentary information about the place of articulation and speech segmentation (Pomianos et al., 2003). So far, this technology has been hampered by the high requirements on the captured video frame rate and size as well as the computer processing power, but it might be possible to meet them in TV settings.

For morphologically-rich languages, such as Polish, a significant improvement may come from using morphology-integrated models (Sak et al., 2010) as it is efficient to decompose words into sub-lexical units (the so-called morphs) and apply them as tokens in the lexicon and the language model. This helps ASR deal with of out-of-vocabulary words (Besacier et al., 2014).

Current ASR systems are only able to recognize word forms that they know (that are included in the system's lexicon). The system either recognizes a word as a whole or it does not. If an ASR system is trained to understand morphology of the language, it can start to work at sub-word level. This means that it can recognize the root of the word and then combine it with a prefix, suffix or other inflectional ending. This way ASR will be able to build words from ready-made morphological blocks and, as a result, the system might successfully recognize out-of-vocabulary word forms, which would be a welcome innovation as out-of-vocabulary word forms are challenging in respeaking.

However, morphology-integrated models also come with additional challenges in speech decoding (a high phonetic ambiguity of sub-word units) as well as higher order n-grams (5- to 10 grams), which are required to capture grammatical dependencies. So far, morpheme-based models have been successfully applied to Finnish (Besacier et al., 2014) and Turkish (Sak et al., 2010). As of 2021, the companies behind Polish ASR systems Newton Dictate[41] and VoiceLab Dictate[42] both state that they consider implementing morphology-integrated models in future version of their software.

---

41 Personal communication with Krzysztof Struk, a sales representative of Newton Technologies in Poland.
42 Personal communication with Jacek Kawalec, the vice-president of VoiceLab.

Chapter 4: User expectations

Nida (2003) points out that translations must be perceived taking into account the audiences for which they are produced. Neves (2005, p. 124) observes that in the case of SDH "hearing translators rarely have true knowledge of the cognitive and social environment of their target audience." Thus, any attempt at preparing or analysing (live) subtitling requires awareness of who are the recipients and how they "read" audiovisual texts.

In this chapter, I look for answers to the following questions: Who are the users? What are their needs and expectations? How live subtitles can best address those needs? And what to do when users have conflicting expectations? In the following sections we will look at the characteristics of various groups of users, which will be followed by the analysis of their diverse needs and expectations. Finally, the chapter will close with a reflection of the role that the users (should) play in live subtitling as stakeholders.

4.1. Who uses (live) subtitling?

SDH in general can be used by everybody and can probably benefit most viewers. Same-language subtitling has been used with great success to boost literacy in India (Kothari et al., 2000). And user research conducted for Ofcom in the UK in 2006 showed that out of 7.5 million people using TV subtitles, 6 million did not have a hearing impairment (Romero Fresco, 2011). Polls from the Flemish public television VRT indicate that over 70% of the people using closed captions hear normally (Waes et al., 2013). Many viewers can benefit from subtitles in noisy environments and public places such as bars, restaurants, train or metro stations (Robson, 2004). Subtitles can also be used as an educational tool (Vanderplank, 2016) and can greatly help immigrants or other learners of the language in which the subtitles are presented.

However, while live subtitling (and SDH, in general) can be used by everybody, it is primarily addressed at viewers with hearing impairment. As opposed to other viewers for whom subtitling is an aid that makes it easier or more comfortable for them to follow the audiovisual content, for some hearing impaired viewers lack of subtitling is a barrier that that prevents them from being able to understand the content, benefit from it or enjoy it. In other words, it renders the content inaccessible to them. As a result, surely, the needs of the hearing impaired viewers should take precedence over the needs of other, secondary audiences. However, there is no clear set of needs that all hearing impaired viewers have.

According to Neves (2008, p. 131) one of fallacies about SDH is a belief that "SDH addressees make up one cohesive group". In fact, SDH caters to a wide range of viewers whose needs and expectations are varied and, in some cases, conflicting. To begin with, the Deaf audience itself is not a homogeneous group. Fairly obviously, it consists of people who have a profound hearing loss from birth. Less obviously perhaps, it also includes people with varying degrees of hearing loss acquired later in life. The members of the first group, usually referred to by using "Deaf" with a capital "D"[43], primarily use sign language for communication as it is their mother tongue. As a result, they may be on average less fluent in reading subtitles (Neves, 2005). The people in the second group, i.e. those with acquired hearing loss, conventionally referred to by using "deaf" with lower case "d", are more likely to have received an education within the hearing community and consequently have better reading skills. Thus, the term "d/Deaf" is used to highlight the difference between two distinct groups: people who are Deaf but who belong to the social context of the hearing majority and consider the oral language as their mother tongue, and the Deaf, a social and linguistic minority who use a sign language and for whom the oral language is either their second language or a foreign language (Neves, 2008; Szarkowska, 2008). Finally, the third group are the hard of hearing who usually have some degree of residual hearing. A significant number of the hard of hearing develop hearing problems with age (Neves, 2005). This group will be considerably larger in the future due to population ageing. According to European statistical office Eurostat, people aged 65 years or over will account for 29.5% of the EU population by 2060 and the number of people aged 80 years or above will almost triple.[44] In the US, 10 million people are hard of hearing, while close to one million are functionally Deaf (defined as unable to hear conversations even with the use of a hearing aid) (Romero Fresco, 2011, p. 9). The European Federation of Hard of Hearing People claims that at least 51 million Europeans have some hearing impairment (approximately 9% of the inhabitants of the EU)[45]. That seems a low estimate when compared to the statistics from the UK where 16% of the population is believed to have hearing impairment (Zarate, 2021). In *The World*

---

43   This spelling convention was originally suggested in the US by James Woodward (1972) and developed by Carol Padden (1980). For more information see Neves, 2005.

44   https://ec.europa.eu/eurostat/documents/4031688/5930084/KS-FM-13-002-EN.PDF/37dc8192-c5df-49b3-98a6-2b005beb75bf?version%20=1.0 (accessed on February 29, 2024)

45   https://efhoh.org/wp-content/uploads/2017/04/Hearing-Loss-Statistics-AGM-2015.pdf (Accessed on February 29, 2024)

Hearing Report the World Health Organization (2021) estimates that globally 15% of adults have hearing loss and by 2050 as many as 2.5 billion people are projected to have some degree of hearing loss. In Poland, as of 2019, according to Polish Main Statistical Office, 4% of the population uses hearing aids while 8% struggles with hearing a conversation in a quiet environment (GUS, 2021). Szarkowska (2010) estimates the number of hearing impaired Poles at roughly four million, on the assumption that 10% of any population has problems with hearing.

4.2. User groups and their characteristics

So far, we have discussed three groups. However, further differentiation can be done. According to Neves (2008), at least five categories of Deaf viewers can be identified:

– pre-lingually and post-lingually deaf;
– oralising and signing deaf;
– deaf who feel they belong to hearing majority social group
– Deaf who assume themselves as a linguistic minority and for whom the written text is a second language [whom Lambourne (2006) calls "a minority of a minority"]
– deafened viewers who have residual hearing and/or hearing memory.

It should be noted that the categorization in the groups can be blurry. While Deafness can be measured audiologically, it is also a social phenomenon and an issue of language use (Ladd, 2003; Mliczak, 2019). For some people being Deaf is a matter of belonging to a community with its own language and culture. As a result, self-identification has to do at least as much with a sense of identity as with a medical status of hearing loss. Among people who self-identify as Deaf or hard of hearing there are varying degrees of hearing loss. Thus, it is possible to encounter people who self-identify as Deaf and yet from a functional perspective they could be considered hearing individuals (for instance, thanks to the use of an implant that allows them to comfortably participate in spoken interactions). On the other hand, an older person can be considered functionally Deaf due to profound hearing loss linked with ageing but can still self-identify as a hard of hearing or even a hearing individual.

And as many of these groups are heterogenous in themselves (see Zarate, 2021), perhaps even more sub-groups could be distinguished (Gambier, 2018). For instance, those Deaf viewers who use sign language as their first language can have varying levels of proficiency in their second language that will impact their comprehension of written texts. And if they have low proficiency in their second language, they will probably have a stronger preference for using sign language interpreting (as opposed to subtitling). Indeed, some might not be able to follow SDH at all (Jankowska, 2020) unless it is simplified. Whereas, if they have high proficiency, they might be more open to using subtitling.

Irrespective of the number of groups that we distinguish, the crucial matter is that the members of these groups differ significantly in their needs as well as their reading skills, which depend to a large extent on the nature of their hearing loss (Linde & Kay, 1999). Indeed, a BBC white paper found "a significant diversity in the needs of different subtitle users" (Armstrong et al., 2015, p. 10). Let us know examine what these needs are.

4.3. User needs and expectations

Some subtitling needs are surely universal and shared by all viewers. In regard to live subtitling, Ofcom (2005) identified two basic needs (see Fig. 18): having more subtitled programmes to choose from and subtitles being provided in a reliable way (available when promised). However, many other needs will be more or less important depending on the group of users.

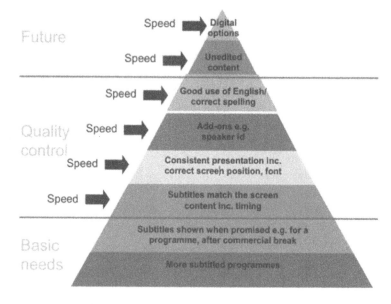

Fig. 18: *Hierarchy of subtitling needs (Ofcom, 2005)*

Making TV Accessible, a report published by the International Telecommunications Union, (ITU, 2011) points out that viewing television with subtitles is dependent on being a proficient reader and reading proficiency can vary enormously between the groups described above. In the context of Deaf viewers, as pointed out in the previous section, they are reading subtitles in what is for them a second language (with sign language being their first language and preferred method of communication). Also, the speed at which viewers are able to read is not the same as "the reading speed at which viewing experience is comfortable" (ITU, 2011, p. 5). The report warns that even in countries with high literacy rates "as many as 10 to 20 per cent [of viewers] will not be able to follow on-screen texts including captioning unless there is some degree of language condensation to bring the required reading speed down to acceptable levels".

Apart from reading speeds, Neves (2008, p. 131) enumerates other differences between both groups. According to her, both groups have different preferences concerning the kind of subtitling they want (e.g. edited, verbatim) and they relate to sound in different ways. Gambier (2018) goes further by pointing out different variables that can affect viewers needs such as age, sex, education, reading proficiency, reading habits, typical reading speed, oral and reading comprehension, frequency and volume of AVT consumption, AVT habits and command of foreign languages etc.

Given the diverse needs of the users, how should providers of subtitling make decisions on how to adapt their subtitles? And what to do if these needs are conflicting? One solution is to imagine what Gambier (2018) calls an "ideal viewer". For instance, subtitlers might conclude that their primary audience are the Heard of Hearing viewers who are proficient in the language of the subtitles (assuming that Deaf viewers will tend to use sign language interpreting instead of subtitles). This approach is risky as the ideal viewer might turn out to be different from the "empirical viewer" (i.e. the actual audience).

Another approach is to look for the lowest common denominator, trying to accommodate as wide audience as possible. This is often done with relation to subtitle speed. Pedersen (2011, p. 133) quotes an employee of SVT, Swedish public service broadcaster, as claiming that their goal is making subtitles that "even every little old woman in every rural cottage" has enough time to read comfortably. As Neves (2005: 126) puts it, having awareness of different needs will help subtitlers to decide about issues such as the amount of information to be presented in SDH, the way the information should be structured, and the linguistic and stylistic devices used to present the information. According to Gutt (2000, p. 32), the overall goal of translation is to avoid placing an extra cognitive effort on the viewers and make it easier for them to arrive at the intended interpretation. Translation should "yield adequate contextual effects at minimal processing cost". From this perspective, creating slower, more condensed subtitling could be seen as indispensable for some viewers but beneficial to all of them. In practise, however, this is exactly one of the areas where D/HOH viewers' attitudes to subtitles vary most: the issue of verbatim vs. edited subtitles. ITU report observes that viewers are often unaware of the way subtitles are produced and "they may be suspicious of linguistics condensation" (ITU, 2011, p. 5), which they perceive as changing the intended meaning.

A yet another approach is the personalisation of subtitling. Upon the analysis of the linguistic profiles of various user groups, it becomes clear that one set of subtitles may not serve adequately the needs of all viewers, a conclusion that was drawn up by most scholars investigating the issue. For example, Gottlieb (1997, p. 129) proposed that for a film or a television programme various subtitle versions should be produced. According to him, this could mean different "levels" of subtitling, from fast, uncondensed subtitling through normal speed to slow, heavily condensed subtitling for slow readers. Szarkowska (2009, p. 197) notes that "the best solution may be to provide both edited and verbatim subtitles for viewers to choose from". Künstler and Butkiewicz (2019) suggest that one subtitle version should be made to satisfy the needs of spoken language users with hearing problems, with the other version tailored to the needs of the Deaf people for whom sign language is their mother tongue. The latter can be called "the version for oral language learners" (Künstler & Butkiewicz, 2019, p. 11).

Producing two versions of subtitles (or three, if subtitling is used instead of dubbing or voice-over for translating foreign broadcasts) and making them available simultaneously was traditionally thought to be difficult to implement given the technical and economical restraints. It should be noted, however, that such practice was implemented in the US by PBS for children's cartoons (Szarkowska, 2009). A white paper published by BBC (Armstrong et al., 2015) also recommended more personalisation of subtitling, which is now much easier to achieve on streaming platforms. Indeed, as of early 2022, Netflix is making some of its new programming available with both interlingual SDH and interlingual non-SDH subtitles in several languages[46].

---

46   For instance, viewers of an English-speaking Netflix series *Bridgerton* can choose either interlingual subtitles or interlingual SDH in languages such as Spanish and Italian (on top of being able to choose SDH in English).

4.4. The role of users as stakeholders

Given the shift to user-centred approach in media accessibility, as discussed in Section 1.4, users of subtitling have an important role to play as stakeholders in the world of subtitling. Researchers have long been reaching out to users through reception studies or questionnaires (Di Giovanni, 2020; Romero Fresco, 2015; Szarkowska, 2010) and some broadcasters make efforts to elicit viewers feedback (Armstrong et al., 2015). In Canada, attempts have been made at involving the users in the process of quality assessment by training them as NER evaluators (Romero Fresco, 2021).

Users themselves often take to the Internet and especially to the social media to make their voices heard. In 2017, following an Internet petition by Deaf viewers, a Polish broadcaster Polsat decided to provide live subtitles for a local edition of the *Dancing with the Stars* franchise, which featured a Deaf dancer (Szczygielska & Dutka, 2019). Deaf users of subtitling also participated in creating a Napisy Plus initiative (literally "*Subtitling Plus*", https://www.facebook.com/napisyp lus//) that aims to promote subtitling and educate people about SDH and other access services. It includes a website with educational content as well as various social media profiles. A Facebook group "Media Napisy PJM" (literally "Media, Subtitles and Polish Sign Language") is an example of a place where users of SDH and sign language interpreting share information about audiovisual content. The group often features complaints about subtitling or sign language interpreting not being available for some programming, about errors in subtitling or about the sign language interpreter being too small on screen.

While social media groups can help users organize themselves, they can often turn into echo chambers where users complain to each other instead of reaching out to the regulator or the broadcaster. However, finding a way to get in touch with broadcasters can often be hard for users. As part of her research in subtitling quality, Fresno (2019) reached out to six major US broadcasters; none of them responded. In the Polish context, as of 2022, neither of the three major broadcasters actively seeks feedback from users of subtitling. In fact, the websites of both Polsat News and TVN24 does not provide any way for viewers to pass on feedback or reach out to the station in any way. Only the state broadcaster TVP provides a feedback form for viewers.[47] In the case of all three broadcasters, there

---

47 Available at: https://www.tvp.pl/kontakt. TVP also provides an automated phone line where viewers can record messages with feedback on the broadcaster's programming but this point of contact is not accessible to the Deaf viewers.

is also no way to contact the departments that prepare subtitling (if it is done in-house) or handle procurement of external subtitling services.

To help the users play an active role as stakeholders, it is the task of the regulators, the broadcasters and the researchers have to be willing to listen to users, learn from their feedback and adapt to their needs as well as help users achieve a more nuanced understanding of the quality of live subtitling. Users, in turn, should be willing to learn about the intricacies of subtitling so that they can make more nuanced evaluations of the quality of the services (Romero Fresco, 2021). They should also support or actively engage in organizations that represent them so as to be able to lobby the regulator and the broadcasters more effectively. Finally, users should also be open to taking part in reception research.

Chapter 5: Quality assessment in live subtitling

> *"To those in translation management, the concept [of quality] is often associated with processes, workflows and deadlines. To professionals, quality is often a balancing act between input and efficiency. To academics, it is often a question of equivalence and language use" (Pedersen, 2017, p. 210).*

In this chapter, I will discuss what quality means in the context of live subtitles and how it can be conceptualized as well as measured. After identifying and describing various dimensions of live subtitling quality, both linguistic and technical ones, I will discuss existing quality metrics such as the NER model, latency, reduction rate and subtitle speed. I will also propose new metrics for assessing the quality of text segmentation as well as measuring gaps between consecutive subtitles. This will be followed by a discussion on the differences between subjective perceptions and objective measurements and a summary of the current knowledge on the impact of different live subtitling workflows on the quality of subtitles.

5.1. Challenges involved in assessing the quality of live subtitling

An intrinsic challenge in the assessment of translation quality is that the notion of quality is elusive. One way of looking at quality is referring to national or international translation standards such as the International Standard for Translation ISO 17100. However, the translation standards do not take into account the characteristics of live subtitling. And, most importantly, they focus on the process and are not helpful when evaluating the quality of the product.

Another challenge is subjectivity as scoring decisions are subjective to some degree (Romero Fresco & Pöchhacker, 2018). Similarly to other forms of translation such as interpreting, live subtitling involves paraphrase and assessing paraphrasing (even intralingual one) can be difficult to score (Chmiel et al., 2018). This is because there is no single rendering or way of paraphrasing that is correct; instead many different versions might be acceptable. As a result, "there is no single end product to serve as a standard for objective assessment. [...] Consequently, no absolutely impartial standards or sets of criteria can be applied to measure or assess the quality of a translation" (Graham, 2016, p. 59). In other words, the text within live subtitles can be phrased in various different ways and still express the same meaning. In most cases, it is not possible to say that only one particular way is correct and live subtitles are only acceptable if done this exact way. Therefore, it is not possible to fully automate the assessment of live subtitles; the involvement of human assessors is needed to judge whether live subtitles are accurate or not.

In recent years various shifts occurred in how quality is perceived: from quality as perfection (no errors, no defects) to the product being fit for purpose (Romero Fresco & Pöchhacker, 2018) and from maker-centred to user-centred perspective on quality (Greco & Jankowska, 2019; Jankowska, 2020). Live subtitling can also be evaluated as a service (as opposed to just a process or a product), in which case the user satisfaction (see Chapter 4 for a discussion of user needs and expectations) and communicative effectiveness need to be taken into account (Romero Fresco & Pöchhacker, 2018).

Even though the research into quality parameters and procedures can be challenging and, at least within the domain of audiovisual translation, it may be lagging behind what?, in AVT practice quality is a major issue as "quality management, quality assurance and quality control [...] are central to most areas of translation practice" (Robert & Remael, 2016, p. 28). However elusive and complex, quality assessment of the subtitled product is not only possible but is in fact carried out daily (Romero Fresco & Pöchhacker, 2018).

Quality in subtitling in general and in live subtitling in particular is multidimensional (Greco & Jankowska, 2020) or polyhedral (Fresno, 2019), that is there are various dimensions or factors that contribute to the overall quality of subtitles and the overall experience of using subtitles. Quality is not only about meaning but also professional norms, including form and delivery (Romero Fresco & Pöchhacker, 2018). As some dimensions of live subtitling quality are easier to identify and measure, they have traditionally received more attention than others. The present research aims at analysing as many quality dimensions as possible, including those that have not received much attention in the past. Another aim is to address the so-called Maker-Expert-User-Gap through "validating existing services and suggesting possible improvements (...) systematizing practices and basing them on evidence rather than intuition" (Jankowska, 2020, p. 245).

Below I will try to identify and describe dimensions of quality in live subtitling as well as characterize the existing metrics that can be used to analyse those dimensions. I will also try to propose new metrics.

5.2. Identifying dimensions of live subtitling quality

There are various quality dimensions already proposed in the literature. There is a wide agreement that subtitles in general must appear in synchrony with the image and dialogue, provide a semantically adequate account of the source dialogue (accuracy), and remain displayed on screen long enough for the viewers to be able to read them (Díaz Cintas & Remael, 2007; Saerens et al., 2020). These three dimensions can be referred to as synchronicity, accuracy and subtitle display rate.

Gambier (2018, pp. 54–55) mentions five quality dimensions of AVT in general: acceptability, legibility, readability, synchronicity and relevance. Robert and Remael (2016) put forward four subtitle translation quality parameters: (1) content and meaning transfer (that includes accuracy, completeness and logic); (2) grammar, spelling and punctuation; (3) readability (i.e. how easy it is to comprehend subtitles and is there coherence between them; for instance, if the text had to be condensed or parts of it have been omitted, is it still coherent); (4) appropriateness (using appropriate register and dealing correctly with cultural nuances). They also mention technical requirements related to formatting and segmentation (for instance, the text should be divided into subtitles depending on sense block or grammatical units, and, ideally, each subtitle should be self-contained), spotting (the synchronicity with the audio, minimum and maximum duration of subtitles, minimum gap between subtitles, maximum number of lines). Pedersen (2017) in his FAR model, designed for assessing pre-recorded interlingual subtitles, divides quality into three areas: functional equivalence, acceptability and readability.

Some media regulators put forward specific quality parameters in their guidelines on subtitling. For instance, the American regulator, FCC, identifies four parameters: accuracy (that includes not only faithfully expressing the ideas but also identifying speakers), synchrony (subtitles should match the dialogue and sounds but also being displayed at a readable speed), completeness (subtitles should be provided for the entire programme) and adequate placement (subtitles should not obscure onscreen information) (FCC, 2014).

In its Television Captioning Standard from 2013, ACME, the counterpart of FCC in Australia, lists three quality parameters: readability (text colour and font, segmentation, punctuation, positioning and number of lines), accuracy (representing the actual meaning of dialogues, sounds and music) and comprehensibility (speaker identification, subtitle display time, synchrony with the audio, correct spelling and shot changes) (Romero-Fresco, 2021). While the FCC and ACME refer to both pre-recorded and live subtitles, the British regulator Ofcom established three key quality dimensions for live subtitling in particular: speed, latency and accuracy (Ofcom, 2015).

To sum up, live subtitling quality is indeed multi-dimensional and there is a long list of specific quality parameters that could be discussed. Depending on the author or the organization, these might be conceptualized and grouped differently (for instance, subtitle display time is a part of synchrony for FCC, comprehensibility for ACME, and Ofcom conceptualizes it as a separate category that it calls "speed"). From the perspective of linguistics, one way to discuss quality dimensions is to divide them into linguistic and technical dimensions. The linguistic dimensions comprise grammar, spelling (including capitalization), punctuation and text segmentation (including the division of text into subtitles as well as the line breaks within subtitles), accuracy and the presence of SDH-specific elements such speaker IDs or sound descriptions.

Technical dimensions encompass synchronicity (including subtitle latency and gaps between consecutive subtitles), subtitle display time (including respecting minimum and maximum display time), subtitle speed, subtitle positioning and the visual aspect of subtitles (including the formatting, font, the colour and the size of the text).

In a survey of AVT practitioners, Robert and Remael (2016) found that while subtitlers claim to pay attention to all the quality parameters, the clients focus much more on the technical than on the linguistic parameters. However, in live subtitling research it is accuracy that received most attention so far. In the sections below, I will discuss linguistic and technical parameters of live subtitling quality in more detail, starting with accuracy. This will be followed by the discussion on how to measure these parameters.

5.3. Linguistic dimensions of live subtitling quality

In this section, I will discuss linguistic dimensions of live subtitling quality such as accuracy, grammar, spelling, punctuation and text segmentation.

5.3.1. Accuracy

As we saw above, accuracy is understood as a faithful representation of the content, including dialogues as well as sounds and music. When it comes to dialogues, there are two approaches to accuracy: verbatim and sensatim (Eugeni, 2008; Oncins et al., 2019). Within the verbatim approach, the subtitles are considered accurate if they include the same words as the audio. Any departure from the exact phrasing or word choices of the utterances is considered inaccurate.

Within the sensatim approach, what counts is the informational content of the subtitles. If subtitles include fewer words or different words than the original utterances, they can still be considered accurate as long as they express the same meaning. In the example below, the subtitle would be considered accurate within the sensatim approach (as it expresses the same meaning) and inaccurate in the verbatim approach (as the words are not all the same).

Audio	Subtitle
We all sort of need the same things.	Everybody needs the same thing.

In the US, Canada and Australia, there is a strong tradition in SDH of viewing accuracy as literality; subtitles need to verbatim (i.e. include all of the words of the original message) (FCC, 2014; Fresno, 2019). The European tradition allows for editing. Subtitles are still viewed as accurate as long as the same meaning is expressed, even if the subtitle does not include all the words (Fresno & Sepielak, 2020). In this book, whenever accuracy is mentioned, it will be understood in line with the sensatim approach unless explicitly indicated otherwise.

5.3.2. Grammar, spelling and punctuation

Correct spelling and grammar contribute to greater readability (Robert & Remael, 2016), making it easier for viewers to process the text. Grammar, spelling or punctuation errors can draw the attention of the viewers and distract it from the content. Given the transient nature of subtitles, any distraction or difficulty in processing the subtitles might mean that a subtitle will disappear before the viewer is able to successfully process it and understand the underlying information (Kruger et al., 2015; Kruger et al., 2022; Liao et al., 2021).

Regarding grammar and punctuation, it has long been recommended that subtitlers should try to create subtitles that include self-contained syntactic units (Díaz Cintas & Remael, 2007; Ivarsson & Carroll, 1998; Karamitroglou, 1998; Robert & Remael, 2017). The ideal situation is when a sentence starts and ends inside one subtitle so that the viewer can process the entire sentence at the same time rather than wait for the rest of it to appear (or has to remember the previous part of the sentence that has already disappeared from screen). Another related recommendation is to avoid long, complex sentences. While achieving this all the time is not feasible, through rephrasing the text the subtitler can simplify long sentences into shorter ones.

The importance of this quality dimension becomes apparent when subtitles are created through automatic speech recognition that is not able to simplify the syntax. While some systems attempt to add automatic punctuation, they do not get it right in all the cases, resulting in complex, long sentences without punctuation or incorrect and confusing usage of punctuation marks. This makes it harder for viewers to process the text as either they have to work out themselves where a sentence starts and ends, or they might be confused by a surprising full stop in the middle of a sentence.

5.3.3. Text segmentation

While subtitles should comprise self-contained syntactic units, this is not always possible and so there are cases of one sentence spanning two or more subtitles. Also, within two-line subtitle the text needs to be divided between these two lines. This raises the need for segmenting the text, which is deciding when a new line or a new subtitle should start. There is consensus that line breaks should occur at natural syntactic boundaries (Díaz Cintas & Remael, 2007; Gerber-Morón & Szarkowska, 2018; Perego, 2008; Rajendran et al., 2013; Szarkowska & Gerber-Morón, 2019) such as between clauses and that words and phrases which are strongly linked syntactically should not be separated between lines and (which is considered even more important) between subtitles. The stronger the syntactic link between words, the more serious error it is to separate these. For instance, separating "not" and a verb or separating parts of a complex verb (e.g. "have done") is considered a serious segmentation error.

   Due to time pressure in live subtitling, there is a temptation to disregard text segmentation as less important. In live subtitling workflows that involve just one subtitler, it might be particularly difficult for him or her to control text segmentation. It is much easier to do this in workflows that involve a team of two or three subtitlers working simultaneously. Thus, there is a number of approaches to text segmentation in live subtitling. One way is to relinquish control altogether. The segmentation is then fully decided by the software: new words are added to the existing line up until the maximum number of characters available in a line and then the line break occurs. Once a two-line subtitle fills with text, a new subtitle will begin. The way software controls segmentation can also be improved by adding rules. For instance, the software can be programmed to always force line breaks after certain characters such as full stops, question marks or colons. Live subtitlers can also take a more active role and enforce the line break or the end of the subtitle through a voice command or by pressing a key. Another approach is for live subtitlers to manually control segmentation, in which case they can either aim for perfect segmentation or can limit themselves to just avoiding most serious segmentation errors.

5.4. Technical dimensions of live subtitling quality

Technical dimensions include synchronicity (including subtitle latency and the gaps between subtitles), subtitle display time (including respecting minimum and maximum display time), subtitle display speed, subtitle positioning, legibility and readability (including the formatting, font, the colour and the size of the text).

5.4.1. Synchronicity and latency

Perhaps the most obvious technical dimension of subtitling quality is synchronicity, which is having subtitles appear in sync with the dialogues. In a survey of subtitling professionals, synchronicity was the feature of ideal subtitles that was most often mentioned by participants (Díaz Cintas et al., 2021). To put it simply, a subtitle should appear when a speaker starts saying an utterance and this subtitle should disappear when the speaker stops. In fact, it is far more complex than that as the timing of subtitles needs to take into account rules regarding shot changes and the maximum and minimum duration of subtitles, minimum gaps between subtitles as well as chaining (Díaz Cintas & Remael, 2007). The timing of subtitles also needs to take into account subtitle speed (discussed in more detail below).

While in pre-recorded subtitling the expectation is to achieve full synchronicity, in live subtitling this is often seen as difficult or not feasible, and the fact that there is some latency is perceived by many as unavoidable. The latency in live subtitling is understood as the "the time between the moment something has been said and the actual moment the subtitle appears on screen" (Saerens et al., 2020, p. 4). Subtitle latency depends on a number of factors; the most important being the method of creating live subtitles and the time it takes to produce each subtitle. The lower the latency, the better as high latency makes it hard for viewers to follow subtitles.

However, while there is a general agreement that the less latency, the better, there is no clear cut-off point after which one can say that latency is unacceptable. Indeed, it might depend on the type of content that is subtitled. Some media regulators do provide guidelines. Initially, Ofcom recommended that the latency should not be higher than 3 seconds (Ofcom, 2017) even though no broadcaster was able to achieve that when the regulator assessed latency (Ofcom, 2015). Later on, the recommendation was updated to 6 seconds. Spanish AENOR recommends a maximum of 8 seconds and the French Conseil Supérieur de l'Audiovisuel set the maximum latency to 10 seconds (Fresno, 2019).

5.4.2. Subtitle speed

One of the most important technical dimensions of live subtitling quality is subtitle display time, which is inextricably linked to the subtitle speed, also referred to as the reading speed of subtitles. Subtitle speed has to do with how long a subtitle is displayed on screen and how much time viewers have to read the subtitle relative to the text within this subtitle (Fresno & Sepielak, 2020; Szarkowska, Silva, & Orrego-Carmona, 2021). Subtitle speed is usually expressed as words per minute (wpm) or characters per second (cps). A survey of subtitlers found that characters per second is now the preferred unit, used by 117 out of 138 participants in the survey (Szarkowska, 2016).

The most fundamental principle is for each subtitle to be displayed long enough for viewers to able to read it (Díaz Cintas & Remael, 2007; Szarkowska & Gerber-Morón, 2018). If the subtitle speed is too high, it might mean that a viewer will be unable to read the whole subtitle before it disappears from screen.

While it is clear that very fast speeds can disrupt the watching experience, finding the "ideal" subtitling speed is tricky as people read at different speeds, depending on the individual viewers and the characteristics of subtitled content. For instance, children, particularly younger ones, spend proportionally more time on reading subtitles (Szarkowska, Silva, & Orrego-Carmona, 2021). Depending on the factors such as the viewer's education, AVT habits, proficiency in the language or the knowledge of the topic discussed, some viewers might be able to read faster than others. The speed with which viewers can read can also be affected the complexity of the text itself, including word length and word frequency. Moran (2009) found that viewers reading subtitles containing more high-frequency words had a shorter overall reading time than those subtitles with low-frequency words. Another study showed that viewers spend proportionally more time gazing at two-line subtitles compared to one-liners (Szarkowska, Silva, & Orrego-Carmona, 2021).

The International Telecommunications Union (ITU, 2011) recommends keeping the subtitle speed below 180 words per minute as otherwise some of the viewers will not be able to follow the subtitles. At the same time regular viewing of subtitled television improves literacy. According to the report "same-language-captioning can have a major impact on literacy and reading growth across a broad range of reading abilities". All this makes reading speed one of key issues in subtitling.

Slow subtitles are believed to allow viewers to read comfortably and still have time left to follow on-screen action. However, slower speeds require more condensation, which might make the text less cohesive and more difficult to understand. A more condensed rendition will be less congruous with the original dialogue, which might be noticed by viewers who understand the original language to some degree (Szarkowska & Gerber-Moron, 2018). Fast subtitles, in turn, require viewers to spend more time on the subtitles and less on the images (Romero Fresco, 2012, 2015; Szarkowska, Silva, & Orrego-Carmona, 2021).

Szarkowska (2016) found that the subtitling speeds that were most often used for pre-recorded subtitling ranged from 10 to 17 cps. While the subtitle speeds recommended by regulators for SDH tend to be the same or lower than for pre-recorded subtitling (with the Polish regulator recommending 12 cps), live subtitles tend to be faster than pre-recorded ones and have an ampler speed variation (Fresno & Sepielak, 2020). The effect is that, when watching live subtitles on television, the viewers will encounter higher speeds than the ones they are accustomed to when watching pre-recorded subtitling.

How fast is too fast? In a study on pre-recorded subtitling by Szarkowska and Gerber-Morón the participants were able to cope well with speeds up to 20 cps with no detriment to processing (Szarkowska & Gerber-Morón, 2018). Liao et al. (2021) found that, unlike in the case of 12 or 20 cps, a speed of 28 cps may result in changing viewers' reading and viewing patterns. At this very high speed, viewers spent less time looking at individual words, skipped more words and focused on longer words to obtain the gist of the text. It was also found that their comprehension score dropped significantly.

It is also important to understand that subtitle speed is not the same throughout the show, rather it changes constantly. In verbatim SDH, the speaker's speech rate (i.e. how fast a speaker speaks) will have strong influence on the subtitling speed of verbatim subtitles as the subtitlers will try to follow the speaker's pace. The speaker's speech rate will have less of an impact in edited SDH, where the subtitlers will try to edit down the subtitles to stay under a certain subtitling speed threshold (Fresno & Sepielak, 2020). That is why condensation is considered a key subtitling skill (Szarkowska, Silva, & Orrego-Carmona, 2021).

"For live subtitles to be useful, the viewers need to have enough time to read them" (Saerens et al., 2020, p. 11). But among the various guidelines, only the Spanish norm provides an explicit threshold for live subtitles (at 15 cps). Polish National Broadcasting Council only offers guidance on pre-recorded SDH which should not exceed 12 cps (KRRiT, 2016). And Ofcom (2017) points out that subtitles over 200 wpm (which translates to approximately 17 cps) can be challenging for many viewers.

5.4.3. SDH features: Sound descriptions and speaker identification

While live subtitling can serve many different users, it is often viewed by media regulatory bodies as a live form of SDH. And pre-recorded SDH includes a number of features that help the Deaf and the hard of hearing viewers access content such as descriptions of plot-pertinent sounds and music as well as speaker identification. The latter is particularly important whenever the speaker is not on-screen. While hearing viewers are able to differentiate speakers by the characteristics of their voices, other viewers might need speaker identification to be explicit in the subtitles.

Due to time constraints in live subtitling, it might be more difficult to include these features and subtitlers will have to prioritize what they see as most important. Usually, the speaker identification is considered most important, and it is prioritized (Saerens et al., 2020). Indeed, speaker identification can be even more important in live subtitling. Due to subtitles appearing with latency, the speaker might no longer be speaking or might no longer be shown on screen when his or her utterance appears as a subtitle.

Speakers can be identified in a number of ways: through font colours (with most important speakers having different colours and the utterances of the remaining speakers displayed in white) or name tags (usually names or job titles, usually spelled in all caps and followed by a colon and a space, e.g. ADAM: or PRESIDENT:).

An alternative solution is to indicate that a new speaker starts speaking without identifying who the speaker is. This is usually done using chevrons (see Fig. 19) or dashes and it is most effective in the case of talks when there are two or three speakers, and the viewers can work out easily who the new speaker is.

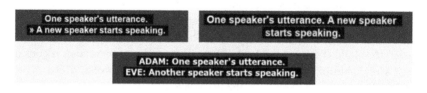

Fig. 19: *Chevrons (left), colours (right; the first sentence in white and the second sentence in yellow) and name tags (middle) are ways to help viewers differentiate which speaker says what (Saerens et al., 2020).*

5.4.4. Legibility and readability

In subtitling, legibility is about the font type, font size and the contrast between the text and the background. While mostly sans-serif fonts are used in subtitling as they are believed to be more legible than serif fonts on low-resolution screens (Díaz Cintas & Remael, 2007), the actual font is usually beyond the control of the subtitlers. In broadcasting, the font depends on the device of the final user, be it a TV decoder or a TV set. In online streaming or OTT TV, it depends on the video player and it can also be customised by the viewer. However, subtitlers and broadcasters can have control over the contrast between the subtitles and the background. To improve it, they can add a black outline to the letters or display subtitles on a black or semi-transparent background.

Readability is about how easy it is to comprehend subtitles and how coherent they are. This can be affected by both technical considerations (for instance, readability is affected by the display mode, discussed in more detail below) as well as linguistic ones (for example, text segmentation).

5.4.5. Subtitle display mode

Apart from subtitle speed, the display mode also plays a role in whether the viewers can follow subtitles comfortably. There are various ways of displaying live subtitles. The block mode consists of displaying one, two or three lines of text and it is similar to how pre-recorded subtitling is displayed. The scrolling mode, in turn, involves displaying one word or one phrase at a time. As new text is created, it is added to the existing text on screen and once there is no more space in a line, the line moves up and the new text appears below, thus creating the scrolling effect (Romero Fresco, 2011).

The scrolling has been developed specifically for live subtitling in an effort to minimize latency as chunks of text can be presented immediately on screen without having to wait for the entire subtitle to be ready. This display mode is most common in English-speaking countries such as the UK, US, Canada and Australia. However, research has shown that the scrolling mode disrupts reading patterns, making viewers spend more time on subtitles (than in the case of block subtitles). Rather than being able to read the entire subtitle at a glance and move to scanning the images, viewers wait for new words to appear (Rajendran et al., 2013; Romero Fresco, 2011).

5.4.6. Subtitle placement

Regarding the positioning of subtitles, whenever a subtitle would cover the speaker's mouth or relevant graphics, its placement should be adjusted so as not to cover the graphics (Díaz Cintas & Remael, 2007). The rationale for this is that subtitles should not hinder viewers' access to information represented graphically or to other on-screen text. From a technical perspective, subtitle placement can be described in terms of pixels or lines (i.e. proportional areas of the screen). As TV sets can have different resolutions and the number of pixels can vary greatly, the safer way to describe the placement of subtitles is through the lines. When changing subtitle placement, subtitlers usually raise them by one or two lines or move them to the top position (the top line, which is the highest area available on screen for subtitles). There are limitations to where subtitles can be placed as only part of the screen is available (known as "safe area"). Subtitles should not appear on the margins of the image are these are considered not safe in a sense that depending on the TV set, they might not be fully displayed, and it would be possible for the subtitle to be partially cut.

5.5. (Not so) objective measures of live subtitling quality

Now that we have discussed different dimensions of live subtitling quality, we will look into ways of analysing them through models and metrics. Various attempts have been made at creating metrics and assessment models that would evaluate the quality of subtitling in an objective way. So far, the research on the quality of live subtitles as a product has been focused on features such as accuracy, latency, subtitle spate, reduction rate and display mode (Romero Fresco & Eugeni, 2020). The analysis came from academics, user associations, broadcasters and regulators. Different models have been proposed to evaluate the quality of live subtitles. Some were based on subtitling theory (Eugeni, 2012), others on the everyday practice of live subtitling (Dumouchel et al., 2012), the automatization of quality assessment (Apone et al., 2010) or the impact of the viewers' comprehension (Romero Fresco & Martínez Pérez, 2015). The following sections will discuss models used most often in pre-recorded and live subtitling.

5.5.1. FAR, WER and WWER

The most comprehensive attempt at creating an assessment model for pre-recorded interlingual subtitling is the FAR model, which introduces three types of errors. Functional equivalence errors (F), acceptance errors (A) and readability errors (R) (Pedersen, 2017). The model offers a number of advantages as it is viewer-centred, includes information useful for training and feedback and can be adapted to specific guidelines. However, it is not suitable for the evaluation of live subtitling. The same is true for metrics-based models used to evaluate translation in general such as the LISA QA metric (applied to machine translation), TAUS and the EU Multidimensional Quality Metrics.

The first attempts to evaluate the quality of live subtitling were done with WER or word error rate (Dumouchel et al., 2012). It is a measure traditionally used in evaluating the quality of speech recognition. It consists in comparing verbatim transcript of speech with the text produced by speech recognition and identifying deletions, substitutions and insertions. While the transcript used as reference needs to be prepared by human editors, the process of comparing the two texts can be done automatically. Any divergence between the two texts (down to a level of a single character) is considered an error. A final score is expressed as a percentage and shows how similar the two texts are. For example, a score of 99% shows that out of 100 characters, 99 were the same and one was different. If the two texts are identical, the WER will produce a 100% score. Thus, WER is well aligned with the verbatim approach to accuracy (as discussed in Section 5.3.1).

The advantage of WER is that as an automated measure, it is very quick to use. The disadvantage is that it does not take into account the meaning. For instance, using a different word that still means the same will be considered inaccurate within the WER assessment. And the other way round, a significant change in meaning will not be properly reflected by WER if it just affects a few characters. Also, with WER it is not possible to differentiate between different kinds of errors. All changes in the text are considered equal and assigned the same weight.

In the example we looked at in the previous section, even though it expresses the same information, so many of the characters have been changed that WER will produce a low score (see Table 1 below). If we understand accuracy in line with the sensatim approach, the WER is actually not a measure of accuracy but of literality (i.e. how verbatim the transcription is). If we change "we" to "they" in the example below, the information will be different and the subtitle will be misleading, and yet it will achieve a higher WER score as the transcription is more verbatim.

Table 1: *Example of WER assessment with deletions, substitutions and insertions in bold, and the matching text underlined*

Audio	Subtitle	WER analysis	WER score
We all sort of need the same things.	Everybody needs the same thing.	**[We all sort of] Everybody** needs the same thing**[s]**.	41%
We all sort of need the same things.	They all sort of need the same things.	**[We] They** all sort of need the same things.	88%

WER is objective in a sense that every character in a text can either match the transcription or not and will be considered correct or incorrect. If the analysis is repeated with the same texts, WER will always produce the same score again. However, despite its advantages, WER is just not a good measure of accuracy in live subtitling.

To compensate for the shortcomings of WER, an American NGO, the Carl and Ruth Shapiro Family National Center for Accessible Media, introduced the so-called "weighted word error rate" (WWER), a formula that classifies subtitle errors on the basis of their seriousness and automates the process so that no human intervention is needed to assess subtitle quality (Apone et al., 2010).

While the introduction of different weights for errors is an improvement over WER, the WWER is also not a good measure of accuracy as it does not allow for the same or similar information to be expressed with different words. All forms of paraphrasing are still considered errors. Indeed, this is the limitation of all automatic accuracy measures designed so far; they are unable to determine if the paraphrase is correct or not. As condensation is a crucial aspect of all subtitling, live subtitling included, subtitlers often rephrase and condense the text, using different words or fewer words without (much) loss of information. And up until today monolingual paraphrasing can only be assessed manually by a human evaluator (Romero-Fresco, 2021) because "as soon as paraphrasing comes into play, so does meaning as the *tertium comparationis*, and the need for subjective judgement by the analyst" (Romero Fresco & Pöchhacker, 2018, p. 158).

5.5.2. The NER model

This element of manual assessment was introduced in the NER model that was put forward by Romero Fresco (2011) and then developed by Romero Fresco and Martinez (2015). Similarly to WER or WWER, it also compares two sets of texts (the verbatim transcription and the subtitles) but it assumes a sensa-tim perspective and looks at idea units rather than words. In order to "account for the fact that not all errors have the same origin or impact on the viewers' comprehension" (Romero Fresco & Pöchhacker, 2018), NER includes the division into recognition errors and edition errors (the latter due to errors made by subtitlers rather than speech recognition software). Similarly to WER, the NER is expressed as a percentage. However, it looks at words or phrases rather than at individual characters. NER is meaning-focused in a sense that it takes into account idea units (phrases of up to seven words, usually containing one verb and expressing one coherent information). If the text in the subtitles is rephrased and uses different words but still expresses the same meaning, it will be considered correct or accurate within the NER assessment. On the other hand, even a small change in the text will be considered a serious error if it changes the meaning.

NER introduces three weights for errors depending on their severity (each type of error carries a negative value that is distracted from the final score): minor (-0.25), standard (-0.5) and serious (-1). The assumption behind the NER model is that those three weights reflect how serious an impact an error has on the viewer's experience of watching subtitled content.

A minor error does not affect the understanding of the text. As a viewer, one can easily identify the error and work out the intended meaning.

AUDIO	SUBTITLE[48]
Gordon **Brown** had been the longest continuously serving chancellor of the Exchequer since the 1820s.	Gordon **brown** had been the longest continuously serving chancellor of the Exchequer since the 1820s.

A major error makes it hard for you to understand the text. As a viewer you will be aware that the caption contains such an error, but you will not be able to work out the intended meaning.

AUDIO	SUBTITLE
He's **buy you a bull** asset.	He's **a valuable** asset.

Critical errors result in false information. They could be called "lies" (Romero-Fresco, 2021) as they provide false information and viewers might not be aware they are seeing an error.

AUDIO	SUBTITLE
Funding for hospitals has been cut by **50%** this year.	Funding for hospitals has been cut by **15%** this year.

If we return to the example used previously, we can see that through the NER analysis it is possible to differentiate between a successful paraphrase and an error that changes the meaning of the text.

---

48   The examples come from the presentation on the NER model by Pablo Romero Fresco, which is a part of the online ILSA course available at: http://ka2-ilsa.webs. uvigo.es/

Audio	Subtitle	NER analysis
We all sort of need the same things.	Everybody needs the same thing.	"Everybody" – Correct Edition (-0)
We all sort of need the same things.	**They** all sort of need the same things.	"They" – Critical Error (-1)

The NER score formula (see Fig. 20 below) takes into account the number of words in the respoken text (N), including punctuation marks and speaker identification. It also uses the number of edition (E) and recognition (R) errors identified in the analysis (and multiplied by their weights: 0.25, 0.5 or 1). The errors are subtracted from the number of words and the sum is then divided by the total number of words. Finally, the result is multiplied by 100 to obtain a percentage.

$$Accuracy = \frac{N-E-R}{N} \times 100$$

CE (correct editions):
Assessment:

Fig. 20: *The NER score formula (Romero Fresco & Martínez Pérez, 2015)*

NER tends to produce high numeric values, which can be misleading as only the values above 98% are considered as indicators of acceptable quality, whereas a value of 95% (which might seem a high score) can equal a text that is unreadable. Indeed, Dostępni.eu, Polish accessibility services provider, based on internal analysis, claims that if a respeaker or automatic speech recognition does not achieve a NER score of at least 95% in Polish, it is impossible to apply parallel correction as the correctors will not be able to make sense of the text they see.[49] In this context, Romero Fresco (2016) recommends to also present the NER scores on a 10-point scale (see Table 2 below) and classify values into four groups: substandard (below 98%), acceptable (98–98.49%) good (98.50–98.99%), very good (99–99.49%) and excellent (99.50%–100%).

---

49   Personal communication with Monika Szczygielska from Dostępni.eu.

Table 2: *Recalculation of the NER score to a 10-point scale (Romero Fresco & Pöchhacker, 2018)*

Accuracy rate (%)	10-point scale
<96%	0/10
96.4%	1/10
96.8%	2/10
97.2%	3/10
97.6%	4/10
98.0%	5/10
98.4%	6/10
98.8%	7/10
99.2%	8/10
99.6%	9/10
100%	10/10

The NER model is now widely used as an assessment tool by broadcasters, regulators, researchers and live subtitling companies in a number of countries. In a survey of companies Robert and her colleagues (2019) found the NER score to be the single most used metric when assessing respoken subtitles (80 % of the respondents admitted to using it). But, of course, it does have some limitations. The most obvious ones include the time-consuming nature of NER assessment, a degree of subjectivity involved in it and the fact that (similarly to WER) it can only be used to compare texts within the same language, and thus it is not possible to use it for the assessment of interlingual subtitles. However, Romero Fresco believes that subjectivity "can be mitigated if the model is reliable" (Romero-Fresco, 2021, p. 743), which can be achieved through proper training of assessors and the calculation of inter-rater agreement. And interlingual live subtitling can now be assessed with the use of NERT, an adaptation of the NER model that allows to measure the quality of interlingual live subtitles and distinguishes between editing and translation errors (Romero Fresco & Pöchhacker, 2018).

Another limitation of the NER model has to do with the fact that as live subtitling quality is so multidimensional, it is difficult for any model to include all the different dimensions of quality, let alone calculate that as a single number. When developing the NER model, its authors set out to meet various requirements and some of the aims included to "provide information about not only the accuracy of the subtitles but also other aspects of quality such as delay, position, speed, character identification" and "provide an assessment of quality as well as an overall idea of aspects to be improved, in other words, food for thought as far as training is concerned" (Romero Fresco & Pöchhacker, 2018, p. 150). While all these elements are not part of the NER formula and thus are not reflected in the NER score, they are meant to be a part of NER assessment and should be analysed and included as comments accompanying the NER score. One of the authors of the NER model himself cautions that "it is the final conclusion and not the accuracy rate that represents the quality of a given set of subtitles as assessed using the NER model" (Romero Fresco & Pöchhacker, 2018).

However, many stakeholders do not look beyond the NER score and understand this number as an overall measure of quality of live subtitling. The NER model can then be "seen to provide cold metrics and to reduce the complex issue of quality to a single number" (Romero-Fresco, 2021, p. 743). Greco and Jankowska (2019, p. 7) warn against this risk of "confusing a part for the whole" and "conducting research on some dimension of an MA [media accessibility] service but then drawing conclusions at the general level of quality for that service".

Summing up, the NER score, which as such is a measure of accuracy, should always be complemented by analysing other dimensions of live subtitling quality. And only by looking at multiple dimensions, we can draw conclusions about the overall quality. In the following section, I will look into if and how those other dimensions can be measured.

5.5.3. Measuring subtitle speed

One such important dimension of quality that can be measured objectively is subtitle speed or subtitle display rate (also known as subtitle reading speed) (Díaz Cintas & Remael, 2007; Fresno & Sepielak, 2020; Szarkowska & Gerber-Morón, 2018; Szarkowska, Silva, & Orrego-Carmona, 2021). Subtitle speed is calculated taking into account the number of characters in a subtitle and the duration of this subtitle (i.e. how long it is displayed on screen).

Measuring subtitle speed can be tricky. It is traditionally measured in characters per second (cps) and words per minute (wpm). Characters per second are used more often as it is a more accurate measure across languages (Szarkowska, Silva, & Orrego-Carmona, 2021) as some languages tend to have longer words than others. There is no standard conversion between cps and wpm; the recalculation is usually done on the assumption that an average word is five characters long (Díaz Cintas & Remael, 2007), which is true for English but not necessarily for other languages.

In a methodological paper on calculating subtitle speed, Fresno and Sepielak (2020) analysed various ways in which subtitle speed can be measured and found at least three approaches to measuring subtitle speed: (1) dividing the total number of characters or words in all the subtitles within a given sample by the time that those subtitles are displayed on screen; (2) dividing the total number of characters or words in a set of subtitles by the duration of the video that they accompany; (3) calculating the speed of each subtitle and taking into account the mean of these values. Crucially, there are significant discrepancies, especially between the first and the last approach.

While the two researchers recommend the use of the third method, they also caution that "the ASS alone does not seem to provide clear insights of how fast or slow a set of subtitles are presented to the end users" (Fresno & Sepielak, 2020, p. 11). Thus, the proposed best practise is that subtitle speed should always be reported together with (1) measures of variability such as range or standard deviation; and (2) percentage of slow and fast subtitles in the studies samples; and (3) in experimental research: range of tolerance used in subtitling software when creating subtitless (Fresno & Sepielak, 2020).

5.5.4. Synchronicity: Measuring latency and gaps between subtitles

It is also possible to measure the synchronicity of the subtitles. While live subtitles are usually delayed to some extent, the aim is to minimize the latency (that is the delay between a speaker saying an utterance and the subtitle appearing on screen). The latency is usually expressed in seconds or milliseconds and can be measured in a number of ways. One way is comparing the moment a word is uttered and the moment a subtitle containing this word appears on screen. This can be done manually by playing the video and stopping when one hears a word. A more precise alternative is to create a set of perfectly synced subtitles where a timecode indicates the onset time of speech. (Timecodes are usually expressed in seconds and frames but can be recalculated to milliseconds.) While there still might be some subjectivity involved in deciding which frame is the first frame of the audio, usually possible differences between assessors will not be larger than several frames (that is, a fraction of a second). Interestingly, past studies do not always disclose how exactly latency was calculated (cf. Fresno, 2019).

Measuring latency can be more difficult when the subtitles are presented not as blocks of text but in the scrolling mode. When subtitles appear word by word, it might be necessary to measure the latency for each word separately. Another possible approach would be to select words at regular intervals and measure the latency for these specific words (which is the approach traditionally used to measure the ear voice span in the research on interpreting, but is has also been applied to respeaking, see Chmiel et al., 2017). However, this might be problematic as some of the words from the audio might not appear in subtitles or, vice versa, some words that are in the subtitles might not be in the audio.

Another aspect of synchronicity is the gap between subtitles. As per subtitling guidelines, there should always be a minimum gap between two consecutive subtitles (Díaz Cintas & Remael, 2007). The minimum gap that is usually recommended is 2 to 4 frames. The rationale for the minimum gap is that it allows the eye to register a slight movement on screen (one subtitle disappearing and another appearing). Movement is one of the strongest gaze attractors (Holmqvist et al., 2015) and thus the minimum gap between subtitles helps the eyes register that a subtitle has changed. If the eyes are fixated on the image, noticing a subtitle change will initiate a movement (a "saccade") towards the subtitle area and the eyes will start scanning the new subtitle. If there is no minimum gap, viewers might not notice that there is a new subtitle on screen (especially if a two-line subtitle changes into another two-line subtitle with a similar number of characters or a one-liner changes into another one liner). Instead of reading the new subtitles, viewers will continue looking at the image.

The minimum gap is related to the practice of chaining. Various subtitling guidelines recommend chaining in order to close short gaps between the subtitles. "Closing" the gaps is understood as shortening them to the minimum gap and depending on the guidelines gaps of up to one second or up to 12 frames (approx. half a second in 25 frames per second video material) are considered short and should be closed. Closing these gaps (chaining) is achieved through extending the out-time of the previous subtitle so that it ends just before the following subtitle (always respecting the minimum gap).

The gap between subtitles has not been analysed in any known previous studies on live subtitling. One might argue that it is because in the case of continuous speech, there is always a continuous flow of live subtitles, one subtitle after another, respecting the minimum gap. And when there are longer gaps between the subtitles that is because there is a pause in speech. However, in the research presented here this was found not to be true. There were numerous cases of longer gaps between subtitles despite continuous speech. This shows that gaps between subtitles do require scrutiny in research on live subtitles.

Gaps between consecutive subtitles can be measured by using the timecodes of subtitles and comparing the out-time of each subtitle with the in-time of the following subtitle. This can be achieved by using subtitling software to export a subtitle file as a spreadsheet in which the in-times and out-times of subtitles are expressed in milliseconds and placed in separate columns. A formula can then calculate the gap between consecutive subtitles. The gap can be calculated for all but one subtitle as the last subtitle in the file will have to be excluded (it will have no following subtitle that could be used for reference).

5.5.5. Measuring text segmentation

As the NER model does not take into account text segmentation errors and there is no other established metric that would allow researchers to measure the quality of text segmentation in subtitles, in this book I propose a novel approach to study text segmentation in subtitling.

The proposed segmentation score aims to provide a single numeric value that can be used to compare the quality of text segmentation between samples of subtitling. The assessment involves classifying the segmentation errors into three categories and assigning weights to errors depending on the severity of each error. The same weights are used as in the case of the NER model: 1, 0.5 and 0.25. Indeed, the assessment can be performed in parallel to the NER assessment, within the same score sheet.

To assess the quality of text segmentation, all the text segmentation errors need to be identified and divided into three categories labelled as A, B or C. Type A errors include syntactic phrases (such as the verb and "not") being split between two different subtitles. As discussed previously in Section 5.5.5, these errors are considered most serious and thus are assigned the weight of 1 (see Fig. 22 for examples of each type of errors). Type B errors involve situations when one sentence was split into two subtitles unnecessarily or parts of two sentences were merged into one subtitle. For instance, the ending of a sentence and the beginning of another sentence were put together in one subtitle, whereas it was possible to have one full sentence per each subtitle. Type B errors violate the rule that each subtitle should be syntactically self-contained (Díaz Cintas & Remael, 2007) and are assigned the weight of 0.5. Finally, type C errors are similar to type A as they also refer to situations where words that strongly linked semantically are split. However, in the case of type A errors the words are split between two subtitles, whereas a type C error involves words being split between two lines (but still displayed in the same subtitle). Type C errors are considered least serious and assigned the weight of 0.25.

Of course, the weights assigned to errors are arbitrary to some degree. While clearly type A errors are more serious than type C errors, it cannot be argued that type B errors (with the weight of 0.5) are *exactly* twice as serious as type C errors (with the weight of 0.25). Still, assigning the weights allows for a more nuanced assessment of segmentation than in the case of just summing up the number of all the errors without distinguishing their severity.

The segmentation score is calculated through multiplying each error by its weight and summing up the values of all the errors in the subtitles. The lower the score, the fewer segmentation errors were found in the assessment, and the higher the quality of text segmentation.

Fig. 22: *Examples of type A, type B and type C text segmentation errors*

Note. Type A error. The phrase "nie będzie", which includes "not" and a verb, is split between two subtitles. Splitting words that are strongly linked syntactically and dividing them between two subtitles is considered a serious segmentation error.

Note. Type B error. The two sentences are segmented in such a way that the last two words of the first sentence ("trzykrotnie nożem") are displayed together with the following sentence. The segmentation could be improved by dividing the first sentence into two separate subtitles (the second line of the subtitle on the left would be displayed together with the remaining two words; the second sentence would be a new subtitle altogether).

Note. Type C error. The word "się" (at the end of the second line) is strongly linked syntactically with the verb "zgodzić" (in the third line) and both words should be kept in the same line.

5.5.6. Measuring other quality parameters

While no specific metrics or established measuring practices exist for other quality features, many of these can be checked manually by watching subtitled videos and taking note of these parameters. This is the case of the presentation mode (are subtitles displayed as blocks of text or scrolling text?) or placement (do subtitles cover on-screen graphics?).

With other parameters, the analysis can be automated to some degree. For instance, checking for the presence of SDH-specific features such as speaker identifiers or sound descriptions can be done manually but it is also possible to search for them in the corpus of subtitles. However, only the manual analysis combined with actually watching the video make it possible to verify if sound descriptions are not missing for pertinent sounds or if speakers are identified correctly.

Finally, legibility and readability can also be analysed in a number of ways. Manually, by checking the font and the size of the text as well as the presence of outline or black or semi-transparent background. There are automated tools that can measure the contrast between the subtitles and the background. And readability indices can be used to assess the difficulty of understanding the text.

All the metrics and measurements described above are used on the tacit assumption that they provide insight into the quality of live subtitles. But if quality is understood not as an abstract and elusive concept but as being fit for purpose, then an important question appears: do these measures correlate with whether the subtitles are fit for purpose and fulfil the needs and expectations of the target audience?

5.6. Quality perception of users versus objective measures

So far, there has not been much rigorous research into how the objective measures (or metrics such as NER that aim for objectivity) correlate with how viewers subjectively perceive subtitling quality. However, small-scale studies in Poland (Szczygielska & Dutka, 2016) and Canada (Canadian Association of the Deaf [CAD], 2018) did suggest correlation between the NER score and the quality ratings by users. The Polish study compared human-made and automatic subtitling of a parliamentary debate and found that the samples of subtitles which had a higher NER score were also judged by viewers to be of better quality than samples which had a lower NER score. The study had 55 participants that watched 3 video clips of parliamentary debates and answered a questionnaire. They were asked to rate the quality of live subtitling on a scale of 1 to 5, where 5 meant very good and 1 meant very bad. The clip which had the highest NER score (99.47%) received a user rating of 3.60, whereas the clip with the lowest NER score (95.26%) also had the lowest user rating of 2.33.

On top of that, the study analysed the reduction rate of subtitles as well as asked the participants to rate how much editing and simplification they see in the subtitles. Interestingly, a video clip that had verbatim subtitles (with a reduction rate of 0.5%) was rated by 15% of the participants as "highly edited and simplified". This shows that viewers rating does not always coincide with objective reality.

In Canada, as part of a research project funded by the Canadian media regulator, an on-line questionnaire was conducted among 330 Deaf or hard of hearing participants and 220 hearing participants. The participants were asked to watch eight subtitled video segments and the results showed "directional indication that satisfaction increases with NER score", however, the authors concluded that more video samples would need to be tested to "yield a scientifically valid result" (CAD, 2018, p. 8).

It is important to point out here that all the measures described in the previous section look at one or several specific dimensions of quality and do not take into account other dimensions. Thus, subtitles might have a high NER score, showing they are accurate and represent the content faithfully but at the same time viewers might evaluate them as low quality subtitles if, for instance, the latency is very high. Even very accurate subtitles will not be satisfactory to viewers if they appear with a delay of 20 seconds.

In the Polish study discussed above (Szczygielska & Dutka, 2016) the participants were also provided with a list of quality parameters and asked to arrange them according to their importance. The participants prioritized legibility (probably meant as readability),[50] literality (the subtitles being verbatim) and

---

50 Legibility and readability seem to sometimes be used interchangeably in live subtitling research. However, if the legibility is defined as a measure of how easy it is to distinguish between letters in a typeface and readability is a measure of how easy it is to decipher, process and understand text, then the questionnaire used in the study referred to readability and the use of term "legibility" is probably a mistranslation from Polish.

presented with a low latency. Grammar and spelling, in turn, were judged to be least important (see Fig. 23).

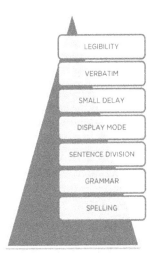

Fig. 23: *Quality parameters as prioritised by users (starting from the most important at the top) (Szczygielska & Dutka, 2016)*

But even if we can agree on most important quality criteria, the weight given to them varies. Depending on how an individual user prioritizes quality dimensions, his or her evaluation of live subtitles will align or misalign with a given quality metric. Quality parameters are also relative because they can depend on several factors, such as time, place, context of communication, genre or the target user (Robert & Remael, 2016).

For instance, subtitles with an acceptable subtitle speed can be evaluated by viewers negatively if they feel that they are missing information. If a viewer believes that subtitles should be verbatim, he or she might reject condensed subtitles as unacceptable, even if they are skilfully condensed and no information is actually missing. The Deaf viewers who cannot compare the subtitles with the audio might form their opinions based on what they are told by their family members or friends. If they are told that some words are missing, some of them might assume that the quality is not satisfactory. Some hard of hearing viewers might use lip-reading to recognize some of the spoken words and if they do not see such words in subtitles, they will consider the subtitles to be inaccurate.

5.7. The impact of editing live subtitles on quality: Live correction

The quality of live subtitling is also affected by various factors. First of all, it depends on the efficacy of the method used to produce live subtitling. For instance, in the case of respeaking it depends on the accuracy of the speech recognition system (how well the system recognizes the words) and the skill and training of the respeakers (how well they can interact with the software by dictating words; and how skilfully they can rephrase the content). Improvements to the systems used and better training for professionals involved can improve the base quality level of subtitles produced this way.

In any case, it will be impossible to eliminate all the errors and achieve 100% accuracy in this way. What can be done to further improve the quality of live subtitling is to revise and edit the subtitles, what is known as live editing or live correction (Saerens et al., 2020).

Revision and editing are a standard practice in pre-recorded subtitling as most subtitlers revise their work in one or several revision steps with revision understood as the process of looking over translation and making changes as needed to ensure that it is of satisfactory quality (Robert & Remael, 2016). Often, there is an extra revision step performed by another subtitler, referred to as the QC-er.

Performing the revision step live is far more challenging due to time constraints and might actually be more similar to post-editing as done on machine translation than the revision of the pre-recorded subtitling. Live correction consists of reading the text, spotting the errors and correcting as many as possible. It can be done either before the text is presented to the viewers (in this case the viewers just see the final, edited version) or it can be performed even after the text has been shown to viewers (in this case viewers see both versions). It can be done by respeakers themselves who spot and correct the errors (self-correction) or by live editors (parallel correction).

A study by Szczygielska and Dutka (2016) that used NER to evaluate subtitles before and after live correction found that the addition of live correction can greatly improve the NER score. The improvement was between 2 and 3 percentage points for subtitles created through respeaking and between 4 and 7 percentage points for automatic speech recognition. If a respeaker was able to produce subtitles with a NER score above 95%, applying live correction made it possible to increase the NER score to the acceptable threshold of 98% or above. Even though the improvement was far greater for automatic speech recognition, as the base NER score for ASR was very low (between 90% and 92% for all the samples), only one of the four samples reached 98% threshold after live correction. The explanation that was found for why live correction produced a much greater increase in the NER score for automatic speech recognition was that ASR introduced many more serious errors in the text, whereas the respoken subtitled tended to have more minor errors. And correcting serious errors has a bigger impact on the NER score.

It is important to point out that while live correction can increase the accuracy of subtitles, it will also increase latency. As a result, even with live correction it might not be possible to achieve error-free subtitles. If there are numerous errors, trying to correct all of them before viewers see the text will take too much time and can result in an unacceptable latency of the subtitles. Still, live correction minimizes the risk of viewers seeing serious errors.

When discussing live correction, it is important to point out that in the process of creating live subtitling not one but several texts are produced. Eugeni and Marchionne (2014, as quoted by Romero Fresco & Eugeni, 2020) distinguish three types of text: the source text, the mid text, and the target text. The source text is the original text, i.e. the utterances of speakers that respeakers hear. The mid text is what the respeaker produces. And the target text consists of the subtitles as displayed to viewers (including changes made by the editor). While Eugeni and Marchionne stop here, actually the mid-text could be distinguished further in two texts as the speaker can say one thing but the speech recognition can recognize something else.

Eugeni and Marchionne (2014) also distinguish three stages at which editing can happen: pre-editing, peri-editing and post-editing. Pre-editing can happen at the preparation stages when subtitles can train the software to recognize terms or proper names related to the show which is to be subtitled. Peri-editing can be done by respeakers who rephrase the mid-text to avoid using a term that they suspect might not be included in the software vocabulary or is a term that tends to be misrecognized. Also, they can rephrase the text to shorten it in an effort to lower subtitle display rate. Finally, post-editing is done by the editor who makes changes in the mid text before it is displayed to viewers as the target text.

5.8. The impact of workflows and procedures on live subtitling quality: Good practices

While in this work we are focusing on the quality of the product and how it can be best analysed, quality can also be discussed in terms of a process. The process of creating live subtitles can be organized in a number of ways resulting in many possible workflows. It is not possible to identify one and only ideal workflow as each workflow involves trade-offs. Still, there are some recognized good practices that are believed to contribute to better quality of the final product.

The guidelines produced by the ILSA Project recommend that live subtitles produced through respeaking should be corrected before they are displayed on screen. Depending on the difficulty of the task, the correction "can be done by the respeaker (self-correction) or by a live editor" (Saerens et al., 2020, p. 10). In either case, live correction can improve the accuracy of subtitles and minimize the number of errors, contributing to better quality. Self-correction is better than no correction and parallel correction is likely to have an even greater impact on quality.

Self-correction can be used for slow-paced shows in languages such as English, where there are not that many misrecognitions. In such a scenario, the respeaker has enough time to pause respeaking, correct the errors and resume respeaking. However, fast-spoken programmes and topics where speech recognition tends to produce many misrecognitions will require parallel correction as any pauses in respeaking might result in loss of content. Parallel correction allows the respeaker to focus on respeaking only, as the editor carries out the other tasks. It is also indispensable in "highly inflected languages such as French, Polish, Russian or Turkish" (Saerens et al., 2020, p. 10) where there is more room for misrecognitions.

Another recommendation is to use semi-live subtitling whenever possible as this allows more time for subtitles to be revised and minimizes the space for error. Also, when the subtitles are pre-prepared, they can be displayed with "little or no latency" (Saerens et al., 2020, p. 6) and it is easier to control subtitle speed.

The latency can also be minimized in a number of other ways. The most effective is introducing what is known in broadcasting as antenna delay. It is an additional delay that a broadcaster introduces before broadcasting the TV signal. When the live audio and video are recorded, they are not broadcast immediately but after a certain delay, which can vary from several seconds to more than a minute. While the signal is broadcast with a delay, the subtitling team receives it immediately. This way the latency of subtitles can be minimized.

If there is no antenna delay, the latency of the subtitles will roughly equal the time it takes to prepare them (see Fig. 24). If it takes 10 seconds to produce a subtitle, we can assume this subtitle will be displayed with a 10 second latency (10 seconds after the speaker started saying the utterance which is in the subtitle).[51]

---

51 Please note this is a slight simplification used here for the clarity of the example. In practice, it might be possible to gain a little time even when no antenna delay is

If the broadcaster adds an antenna delay of 5 seconds, the latency will be short-ened to 5 seconds. With an antenna delay of 10 seconds, the latency can be min-imized to zero (see Fig. 24).

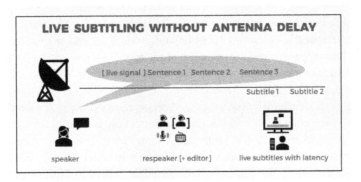

Fig. 24: *Model of live subtitling without antenna delay (Saerens et al., 2020)*

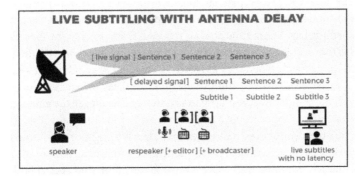

Fig. 25: *Model of live subtitling with antenna delay (Saerens et al., 2020)*

introduced. If live subtitlers receive the signal directly from the studio where the show is being recorded (instead of relying on the broadcast signal that viewers receive), it is possible to gain one or two seconds, which is the time it takes for the signal to be processed and broadcast even when no antenna delay is added.

It is important to point out that the time it takes to produce a subtitle is not the same throughout the broadcast; it varies due to many factors. For instance, the respeaker might have a lower or higher ear voice span (EVS) and the EVS tends to vary over time (Chmiel et al., 2018). Thus, the respeaker might start repeating one sentence a second after the speaker started it; for another sentence it might take the respeaker two or three seconds to start repeating it. The speech recognition systems will also process the audio and produce the text at a different rate, depending on pauses and the structure of the text. If there is a live editor, he or she might take more or less time to spot an error and fix it. All this results in a latency that is changing all the time.

That is the reason why introducing short antenna delay (5–10 seconds) can minimize the latency but will not make subtitles appear in perfect sync. As the time it takes to create each subtitle varies, some subtitles will have more or less latency (some might even have a negative latency, in which case the subtitle will appear even before the speaker starts speaking; something that broadcasters prefer to avoid as it might make viewers doubt if they are indeed watching a live show).

An approach that does permit (near-)perfect sync is introducing long antenna delay (for instance, one minute) that changes a live broadcast into as-live broadcast. This allows to pre-prepare subtitles and then cue them in manually, in a similar fashion as it is done in semi-live subtitling. In this scenario, the respeaker and the editor have more time at their disposal, and, potentially, they can correct all errors and include as verbatim content as possible. The subtitles are not released immediately when they are ready, instead another subtitler (sometimes referred to as "broadcaster") can use the antenna delay to synchronise the subtitles with the programme, resulting in no latency. The bigger the antenna delay, the better the quality of the live subtitles provided for the end users. And the viewers are usually not even aware that they are watching an as-live broadcast.

Regarding latency, the ILSA Project guidelines recommend adding an antenna delay of up to 2 minutes and a have a separate operator who cues subtitles. For news broadcasting, where it might not be desirable to have long antenna delay, the recommendation is to add a delay of 10 seconds (Saerens et al., 2020).

The ILSA guidelines also draw attention to other aspects of the process that can impact the quality of the final product. These include the working conditions of live subtitlers: proper sound insulation of the rooms they are working in, good sound quality, a video monitor showing the TV output so that they can control if the subtitles are broadcast correctly, visual contact with the rest of the team that allows the subtitler to signal the need for back-up or change of roles, good air conditioning and regular breaks. The guidelines note that making live subtitlers work longer without breaks "will have a serious impact on the quality of the subtitles" (Saerens et al., 2020, p. 19).

Even if all care is taken to ensure high quality of live subtitles, they cannot match the quality possible with pre-recorded subtitling. Due to this, the guidelines advise against producing live subtitled for content that is scripted or pre-recorded. Instead, the subtitles should be prepared in advance, thus allowing for more time to work on them and higher quality. Some broadcasters might be tempted to use live subtitling in these cases as it might be easier and less costly to do. Semi-live subtitling requires giving subtitlers access to the scripts or the news system. And in some English-speaking countries pre-recorded subtitling might actually be more expensive than live subtitling.

Regarding the positioning of subtitles, whenever a subtitle would cover the speaker's mouth or relevant graphics, the best practice is to raise such a subtitle so that it appears either one or two lines higher on the screen or it appears at the top of the image (Saerens et al., 2020). If this is not possible, the alternative is to adjust the default position of all the subtitles, in such a way that in most cases the subtitles would not cover graphics and text used in the lower third of the screen. When subtitles cover the speaker's mouth, this has a negative impact on quality for those viewers to rely on lip reading to better understand the utterances.

Regarding legibility, subtitles should be displayed on the so-called "black box" (black rectangular background), semi-transparent background or with a black outline so as to improve the contrast. This is because white text can have poor legibility when presented on light-coloured backgrounds. For instance, if the news presenter is wearing white clothes, white subtitles will be illegible unless they have an outline or black background added.

Chapter 6: The quality of live subtitles on TV news channels in Poland

6.1. The rationale for the study

The Polish regulations on media accessibility impose a compulsory subtitling quota, which in 2020 was raised to 25% of all TV programming. As of 2022, the quota increased to 35%. It is set to raise to 50% by 2024 (KRRiT, 2018; Szczygielska, 2019). Thanks to the increase of the subtitling quota, Polish viewers now have access to far more subtitling on television, including live and semi-live subtitles for live TV content. As the quantity of live subtitling increases, it is time to focus on its quality. In this context, the study aims to investigate the quality of live subtitling on the news channels in Poland by looking at various dimensions of quality over a longer period of time.

The following research questions were formulated: (1) Do the Deaf and the hard of hearing viewers have effective access to news television thanks to live subtitling provided, that is, whether the subtitles which are currently provided reflect the content accurately and are intelligible? (2) Does the quality of live subtitling differ between broadcasters? (3) Does the quality differ between live subtitling and semi-live subtitling? And: (4) Does the quality increase or decrease over time as broadcasters gain more experience in providing live subtitles? All the three major Polish TV news channels were taken into account: TVP Info (run by the public broadcaster) and private-owned TVN24 and Polsat News.

6.2. Method

For the needs of the study I collected a corpus of live and semi-live subtitles based on recordings of 96 live TV shows across three quarters (Q2 2021, Q3 2021 and Q1 2022) with 32 shows recorded each quarter. For each show, a sample (an excerpt of around 10 minutes) was selected and analysed (the total duration of all samples was 970 minutes). The verbatim transcripts of each show were also prepared. The corpus included the text of each subtitle as well the subtitle in-time, out-time, its duration and subtitle length (the number of characters in a subtitle). I then used the NER model (as a measure of accuracy) and other established metrics of live subtitling quality such as latency, subtitle speed, reduction rate as well as specially developed metrics on gaps between consecutive subtitles and text segmentation to evaluate various quality dimensions of samples of live and semi-live subtitles. The metrics were used in line with the standards set in previous research (Fresno, 2019; Fresno & Sepielak, 2020; Romero Fresco, 2016; Romero Fresco & Martínez Pérez, 2015; Szarkowska, Barreto Silva, & Orrego-Carmona, 2021; Szarkowska & Gerber-Morón, 2018).

Altogether, seven metrics were used in the study:

(1) **NER score.** For each TV show, a score sheet was prepared that included the subtitles and the verbatim transcript. Trained NER assessors compared the subtitles with the verbatim transcript and identified errors. These included, missing or inaccurate information as well as grammar or spelling mistakes. Each error was classified as per the NER model and assigned a weight of 0.25, 0.5 or 1. The total value of all the errors was subtracted from the total number of words in all the subtitles in the sample and the resulting number was divided by the total number of words. The final value (NER score) is expressed as percentage. The higher the NER score, the higher the accuracy of the subtitles that were analysed (see Chapter 5 for a more detailed discussion of the NER model as well as other quality metrics).

(2) **Subtitle latency.** Subtitle latency is the time difference between a speaker starting to say an utterance and the moment the subtitle appears on screen. Latency was measured in milliseconds by comparing two subtitle files: one that reflected real-life subtitles as broadcast by the TV station and another that was re-synced to match the original audio. For each subtitle, the in-time of the real-life subtitle (the moment when the subtitle appeared on screen) was compared with the in-time of the re-synced subtitle (the moment the first word in this subtitle was being uttered by the speaker) and the time difference between the two was calculated in milliseconds.

(3) **Gaps between consecutive subtitles.** In case of continuous speech, consecutive subtitles should appear one after another, respecting the minimum technical gap of a few frames. However, longer gaps have been observed between some consecutive subtitles when analysing the recordings of TV shows. Therefore, a new metric was set up to examine gaps between subtitles. Gaps were measured by comparing the out-time of one subtitle with the in-time of the following subtitle; the time difference was calculated in milliseconds.

(4) **Subtitle speed.** Subtitle speed has to do with how long a subtitle is displayed on screen and how much time viewers have to read the subtitle relative to the text within this subtitle. It was measured in characters per second (cps). For each subtitle, all the characters (including letters, punctuation and spaces) were counted, and the number of characters was divided by the duration of the subtitle.

(5) **Reduction rate.** The number of characters was counted for each subtitle file as well as the respective verbatim transcription. The reduction rate was calculated by taking the number of characters in the verbatim transcription and subtracting the number of characters in the subtitles. This was then re-calculated as a percentage to show how much text reduction occurred in sub-titles (i.e. how much fewer characters there were in subtitles as compared to the verbatim transcript).

(6) **Segmentation score**. It is a new metric proposed for measuring the quality of text segmentation in subtitling. Three types of segmentation errors were iden-tified in subtitles and assigned weights, depending on the severity of the error. Type A errors involved words that are strongly linked syntactically (such as "not" and the verb) being split between two different subtitles. These errors are assigned the weight of 1. Type B errors involved subtitles that were split or merged unnecessarily. For instance, the ending of a sentence and the begin-ning of another sentence were put together in one subtitle, whereas it was possible to have one full sentence per subtitles. Type B errors were assigned the weight of 0.5. Type C errors also involved words that are strongly linked syntactically (as Type A). This error type received the weight of 0.25 and was identified when such words were split between the two lines of one subtitle. The segmentation score was calculated by summing up the total number of errors as multiplied by their weights. Thus, the segmentation score of zero indicates perfect text segmentation and the higher the score, the more text segmentation errors were present in subtitles.

(7) **Speech rate.** While speech rate is not a metric of subtitle quality *per se*, it reflects how fast speakers talk in a TV show. Faster speech rates can mean that creating live subtitles is more challenging and thus it is important to con-trol for speech rate in the analysis of the previous six quality metrics. Speech rate was measured by counting the total number of words in the verbatim transcript of the sample from each TV show. The number of words was then divided by the duration of the sample in seconds. Speech rate is expressed in words per minute.

All the data gathered in the study was organized into two datasets (see Appendix). The show-level dataset included data that was available for each sample (i.e. excerpt of a TV show) such as the reduction rate, the NER score, the number of characters in the verbatim transcript as well as in the subtitles for the sample. This dataset consisted of 96 rows, one for each sample (i.e. excerpt of a TV show). The subtitle-level dataset, in turn, had 13,620 rows of data, one per each subtitle in the study and included data that was available for each individual subtitle such as in-time, out-time, subtitle duration (measured in milliseconds), subtitle length (measured in the number of characters including spaces and punctuation) or subtitle speed (measured in characters per second, cps). Both datasets were used to produce descriptive statistics and were then analysed with various statistical methods including analysis of variance (ANOVA), analysis of covariance (ANCOVA), correlation and linear mixed models, with the choice of the method determined by the dependent variables and research question.

6.3. Materials

The subtitling quota as set by the Polish regulations on media accessibility is calculated and reported per quarter (see Section 2.3 for a detailed discussion of the Polish regulatory framework). Taking this into account, and with the aim of being able to look into the quality of live subtitling over a longer period of time, three weekly sampling exercises were carried out, collecting samples of the news broadcasts and political chat show from April 2021, July and August 2021 and January 2022. The samples collected in the study make it possible to compare the quality across three different quarters and two years (Q2 and Q3 in 2021 and Q1 in 2022).

Some of the recordings used in the study were contributed by the Polish National Broadcasting Council. The Council agreed to record TV news channels for a week in June 2021 and again in July 2022. However, due to either the source of signal or the method of recording used by the Council, the recordings included live subtitling only for one of the channels: TVP Info. For the other channels, only the audio and video were recorded, but not subtitles. For this reason, the recordings from June 2021 were not used in the study (as only one station had subtitles). In July, I made back-up recordings to use in case the recordings made by the Council could not be used. This way, the Council's recordings from the July 2021 (with subtitles available only on TVP Info) were supplemented by the back-up recordings of the other two channels.

Overall, all the recordings come from three different sources: the Council, the OTT TV provider (Orange) and cable TV provider (UPC). The recordings of the same show from different sources were compared to show that while depending on the source of the recording, the size, the font, and the position of the subtitles on screen varied, there were no differences to other aspects of subtitling quality. Most crucially, the latency of subtitles was the same no matter the source of the recording.

For all three sampling exercises, the recordings of various news shows and political talks were made over a period of 7 days. However, some of the recordings had to be discarded for either a technical error (recording was not done correctly, the file got corrupted or the recording featured only video but not audio) or because the show did not have live subtitles (either because the broadcaster did not provide them or there was a malfunction at the broadcaster or at the TV signal provider). While the shows that were recorded for the study were always labelled by broadcasters as including live subtitling, on some dates there were no subtitles available.

Out of the available recordings, samples were selected so that for each quarter and each TV station, there are samples of one news bulletin and one political chat show from 5 days. This means that, as a principle, two samples were analysed per station per day. Samples were classified as live or semi-live and the semi-live samples of news bulletins were selected in such a way as to only include semi-live subtitling. However, as news bulletins occasionally include unscripted live interaction (such as a conversation with a correspondent), on the days where news bulletins included a longer unscripted interaction, two samples were cut out: one with semi-live subtitling and the other with live subtitling. Altogether, 32 samples were analysed from each quarter and a total of 96 samples were analysed in the study.

The samples analysed in the study were made between 19 April and 23 April and then between 28 July and 2 August in 2021. In 2022, most of the recordings were made between 5 January and 13 January. As some recordings had to be discarded from the January 2021 (due to technical malfunction and some recordings having no audio), additional recordings were also made on 27 January 2022.

The aim was to include one flagship news bulletin for each news channel. The flagship news bulletins in Poland are *Wiadomości* (TVP), *Wydarzenia* (Polsat) and *Fakty* (TVN). Both TVP and Polsat broadcast the prime-time editions of their flagship news bulletins simultaneously, both on their main channels as well as on their news channels (TVP Info and Polsat News, respectively). However, prime-time edition of *Fakty* is only available on the TVN's main channel, and it is not broadcast on its news channel TVN24. Furthermore, when the samples were being collected, the broadcaster did not provide subtitles for this show on TVN.[52] TVN24 broadcast other news bulletins, but those are not subtitled either (see Table 3 for a summary). TVN is able not to subtitle its news shows as it can meet the compulsory subtitling quota by providing subtitles for pre-recorded programming such as feature films and television series. This way it can avoid

---

52 As of April 2022, TVN still does not subtitle its flagship news show *Fakty*.

subtitling live programming. Such an approach is more difficult for news channels, as most of their programming is live rather than pre-recorded.

Table 3: *Flagship news bulletins by three main Polish broadcasters*

TV channels	TVP / TVP Info	Polsat / Polsat News	TVN
News bulletin	*Wiadomości*	*Wydarzenia*	*Fakty*
Subtitles availability	subtitled on TVP and TVP Info	subtitled on Polsat News but not on Polsat	not subtitled

All the news bulletins follow a similar format. There is one newsreader in the
studio who welcomes the audience and then introduces short news segments by
reading out from the teleprompter. Each news segment is usually several minutes
long. The segment is pre-recorded and narrated by a journalist who prepared
it. Segments feature short soundbites from politicians, experts, or members of
the public, interlaced with the narration. Occasionally, there are short segments
consisting of graphics or photos, which are narrated by the newsreader. Most
of the news bulletin is scripted. On occasions, when an important news story
is unfolding, the newsreader might talk live with a correspondent, or the newsreader might make unscripted comments in reaction to a news story.

Apart from news bulletins, the aim of the study was to include one prime-
time unscripted news show, this way representing two most common news TV
genres. The rationale behind the decision to record news bulletins and political talk shows was to represent different news genres, and also to include both
semi-live and live subtitling. In the case of news bulletins which are scripted, it
is usually possible to provide semi-live subtitling (using the texts available in
the news systems and read out by the presenter from the teleprompter as well as
transcripts of the video materials which are also included in the news system).
Political talk shows are not scripted, and thus semi-live subtitling is impossible.

All the three broadcasters have a talk show that follows their flagship news
bulletin and offers to provide more depth on stories of the day through talks with
politicians or experts. TVP Info airs *Gość Wiadomości* (that follows the news bulletin *Wiadomości*), Polsat News broadcasts *Gość Wydarzeń* (after *Wydarzenia*)
and TVN24 airs *Fakty po Faktach* (after *Fakty*, which is aired on TVN). This
show is then followed by *Kropka nad i*, another political talk show. As TVN24
did not subtitle its prime-time news bulletins (or, indeed, did not provide semi-
live subtitling at all), both talk shows were included in the study to have at least
two samples for this broadcaster from each day.

Both *Gość Wiadomości* and *Gość Wydarzeń* follow a similar format. They last between 10 and 15 minutes, and the journalist holds a one-on-one discussion with one guest, usually a politician. On some days, instead of a longer discussion with one guest, *Gość Wydarzeń* includes two shorter discussions with two guests, one after another. In turn, *Gość Wiadomości* occasionally features talks with two guests at once (typically a representative of the ruling part and a representative of one of the opposing parties). *Fakty po Faktach* is longer and lasts between 20 and 30 minutes and has a larger number of guests as it can include discussions on various topics. It is followed by *Kropka nad i*, which usually has two guests.

Whenever a particular show was not available due to changes in TV scheduling, another show that aired in the same broadcasting slot was recorded. For instance, on 31 July 2021 due to the Tokyo Olympics *Kropka nad i* was not broadcast, substituted by a live talk show on the Olympics. So for this particular day the sample of this show was analysed. (Other such substitutes on TVN24 include *Sprawdzam*, *Tak jest* and *Czarno na białym*.) Also, on two days when the subtitling was not available for *Wiadomości*, samples were collected from other news bulletins on TVP Info (*Panorama* and *Teleexpress*). For a similar reason, one sample was collected from Polsat News evening news bulletin *Wydarzenia* broadcast at 21:50 CET (instead of the main edition at 18:50). See Table 4 for a summary.

Table 4: *Names of the shows recorded in the study*

	TVP Info	Polsat News	TVN24
News bulletin	*Wiadomości*, *Teleexpress*, *Panorama*	*Wydarzenia (18:50)*, *Wydarzenia (21:50)*	(-)
Chat show	*Gość Wiadomości*	*Gość Wydarzeń*	*Fakty po Faktach*, *Kropka nad i*, *Sprawdzam*, *Tak jest*, *Czarno na białym*, *Tokyo 2020*

For each show analysed in the study, a sample of between 10 and 11 minutes was cut out of the recording. The samples were extracted in such a way so as to start and end with complete sentences and include at least 10 minutes of the show. The samples usually start with the first sentence in the show and end once a news item ends or a speaker in a political talk finishes a thought. When it comes to samples from news bulletins, it was found that both TVP Info and

Polsat News provide semi-live subtitling for these bulletins. However, on some days news bulletins might include unscripted content (such as a short live discussion with a foreign correspondent), in which case the broadcasters switch to live subtitling. Whenever this happened, the sample was cut out in such a way as to include only semi-live subtitling and omit the live part. Samples of live subtitling from news were also cut out to be analysed separately.

6.4. Procedure

For each video sample a verbatim transcript was prepared. Based on the transcript, it was possible to count the number of words and the number of characters in a sample as well as calculate the speech rate. The transcript also served as reference to compare the subtitles with. To be able to look into subtitle quality, it was necessary to get hold of subtitling files. However, broadcasters are reluctant to share subtitling files for research and if they use external subtitling providers, those companies might not be able to share subtitling files for legal reasons (either because of not holding the copyright or being forbidden from sharing the files in the contract with the broadcaster). Fresno (2019) encountered a similar situation in the US where she requested subtitle files from all the major broadcasters and none of them responded. I contacted the technicians at the National Broadcasting Council but they did not have the know-how on how to extract subtitle files from recordings as they have never before been asked to record subtitle files. Additional attempts at extracting the subtitles from the video failed. Decoding subtitles from live TV signal was only possible through a TV card (additional hardware installed in a computer) and only when using non-coded terrestrial or satellite signals. However, I had the terrestrial signal available for only one of the channels (TVP Info) and I did not have access to the satellite signal. I attempted making the recordings with cable TV decoders and while they do record subtitles as separate files, it is impossible to transfer these files to a computer for analysis as the files are coded and can be reproduced only on the decoder that recorded them. Additional attempt was made at extracting the subtitles through OCR software that can recognize letter shapes and can turn images into text. Unfortunately, the results were not satisfactory as too many letters were recognized incorrectly.

The final solution was to essentially reverse engineer the subtitle files based on video recordings. This was done be manually creating subtitle files using the subtitling software EZTitles 6 based on the recording of each show. Subtitles that were created include exactly the same text that the subtitles on the recording and they are synced to appear and disappear exactly at the same time as the original subtitles. This way we can assume that the files are identical to the files that would have been saved at the broadcaster's premises, assuming that live subtitles are archived.

The subtitles were then saved as .SRT files as well as exported as spreadsheets that included the text of each subtitle and its in-times and out-times expressed in milliseconds. This made it possible to calculate the gap between each subtitle and the following one (which was done by taking the out-time of each subtitle and subtracting it from the in-time of the following subtitle, arriving at the gap between the two subtitles expressed in milliseconds).

The .SRT files were then analysed through BlackBox, software designed by Gonzalez-Iglesias Gonzalez at the University of Salamanca to analyse subtitling files. BlackBox calculated the subtitle speed for each subtitle as well as the number of characters in each subtitle. The calculation methods used by BlackBox are in line with the recommendations by Fresno and Sepielak (2020). The results of the BlackBox analysis for each sample were saved as a spreadsheet.

The subtitle files were then re-synced in EZTitles 6 in a such a way that each subtitle starts exactly at the moment when a speaker starts uttering the first word in this subtitle. Such new subtitles which are now in perfect sync with the audio were also saved as .SRT files as well as exported as spreadsheets with the text of the subtitle and the values in milliseconds for in-times.

The two spreadsheets (one with data for real-life subtitles and the other with data for re-synced subtitles) were then merged and by taking into account the in-time values of real-life subtitles and the in-time values of re-synced subtitles, it was possible to calculate the latency of each subtitle, expressed in milliseconds.

The number of words and the number of characters were also calculated for each subtitle file as well as the respective verbatim transcription. Finally, the number of characters was used for analysis (as more accurate than the number of words). The text reduction rate was calculated by taking the number of characters in the verbatim transcription and subtracting the number of characters in the subtitle. This was then re-calculated as a percentage to show how much text reduction occurred in subtitles.

In another step, the NER score sheets were prepared. They were based on the score sheets used by the Global Alliance of Speech-to-Text Captioning in its NCSP certification.[53] The verbatim transcripts were pasted into the score sheets,

---

53   The NCSP score sheets were designed by Chris Ales with input from Łukasz Dutka and were based on the score sheets used within the LIRICS certification and shared by Pablo Romero Fresco.

divided into idea units and then manually aligned with the subtitles. Whenever needed, the rows containing the transcript were merged or split so as to better align them with the subtitles. The score sheets included columns for the assessors to indicate errors, add comments and indicate weights for errors. The spreadsheet formulas then summed up all the errors and calculated the NER score. Each score sheet was filled in by one assessor and then reviewed by another one. Four assessors were recruited for the study, and these were experienced live subtitlers who received training in the use of the NER model.

In the process of adapting the score sheets, several changes were made. First of all, while the NER model distinguishes between edition and recognition errors (which is important for training purposes and can serve as useful feedback for respeakers), this distinction does not affect the final NER score as both kinds of errors have the same weights. It turned out to be tricky for assessors to decide whether something is an edition or recognition error and they felt they needed access to the recording of the respeaker's voice or its transcription to be able to tell with certainty whether the error was caused by the respeaker or by the software. It was not possible to get such resources for the research presented here and in any case trying to work out the source of the errors made NER assessment even more time-consuming. Consequently, as the focus of the present work was on the quality of live subtitles as a final product, the assessors were asked not to differentiate between these two types of errors.[54] (The assessors still reported that the analysis was rather time-consuming as they needed from 1 to 2 hours to assess a 10-minute sample of live subtitles). This decision did not affect the final NER scores in any way. It does mean, however, that there is no data on what portion of the errors were edition errors as opposed to recognition errors.

On the other hand, while the NER model does not take into account the segmentation errors, the assessors were asked to look for segmentation errors and annotate them separately. While the segmentation errors were annotated in the same score sheet, they were not included in calculating the NER scores and did not affect the NER assessment in any way.

Altogether five assessors participated in the study, including four independent assessors and the author of the study. Two of them assessed semi-live subtitle samples and the other two live subtitles samples, while the author acted as the second assessor of all the samples. All the assessors were experienced live subtitlers but were not involved themselves in creating live subtitles that

---

54   It should be noted that a similar decision was made by Fresno (2019) in her study of live subtitling in the US.

were recorded and analysed in the research presented here. Before the assessment, they were trained on using the NER model and they practiced using it on examples. When performing the assessment, they were asked to use the NER decision-making tree developed by the Canadian regulator (CRTC, 2019). All the assessors participated in six meetings where they discussed errors they had doubts about and aimed to find consistent ways of evaluating errors.

The assessment of each sample was then reviewed by the author who added comments and adjusted error weights if needed. The NER scores were recorded both for the first and second assessment of each sample. In the results below, the final scores are presented (from the second assessment). However, it should be pointed out that the adjustments were minor and never changed the score by more than 0.1%.

All the data was then divided into two data sets and imported for analysis into statistical software IBM SPSS. The first dataset included show-level data such as the NER score or the reduction rate. The second dataset included subtitle-level data such as subtitle speed or latency (as it was possible to calculate these for each individual subtitle). The details of the analysis and the results are reported in the following section.

6.5. Results and discussion

This section will present the results obtained after analysing the corpus of 13,620 subtitles, drawn from 96 samples of live and semi-live subtitles. The objective of the analysis is to answer the research questions (as put forward in Section 6.1) and the same questions will be repeated for various quality dimensions of live subtitling which were operationalized through the use of one or more metrics.

The results are first presented and then analysed separately for each metric starting with the NER score (as a measure of accuracy) and followed by metrics on synchronicity (latency and gaps between consecutive subtitles), subtitle speed, completeness (reduction rate) and text segmentation. The results of each metric are first discussed in terms of descriptive statistics. This is then followed by the analysis of inferential statistics through the use of analysis of variance as well as linear mixed models.

Other characteristics of subtitles such as their placement and the subtitle display mode are also described. And the final section of this chapter discusses all the results together and examines the relation between various quality dimensions of live subtitling. For the sake of conciseness, when reporting the results TVP Info is referred to as "TVP", Polsat News as "Polsat" and TVN24 as "TVN".

6.5.1. Accuracy (NER score)

As discussed in Section 5.3.1, in some territories accuracy is perceived as synonymous with literality. Subtitles that are verbatim transcriptions are seen as more accurate and subtitles which are not verbatim are seen as less accurate. This view is most popular in countries such as the US or Canada where the media regulators favour verbatim subtitles (Fresno, 2019). However, analysing if the subtitles are verbatim would not be very helpful in the European context where subtitles tend to be edited. In fact, this research shows that live subtitles on Polish news TV are far from verbatim (see 8.5.4 for results on the reduction rate in live subtitles), indeed, they are heavily edited. Consequently, for the needs of the research presented here, accuracy is understood not as literality but as expressing the same ideas, but not necessarily with all and exactly the same words.

To measure accuracy, NER score was used. NER score is a result of analysing the subtitles with the use of the NER model, which allows the assessor to accept non-literal phrasing as correct as long as the subtitles express the same information as the transcript of the original speaker (see Section 5.5.2 for a detailed discussion of the NER model). The score is expressed as a percentage and the higher the score, the better the quality of subtitles in terms of their accuracy. NER score tends to produce mostly high values with values above 98% believed to reflect acceptable quality, whereas values below 98 % are thought to reflect bad quality (Romero Fresco, 2021).

Ninety six samples of TV shows with live and semi-live subtitles were analysed with the NER model. The average NER score for all the samples in the study (see Table 5 below) is 97.55%, and as such it is below the acceptable threshold and corresponds to "substandard" quality (3/10)[55]. As expected, semi-live subtitling achieves better accuracy with an average NER score of 99.35% (very good, 8/10), which not only clears the threshold of acceptable quality, but it is actually a very high result corresponding to very good accuracy. When looking at the range of values, even the worst sample of semi-live subtitles is above the 98% threshold (98.16%, acceptable, 5/10). In the case of live subtitling, the average NER score is 96.73 (substandard, 1/10), which is below the threshold of acceptable quality. The range of values for live subtitles is much wider than for semi-live subtitles: it goes from 88.62% (extremely low accuracy, 0/10) to 99.67% (very high accuracy, "excellent" as per the NER model, 9/10).

---

55   See 7.2.2 for the explanation on how the NER score is recalculated into a 10-point scale.

Table 5: *Average NER scores for live and semi-live subtitles in the study*

Type of subtitles	Mean	N	SD	Minimum	Maximum
Live	96.73	66	1.92	88.62	99.67
Semi-live	99.35	30	.41	98.16	99.91
Total	97.55	96	2.01	88.62	99.91

Note. "N" stands for the number of samples (i.e. excerpts of TV shows) that were included in the analysis, whereas "SD" refers to standard deviation.

Interestingly, the average NER score for semi-live news subtitles on Polish news TV (99.35%) is higher than what was found for news programmes in the UK (98.75%). However, the average NER score for live subtitles (96.73%) is lower than the average found by Fresno (2019) in the US for a presidential debate (98.84%)[56], and in the UK for chat shows (97.70%).

Let us now look at the results for each broadcaster (see Table 6 below). Polsat achieves the highest average NER score for live subtitles (97.81%, substandard, 4/10), slightly higher than TVP (97.19%, substandard, 2/10). While both these values are below the threshold of acceptable accuracy, it should be noted that TVN achieves a far worse result (95.90%, substandard, 0/10). Only TVP and Polsat provide semi-live subtitles and both broadcasters achieve very good accuracy: 99.10% (very good, 7/10) and 99.50% (excellent, 8/10) respectively.

Table 6: *Average NER scores for live and semi-live subtitles for TVP, Polsat and TVN*

TV station	Live vs. semi-live	Mean	N	SD	Minimum	Maximum
TVP	Live	97.19	16	1.14	95.02	98.77
	Semi-live	99.10	15	.47	98.16	99.83
	Total	98.15	31	1.34	95.02	99.83
Polsat	Live	97.81	18	1.19	95.30	99.67
	Semi-live	99.50	15	.26	99.12	99.91
	Total	98.58	33	1.23	95.30	99.91
TVN	Live	95.90	32	2.19	88.62	99.06
	Total	95.90	32	2.19	88.62	99.06
Total	Live	96.73	66	1.92	88.62	99.67
	Semi-live	99.35	30	.41	98.16	99.91
	Total	97.55	96	2.01	88.62	99.91

---

56   It is important to bear in mind that it was a one-off high-priority event.

Let us now examine the results quarter by quarter (see Table 7) to check if the stations are improving (i.e. increasing accuracy) over time as the broadcasters are becoming more experienced with providing live subtitling.

Table 7: *Average NER scores by quarter, broadcaster and type of subtitling*

Quarter	TV station	Live vs. semi-live	Mean	N	SD	Minimum	Maximum
Q2 2021	TVP	Live	98.0	5	.63	96.95	98.48
		Semi-live	99.53	5	.15	99.32	99.70
		Total	98.78	10	.90	96.95	99.70
	Polsat	Live	98.39	6	.84	97.18	99.67
		Semi-live	99.82	5	.11	99.67	99.91
		Total	99.04	11	.96	97.18	99.91
	TVN	Live	96.14	11	1.72	92.71	98.46
		Total	96.14	11	1.72	92.71	98.46
	Total	Live	97.18	22	1.68	92.71	99.67
		Semi-live	99.67	10	.19	99.32	99.91
		Total	97.96	32	1.81	92.71	99.91
Q3 2021	TVP	Live	96.80	6	1.50	95.02	98.77
		Semi-live	99.08	5	.62	98.16	99.83
		Total	97.83	11	1.64	95.02	99.83
	Polsat	Live	97.91	6	1.37	95.48	99.05
		Semi-live	99.36	5	.20	99.12	99.61
		Total	98.57	11	1.24	95.48	99.61
	TVN	Live	95.89	10	1.82	93.25	98.81
		Total	95.89	10	1.82	93.25	98.81
	Total	Live	96.69	22	1.77	93.25	99.05
		Semi-live	99.22	10	.46	98.16	99.83
		Total	97.48	32	1.90	93.25	99.83
Q1 2022	TVP	Live	96.83	5	.66	96.26	97.94
		Semi-live	98.95	5	.37	98.43	99.48
		Total	97.89	10	1.23	96.26	99.48
	Polsat	Live	97.12	6	1.11	95.30	98.11
		Semi-live	99.33	5	.10	99.21	99.45
		Total	98.13	11	1.40	95.30	99.45
	TVN	Live	95.67	11	2.96	88.62	99.06
		Total	95.67	11	2.96	88.62	99.06
	Total	Live	96.33	22	2.24	88.62	99.06
		Semi-live	99.14	10	.33	98.43	99.48
		Total	97.21	32	2.28	88.62	99.48

Table 7: Continued

Quarter	TV station	Live vs. semi-live	Mean	N	SD	Minimum	Maximum
Total	TVP	Live	97.19	16	1.14	95.02	98.77
		Semi-live	99.19	15	.47	98.16	99.83
		Total	98.16	31	1.34	95.02	99.83
	Polsat	Live	97.81	18	1.19	95.30	99.67
		Semi-live	99.50	15	.26	99.12	99.91
		Total	98.58	33	1.23	95.30	99.91
	TVN	Live	95.90	32	2.19	88.62	99.06
		Total	95.90	32	2.19	88.62	99.06
	Total	Live	96.73	66	1.91	88.62	99.67
		Semi-live	99.35	30	.41	98.16	99.91
		Total	97.55	96	2.01	88.62	99.91

The results over the three quarters do not indicate improvements in accuracy. In fact, the opposite is true as the average NER score decreases over time. The trend becomes easier to notice when visualized on graphs (see Fig. 26 below for live subtitles and Fig. 27 for semi-live subtitles). Across the three quarters, the NER score for live subtitles for TVP drops from 98% (acceptable, 5/10) to 96.83% (substandard, 2/10). For Polsat it drops from 98.39% (acceptable, 5/10) to 97.12% (substandard, 2/10). And for TVN it drops from 96.14% (substandard, 0/10) to 95.67% (substandard, 0/10).

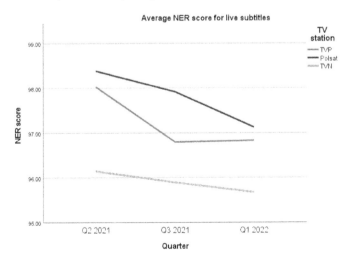

Fig. 26: *Average NER Score for live subtitles across three quarters for all three broadcasters*

The accuracy also decreases in the case of semi-live subtitles (see Fig. 27). For TVP it drops from 99.53% (excellent, 8/10) to 98.95% (good, 7/10). For Polsat it goes down from 99.82% (excellent, 9/10) to 99.33% (very good, 8/10). These are still satisfactory results, however, as they correspond to acceptable accuracy.

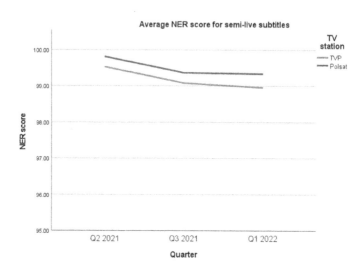

Fig. 27: *Average NER Score for semi-live subtitles across three quarters for TVP and Polsat*

Surprisingly, the average results show a worrying trend of accuracy decreasing over time for all the broadcasters for both live and semi-live subtitles. To check if these results are statistically significant, a 2x2 analysis of covariance (ANCOVA) was carried out with NER score as dependent variable. There were two independent variables: TV station (Polsat, TVP) and Type of subtitling[57] (live vs. semi-live). Speech rate was added as a covariate to account for the potential impact of the speech rate on accuracy. For the needs of this analysis, subtitles from TVN had to be excluded (to be able to compare live and semi-live subtitles, given that TVN only provided live subtitles). Altogether, 63 TV broadcasts were analysed.

The resulting dataset was checked to verify if the data is parametric. The dataset failed the assumption of normality. Log transformation and square root transformation were used in an attempt to improve the dataset, but these

---

57   Terms such as Type of subtitles, Speech rate, Latency or Subtitle speed are capitalized whenever used as names of variables when discussing statistical analysis.

techniques did not normalize the data. Therefore, the non-transformed data was used. To improve the power of the analysis, bootstrapping was performed, which solved the problem with homogeneity of variance and confirmed the results of unbootstrapped tests.

The results of the analysis show a weak (but statistically significant) main effect of TV station on the NER score, $F(1, 59) = 4.78, p = .033, eta^2 = .075$, with higher results for Polsat ($M = 98.67, SE = .158$) than for TVP ($M = 98.17, SE = .162$). As predicted, there was a strong and significant main effect of Type of subtitles on NER score, $F(1, 59) = 59,21, p <.001, eta^2 = .501$, with higher values for semi-live subtitles ($M = 99.32, SE = .157$) than for live subtitles ($M = 97.53, SE = .167$). It should be noted that the estimated means for semi-live subtitles are well above the 98% threshold that indicates acceptable quality according to the NER model (the estimated mean of 99.32 corresponds to very good quality, 8/10), whereas the estimated means for live subtitles are below the acceptable threshold (substandard, 3/10). The estimates are in line with descriptive statistics reported previously.

There is no interaction between the two independent variables: Type of subtitles and TV station ($p = .566$). Surprisingly, there is no effect of Speech rate on NER score ($p = .408$). In other words, whether speakers talked slow or fast did not affect the accuracy of subtitles. The estimated marginal means (see Fig. 28) are reported for the average speech rate of 134.06 words per minute and the estimated means are in line with the descriptive statistics reported previously.

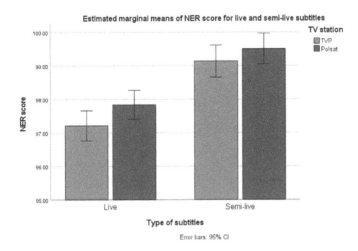

Fig. 28: *Estimated marginal means of NER score for live and semi-live subtitles for TVP and Polsat*

To compare live subtitles between all the three broadcasters, a one-way analysis of covariance (ANCOVA) was carried out with NER score as dependent variable. The independent variable was TV station. Speech rate was included as a covariate. For the needs of this analysis, semi-live subtitles were excluded. Altogether, 66 TV broadcasts were analysed.

The resulting dataset passed the assumption of normality and homogeneity of variance for the data from TVP and Polsat but failed these assumptions for TVN. A closer investigation revealed that is due to on outlier in the TVN data (one broadcast of the chat show *Kropka nad i* had a much lower NER score than other shows; 88.62%). The data for this show was re-checked and was correct. As the data reflects a real variation of accuracy between shows, the outlier was not excluded (see Fig. 29 for the visualization of the outlier).

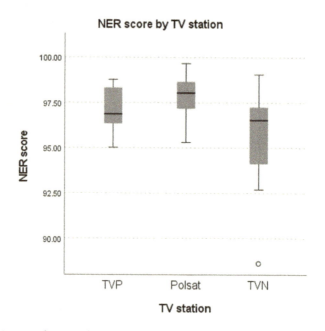

Fig. 29: *Estimated marginal means of NER score for live subtitles on TVP, Polsat and TVN*

A non-parametric equivalent of an independent one-way ANOVA (Kruskal-Wallis Test) showed a strong main effect of TV station on the accuracy of live subtitles, $F(2, 182.97) = 9.40$, $p < .001$, $eta^2 = .233$. Bootstrapping was carried out and confirmed the results. The analysis found a statistically significant difference between Polsat and TVN as well as TVP and TVN in terms of accuracy with higher results for both Polsat ($M = 97.31$, $SE = .435$) and TVP ($M = 97.31$, $SE = .435$). The difference between TVP and Polsat was not significant.

As in the previous analysis, there was no effect of Speech rate on NER score ($p = 0.79$). The estimated marginal means (see Fig. 29 above) are reported for the average speech rate of 131.23 words per minute and the estimated means are in line with the descriptive statistics reported previously.

Summing up the overall results of the analysis of accuracy, both TVP and Polsat provide good quality subtitling of live news content but only for those broadcasts which are subtitled semi-live. In the case of live subtitles on TVP and Polsat, the average accuracy is substandard as per the NER model. This means that subtitles sometimes contain inaccurate or false information as well as errors that make it difficult to work out the meaning of the text. In the case of TVN (which provides only live subtitles), the accuracy is extremely low, which corresponds to "virtually unreadable subtitles" as per the NER model (Romero Fresco, 2021, p. 744). See Fig. 30 for an example of subtitles with low accuracy.

Fig. 30: *Example of subtitles from a political talk show* Gość Wydarzeń *(Polsat) which received a NER score of 95.30% (0/10)*

VERBATIM TRANSCRIPT:	LIVE SUBTITLES:
To dokładnie dlatego są tarcze. Na pewno emeryci nie stracą, bo jest z automatu rewaloryzacja emerytury, jeszcze z jakąś marżą nad inflacją. Więc emeryci i tak będą w lepszej sytuacji.	To jest dlaczego na pewno emerytury emeryci nie stracą było jest z automatu waloryzacja emerytury jeszcze ze chorzy marżą nad inflacją więc i tak w końcu będzie będą lepszej sytuacji.

(English translation)	**(English translation)**
That's exactly why we have shields [Reference to the government's "anti-crisis shields", various initiatives aimed at protecting the citizens from the rising cost of living.] For sure, the pensioners will not lose [due to inflation], because the pensions are automatically revalued, and the increase [of the pensions] is even higher than inflation. And so the pensioners will be in a better situation [than other citizens] anyway.	This is why for sure pensioners will not lose pensions was is automatically valued pension also with sick ones dream over inflation so anyway in the end [it] will [they] will better situation.

When analysing the results across the three quarters (see Fig. 26 discussed previously), there is a worrying trend of decreasing accuracy. Over time, the NER scores get lower for both semi-live and live subtitles. The decrease is most noticeable in the case of live subtitles on TVP and Polsat. In Q2 2021, both broadcasters were able to achieve average NER scores of 98% or above, corresponding to acceptable accuracy. In Q1 2022, both are below the acceptable threshold (when the NER scores are recalculated to a 10-point scale, it is a downgrade from 5/10 to 2/10 for both broadcasters). This result could be explained by broadcasters paying less attention to quality or struggling with training their staff. In the case of Polsat, this could also be explained by changes in the living subtitling workflow (as live subtitles on Polsat also show significant changes over time in other dimensions of quality, which will be discussed in more detail in the following sections).

To explore this trend further, let us look at NER scores for three flagship political chats shows from TVP and Polsat from Q2 2021 (the first analysed quarter) and Q1 2022 (the last analysed quarter). In the case of TVP (see Table 8), 4 out of 5 editions of this show are above the acceptable threshold for accuracy in the first analysed quarter, whereas none of the editions of the show analysed in 2022 are above the threshold. In the case of Polsat (see Table 9), 4 out of 5 editions of the show are above the acceptable threshold in the first analysed quarter, which is true for only 1 out of 5 editions in 2022. As shown above, there was no effect of speech rate on accuracy. Of course, the difference between shows could be explained by more challenging topics or speakers. However, the analysis of variance with NER score as the dependent variable and Show as independent variable, showed no significant effect of Show ($p = .504$). The same was true for Date ($p = .201$). The likely explanation then is that the decrease in accuracy is due to the changes in the workflows or training of the live subtitlers.

Table 8: *NER scores for TVP's flagship political chat show* Gość Wiadomości *in Q2 2021 and in Q1 2022*

Gość Wiadomości (TVP)					
Q2 2021			Q1 2022		
Date	NER	10-point scale	Date	NER	10-point scale
April 19	98.45%	7/10	January 5	96.77%	2/10
April 22	98.26%	6/10	January 10	96.77%	2/10
April 23	98.01%	6/10	January 11	96.26%	1/10
June 23	98.14%	6/10	January 12	97.94%	5/10
June 25	96.95%	3/10	January 13	96.43%	2/10

Table 9: *NER scores for Polsat's flagship political chat show* Gość Wydarzeń *in Q2 2021 and in Q1 2022*

Gość Wydarzeń (Polsat)					
Q2 2021			Q1 2022		
Date	NER	10-point scale	Date	NER	10-point scale
April 19	98.45%	7/10	January 5	96.81%	3/10
April 20	98.58%	7/10	January 7	98.08%	6/10
April 21	97.79%	5/10	January 10	95.30%	0/10
April 22	98.65%	7/10	January 12	98.11%	6/10
April 23	99.67%	10/10	January 13	96.56%	2/10

While the accuracy decreases both on Polsat and on TVP, Polsat still manages to achieve slightly higher NER scores than TVP in the last analysed quarter (Q1 2022). Interestingly, the assessors in their comments in the NER analysis of the Polsat samples from Q1 2022 noted that the live subtitles on Polsat seemed worse than those on TVP and it was very difficult to understand their content. When asked to compare their subjective perception of accuracy between TVP and Polsat in Q1 2022, all assessors agreed that live subtitles on Polsat were less accurate and more difficult to understand than on TVP. However, the average NER scores for live subtitles in Q1 2022 do not reflect this (97.19% for TVP and 97.81% for Polsat).

One explanation of that paradox could be that assessors were simply biased in their perceptions. After all, it is not uncommon for subjective perceptions not to match the objective assessment. However, the analysis of other quality dimensions in the study showed a significant change in the reduction rate for Polsat across quarters (see Section 6.5.5). The reduction rate dropped from 34.14% to 11.10% for live subtitles on Polsat. At the same time the reduction rate increased for the other two broadcasters, reaching 41.57% on TVP and 46.45% on TVN. This gives rise to another possible explanation of why the assessors thought live subtitles on Polsat are less accurate than on TVP despite the NER scores indicating otherwise. The NER score is calculated using the number of words in subtitles (as opposed to the number of words that would be included in a verbatim transcript). Thus, the higher the reduction rate, the fewer words there are in subtitles. And the lower the reduction rate, the more words there are in subtitles. If there are more words in subtitles, the overall significance of each individual error is smaller. This means that potentially live subtitles on Polsat could have more errors than live subtitles on TVP but would still achieve a higher NER score. This could make NER score less reliable when comparing subtitles with high reduction rate to subtitles with low reduction rate.

To explore this possibility, a Pearson correlation was computed with NER score and Reduction rate as the variables. All broadcasters were included, and semi-live subtitles were excluded. The analysis found a highly significant negative correlation, $r = -.563$, $N = 66$, $p < .001$, between NER score and Reduction rate, which means that when Reduction rate decreases, NER increases. It could be argued that this correlation is not surprising.

A lower reduction rate can mean that subtitles are more verbatim and potentially include more information. Consequently, they should be more accurate. However, automatic speech recognition can produce fully verbatim subtitles that might include many errors and might not be very accurate. Also, subtitles can be condensed successfully and have a high reduction rate but still include all the important information and still be very accurate.

To further explore this, Pearson correlations were then computed separately for each station and Reduction rate as the variables. The analysis found a highly significant and very strong negative correlation for TVN, $r = -.809$, $N = 32$, $p < .001$. Also significant but less strong negative correlation was found for TVP, $r = -.556$, $N = 16$, $p = .025$. Interestingly, no significant correlation was found for Polsat, $r = .224$, $N = 18$, $p = .371$. Thus, the analysis refuted the hypothesis that the comparison between different NER scores was less reliable due to differences in the reduction rate (and the NER score being calculated based on a higher number of words).

As there was no link between the reduction rate and NER scores in the case of Polsat, another possible explanation for why assessors thought that live subtitles on Polsat were less accurate than on TVP (despite the NER scores indicating otherwise) could be the difference in subtitle speed. While the average subtitle speed of live subtitles in Q1 2022 on TVP was quite low (11.65 cps), it was very high on Polsat (21.55 cps) (see Section 6.5.4). Lower subtitle speed means viewers have more time to process the text and try to work out the meaning. If two sets of subtitles include a similar number of errors and similar overall accuracy as measured by the NER score, having more time to process subtitles might make it easier for viewers to understand the content and, thus, it can create a subjective impression of higher accuracy on TVP as compared to Polsat.

Returning to the overall results on accuracy, it should be pointed out that the results of this research confirm that semi-live subtitling (as compared to live subtitling) can deliver a much better quality in terms of accuracy. While this is not surprising, it also shows that the two broadcasters that do provide semi-live subtitling (TVP and Polsat) are using this method quite successfully. Thus, live subtitling should not be used for the shows where it is possible to use the semi-live method. For instance, one of the samples for TVN comes from a show *Czarno na białym*, which features a scripted live introduction followed by pre-recorded video materials. In fact, a closer look revealed that the particular edition of the show that was analysed in the study featured a repeat of video materials already used on the show in the past and recorded several months before. This means it was possible to provide semi-live subtitles for this show. This particular sample achieved a NER score of 96.74% (substandard, 2/10). The results of the study show that viewers would have been able to watch the show with much more accurate subtitles if the broadcaster decided to use the semi-live method.

At the same time, the average result for TVN for live subtitles (95.90%, substandard, 0/10) corresponds to quite low accuracy that reflects text that includes so many errors that it is difficult for a viewer to work out the meaning. Such low accuracy might mean that the subtitles bring little actual value to the users. A closer look at the results for this broadcaster reveals that out of 32 shows analysed, only one achieves NER score above the threshold of 98%. To improve the accessibility of its news broadcasts, TVN should start providing semi-live subtitling for news bulletins, while simultaneously improving the accuracy of live subtitles it provides for its other shows.

When analysing accuracy, we have seen that some of the live shows on Polish news channels are of acceptable quality in terms of accuracy. However, the question whether the overall quality of live subtitles is acceptable cannot be answered solely on the basis of accuracy. We will now look at other dimensions of quality, starting with synchronicity, which will be analysed by exploring two parameters: latency and gaps between consecutive subtitles.

6.5.2. Latency

Latency is the time difference between a speaker starting to say an utterance and the moment the subtitle appears on screen (for a more detailed discussion on latency see Section 5.5.4). Subtitle latency depends on a number of factors; the most important being the method of creating live subtitles and the time it takes to produce each subtitle. The latency can be reduced through the use of antenna delay (as explained in Section 5.8).

Subtitle latency can be measured in seconds or milliseconds. Latency can sometimes have a negative value, that is, a subtitle can appear even before the speaker starts speaking. This can sometimes happen in semi-live subtitling where the text of the subtitle is pre-prepared and a subtitler cues in this subtitle too early by mistake. Negative latency can also be linked to the use of antenna delay where subtitlers receive the signal before it is broadcast, thus gaining some time. Generally, the lower the latency, the better as high latency makes it difficult for viewers to follow subtitles. However, negative latency is best avoided as it is also a departure from synchronicity. It can be surprising for viewers and can make them question if they are indeed watching a live show (rather than a pre-recorded one). The British media regulator Ofcom currently recommends that latency should not be higher than 6 seconds, while the Spanish norm allows for 8 seconds and the French media regulator sets the maximum latency to 10 seconds (Romero Fresco, 2016; Fresno, 2019).

Latency tends to differ greatly between semi-live and live subtitling as one of the main advantages of the semi-live method is being able to achieve little or no latency (Saerens et al., 2020). This is confirmed by the results of this research (see Table 10) where the average latency for live subtitles for all the stations was 16.8 seconds, whereas the average latency for semi-live subtitles was just 2.9 seconds. Thus, on average, semi-live subtitling had a latency lower by 13.8 seconds than live subtitling.

Table 10: *Average latency (expressed in milliseconds) for live and semi-live subtitles in the study*

Type of subtitles	Mean (ms)	N	SD	Minimum	Maximum
Live	16,760.96	7,877	7,146.671	-4,138	75,520
Semi-live	2,906.86	5,520	2,472.822	-4,900	42,700
Total	11,052.62	13,397	8,891.024	-4,900	75,520

Let us now look at the range of values. The lowest latency found for both live and semi-live subtitles was negative, that is some subtitles appeared up to almost 5 seconds before audio. As explained above, this might have been due to the use of antenna delay or to errors made by subtitlers who cued in subtitles too early. In the case of live subtitling, negative latency could be explained by situations in which an introduction to an interview is scripted and subtitlers have prepared it beforehand.

A closer look at data revealed that out of 7877 live subtitles in the study, only five subtitles (0.06%) had negative latency. All these were cases where the news presenter or the show host was saying hello to a guest, introducing a guest or introducing a topic. It seems that in these cases the subtitlers had pre-prepared subtitles (either because these introductions where scripted or predictable) and cued them in too early by mistake. In the case of semi-live subtitles, out of 5520 such subtitles in the study 142 (2.57%) had negative latency.

The highest latency found for live subtitles was 75.5 seconds. In the case of semi-live subtitling it was 42.7 seconds. These are extremely high values. Assuming that a latency of more than 20 seconds is extremely high, I checked how many live and semi-live subtitles had latency higher than that. Such high values were outliers in the case of semi-live subtitling but were quite common for live subtitles. While only a fraction of semi-live subtitles (8 subtitles, 0.14% of all) had a latency higher than 20 seconds, this was true for as many as 25.19% of live subtitles (1984 subtitles).

The average latency for live subtitling on Polish news channels (16.76 seconds) is well above the values recommended in the UK, Spain or France. The results are also much higher than the average latency of 6 seconds found in the case of chat shows in the UK (Romero Fresco, 2016) and 6.1 seconds in the case of a presidential debate broadcast on news channels in the US (Fresno, 2019). It is more similar to the latency found in France (11–20s) (Fresno, 2019). On average, after the Polish speaker starts expressing a thought, the viewer needs to wait 16 seconds for the subtitle to appear. Such high average latency and the fact that one fourth of all subtitles had a latency higher than 20 seconds suggest that it might be difficult to follow live news programmes subtitling on Polish TV.

Regarding the semi-live subtitling, the average latency of 2.9 seconds makes for a much more comfortable viewing. Still, there is room for improvement as semi-live subtitling should make it possible to minimize latency even further. Let us now look in more detail at the results for each broadcaster to see if the latency is similar across all the stations (see Table 11).

Table 11: *Mean latency of live and semi-live subtitles in the study*

TV station	Live vs. semi-live	Mean (ms)	N	SD	Minimum	Maximum
TVP	Live	17,288.59	2164	6,451.97	-767	45100
	Semi-live	4,354.17	2352	2,976.58	-4900	42700
	Total	10,552.15	4516	8,143.57	-4900	45100
Polsat	Live	13,984.10	1928	6,878.98	-4138	39534
	Semi-live	1,832.35	3168	1,169.75	-1500	17100
	Total	6,429.79	5096	7,313.35	-4138	39534
TVN	Live	17,873.78	3785	7,286.09	-1367	75520
	Total	17873.78	3785	7,286.09	-1367	75520
Total	Live	16,760.96	7877	7,146.67	-4138	75520
	Semi-live	2,906.86	5520	2,472.82	-4900	42700
	Total	11,052.62	13397	8,891.02	-4900	75520

Both TVP and TVN have a similar average latency (17.2s and 17.8s respectively), while Polsat has a lower latency at roughly 14s. Interestingly, Polsat also has a lower latency in semi-live subtitling than TVP (TVN does not provide semi-live subtitling). This difference might be due to using different workflows as well as having more skilled or experienced subtitlers. The difference might also be due to the use of antenna delay. As of April 2021 (when samples from Q2 2021 were being collected), Polsat was using an antenna delay of 5 seconds.[58] If the other broadcasters did not use antenna delay at that time, that would explain the difference in latency. However, broadcasters do not disclose this information and it is possible the other broadcasters also used antenna delay. It is also not clear if Polsat applied antenna delay in the following quarters as well.

Even though Polsat was able to achieve lower latency than the other broadcasters, none of the stations were able to get close to acceptable levels of latency as recommended by various regulators. (As of 2022, the Polish National Broadcasting Council has not issued any guidance on latency in live subtitling). The broadcasters could argue that they have less experience in delivering live subtitling than TV stations based in countries where the practice is more established. So let us now examine the results quarter by quarter (see Table 12) to see if the stations are improving, i.e. lowering the latency, over time as the broadcasters are becoming more experienced with providing live subtitling.

Table 12: *Mean latency of live subtitling by quarter and broadcaster*

Quarter	TV station	Mean (ms)	N	SD
Q2 2021	TVP	16,074.64	736	6,442.39
	Polsat	9,501.13	949	3,594.00
	TVN	18,341.17	1324	7,426.25
	Total	14,998.74	3009	7,294.14
Q3 2021	TVP	18,184.70	670	6,798.97
	Polsat	11,237.89	133	5,383.21
	TVN	16,369.14	1305	5,203.03
	Total	16,622.45	2108	5,991.09
Q1 2022	TVP	17,675.22	758	5,958.27
	Polsat	19,444.59	846	5,940.12
	TVN	19,037.05	1156	8,719.28
	Total	18,787.96	2760	7,271.34

(Continued)

---

58   Personal communication with Mateusz Hamulczyk, a broadcasting engineer at Polsat.

Table 12: Continued

Quarter	TV station	Mean (ms)	N	SD
Total	TVP	17,288.59	2164	6,451.97
	Polsat	13,984.10	1928	6,878.98
	TVN	17,873.78	3785	7,286.09
	Total	16,760.96	7877	7,146.67

The results over the three quarters do not indicate improvements in latency. In fact, the average latency in Q1 2022 (the third analysed quarter) is higher for all the broadcasters than in Q2 2021 (the first analysed quarter). While the differences in latency across time for TVP and TVN are not that pronounced, the increase in latency for Polsat is noticeable, particularly when visualized on a graph (see Fig. 31).

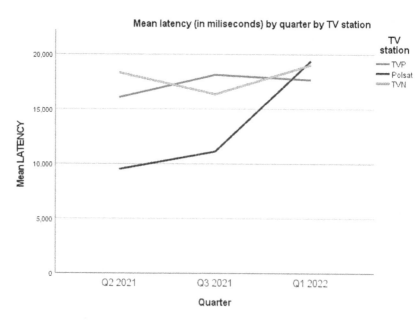

Fig. 31: *Mean latency (in milliseconds) of live subtitles across three quarters for TVP, Polsat and TVN*

The change is surprisingly large for Polsat where the latency increases from 9.5s in Q2 2021 to 11.2s in Q3 2021 until it reaches 19.4s in Q1 2022. When comparing the three quarters, Polsat goes from having the lowest average latency among the three news channels to having the highest average latency. This can be due to a different method of creating live subtitles. (While the broadcasters do not disclose the details of their workflows, the results on accuracy and text reduction also suggest a change in the live subtitling workflow used by this broadcaster.) In part, the increase could also be explained by the broadcaster no longer using antenna delay (which could not be confirmed).

So far, we have looked at averages. As they can be deceptive, Fresno (2019) recommends reporting the percentage of live subtitles that shows delays of or higher than: 6 seconds, 8 seconds, 10 seconds. As the average delay in the Fresno's research on live subtitling on American TV stations was 6.1 seconds, and it is far higher in the research presented here (16.76 seconds), I decided to also report the percentage of captions that show delay of or higher than 15, 20, 25 and 30 seconds (see Table 13).

Table 13: *Percentage of live subtitles within various latency ranges*

	N	%
< 6 seconds	282	3.5%
≥ 6 seconds	7566	94.3%
≥ 8 seconds	7305	9%
≥ 10 seconds	6875	85.7%
≥ 15 seconds	4423	55.1%
≥ 20 seconds	1997	24.9%
≥ 25 seconds	822	10.2%
≥ 30 seconds	326	4.1%
Missing data	174	2.2%

Note. "Missing data" refers to subtitles which are included the corpus, but it was not possible to measure their latency. The content of such subtitles does not match the content of the show (in other words, they include utterances that are not present in the show or have been rephrased to such a degree that it is not possible to match them with the transcript of the show). Therefore, it was not possible to calculate the latency of such subtitles (as they have no point of reference in the transcript of the show).

The results for live subtitles show that very few subtitles have a latency lower than 6 seconds or even 8 seconds with the majority of subtitles falling in the range between 15 and 20 seconds. More than a quarter of all live subtitles on TVP and TVN are above 20 seconds, with Polsat having fewer such subtitles. For comparison with the results from the US, see Fig. 32. And Fig. 33 presents the

percentage of live subtitles on Polish news channels that fall within the ranges
reported by Fresno (2019).

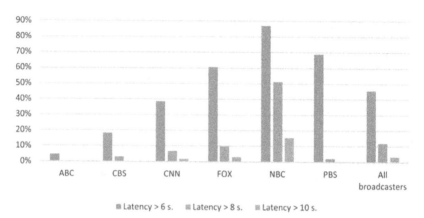

Fig. 32: *Percentage of live subtitles on American television within the three latency ranges reported by Fresno (2019)*

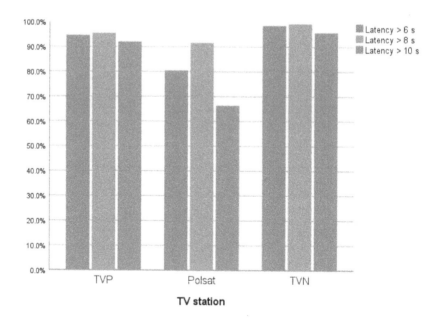

Fig. 33: *Percentage of live subtitles on Polish news channels within the three latency ranges used in the study by Fresno (2019)*

As most of the live subtitles in this research had much higher latency than what was found by Fresno (2019), Fig. 34 below was adapted to present higher latency ranges. As the average latency found in the study was 16.8 s, the following three ranges were selected: above 15 seconds, above 20 seconds and above 25 seconds.

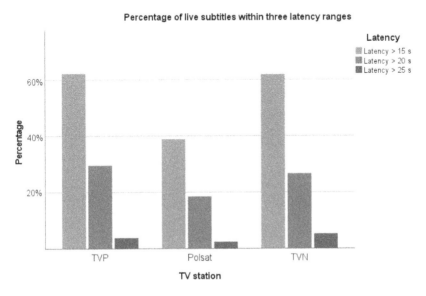

Fig. 34: *Percentage of live subtitles within three latency ranges selected as per the mean latency found in the study*

The histograms below (see Figs. 35 and 36) show the distribution of latency values for live and semi-live subtitles. Predictably, the visualization shows a much wider range of values for live subtitles.

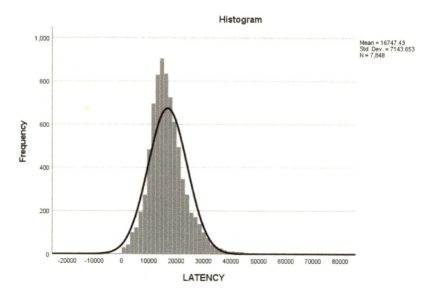

Fig. 35: *The distribution of latency values for live subtitles*

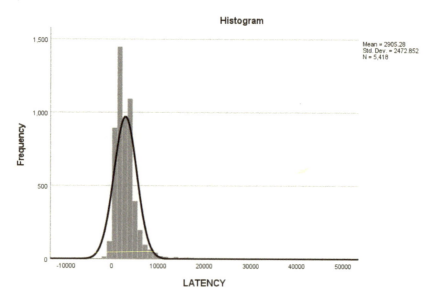

Fig. 36: *The distribution of latency values for semi-live subtitles*

So far, we have looked at descriptive statistics regarding latency (see Table 14 below for the complete results). It should be pointed out that the range of latency values is extremely wide with the highest value found in the study being 76.5 seconds (on TVN). Let us now examine the data with the use of more advanced statistical methods to check if the trends we have identified up until now are statistically significant.

Table 14: *Average latency of live and semi-live subtitles by quarter and TV station*

Quarter	TV station	Live vs. semi-live	Mean	N	Std. Deviation	Minimum	Maximum
Q2 2021	TVP	live	16,074.64	736	6,442.393	0	42,200
		semi-live	4,093.38	770	1,587.159	-4,733	15,400
		Total	9,948.77	1506	7,579.576	-4,733	42,200
	Polsat	live	9,511.15	948	3,582.607	0	24,900
		semi-live	1,627.43	1142	1,216.505	-1,500	11,134
		Total	5,203.40	2090	4,694.521	-1,500	24,900
	TVN	live	18,333.39	1322	7,427.870	0	58,800
		Total	18333.39	1322	7,427.870	0	58,800
	Total	live	14,998.09	3006	7,288.782	0	58,800
		semi-live	2,620.52	1912	1,833.230	-4,733	15,400
		Total	10,185.99	4918	8,377.783	-4,733	58,800
Q3 2021	TVP	live	18,133.81	664	6,775.024	-767	45,100
		semi-live	4,503.29	780	4,269.408	-4,900	42,700
		Total	10,771.06	1444	8,781.226	-4,900	45,100
	Polsat	live	11,126.61	130	5,388.620	-4,138	21,254
		semi-live	2,466.60	996	1,056.769	0	13,934
		Total	3,466.43	1126	3,461.639	-4,138	21,254
	TVN	live	16,368.60	1304	5,204.998	3,966	40,333
		Total	16,368.60	1304	5,204.998	3,966	40,333
	Total	live	16,602.46	2098	5,980.635	-4,138	45,100
		semi-live	3,361.09	1776	3,106.121	-4,900	42,700
		Total	10,532.08	3874	8,205.474	-4,900	45,100
Q1 2022	TVP	live	17,675.22	758	5,958.273	3,033	44,000
		semi-live	4,393.20	785	2,346.872	-3,033	35,800
		Total	10,918.00	1543	8,021.636	-3,033	44,000
	Polsat	live	19,413.20	830	5,940.812	-120	39,534
		semi-live	1,388.80	945	934.344	-1,200	17,100
		Total	9,817.11	1775	9,893.521	-1,200	39,534

(Continued)

Table 14:   Continued

Quarter	TV station	Live vs. semi-live	Mean	N	Std. Deviation	Minimum	Maximum
	TVN	live	19,037.05	1156	8,719.284	-1,367	75,520
		Total	19,037.05	1156	8,719.284	-1,367	75,520
	Total	live	18,774.64	2744	7,277.544	-1,367	75,520
		semi-live	2,752.07	1730	2,283.135	-3,033	35,800
		Total	12,579.05	4474	9,766.833	-3,033	75,520
Total	TVP	live	17,270.44	2158	6,440.913	-767	45,100
		semi-live	4,331.10	2335	2,965.414	-4,900	42,700
		Total	10,545.90	4493	8,141.915	-4,900	45,100
	Polsat	live	13,928.71	1908	6,856.292	-4,138	39,534
		semi-live	1,825.39	3083	1,175.434	-1,500	17,100
		Total	6,452.35	4991	7,308.774	-4,138	39,534
	TVN	live	17,871.03	3782	7,287.363	-1,367	75,520
		Total	17,871.03	3782	7,287.363	-1,367	75,520
	Total	live	16,747.43	7848	7,143.653	-4,138	75,520
		semi-live	2,905.28	5418	2,472.852	-4,900	42,700
		Total	11,094.12	13266	8,887.232	-4,900	75,520

Orero et al. (2018, p. 106) recommend that research data from empirical AVT studies should always be analysed "using appropriate statistical analyses and models" and the results should be reported together with information on how the data was processed, what statistical tests were used, what was the statistical significance and effect size. In the previous section, I used ANOVAs and ANCOVAs as well as Pearson correlations to analyse data on accuracy. While accuracy was calculated on the show level (in other words, NER scores are available for each sample, i.e. a specific set of subtitles from a specific TV show), latency was measured on the subtitle level. In the case of data that is available for each individual subtitle, Silva et al. (2022) advocate for the use of linear mixed models (LMMs) as a more rigorous way to calculate results that are more reliable and fine-grained. In practise, the use of LMMs in the present research makes it possible to look at latency data with more granularity and more statistical rigour. Instead of aggregating subtitle-level measurement into averages for each sample (as would happen with an ANOVA or a t-test), and then comparing the average latency for 96 samples, we can take into account the actual latency calculated for each individual subtitle. Linear mixed models "compute the estimate for each individual score for each item measured" (Silva et al., 2022). In the case of the research presented here, this means that for each sample there are many rows of data, one row per one subtitle. Altogether, the 96 samples analysed in the study include 13,620 data points (rows of data), corresponding to all the subtitles in the study. This makes it possible to better account for variance that is due to the individual characteristics of each subtitle such as its duration or the number of characters. (Table 15 below shows a sample from the dataset used for the linear mixed models in this research. Two different rows of data are included to show how the data was structured.)

Table 15: *Examples of rows of data from the subtitle-level dataset*

Sample	TV station	Date	Quarter	Show	Live vs. semi-live	Subtitle text	Latency	Gap	Character number	Subtitle speed	Subtitle duration
23	2	20220110	2	Fakty po Faktach	0	Jego morderca nie został do dziś osądzony.	23,567	500	41	15.18	2700
31	0	20220105	2	Wiadomości	1	Wspólnoty mieszkaniowe i spółdzielnie zostaną automatycznie objęte regulowanymi taryfami za gaz.	7,3000	18,433	94	21.52	4367

Note. TV stations were coded as 0 (TVP), 1 (Polsat) and 2 (TVN). Quarters were coded as 1 (Q2 2021), 2 (Q3 2021) and 3 (Q1 2022). Live subtitles were coded as 0 and semi-live subtitles as 1. Latency, gap between consecutive subtitles and subtitle duration are expressed in milliseconds. Subtitle speed is expressed in characters per second.

LMMs are called "mixed" as they can contain both fixed and random effects (Meteyard & Davies, 2020). Fixed effects are the variables of primary interest, and they can entered in the models either as factors (for categorical variables) or covariates (for continuous variables). Factors (which are also known as "predictors") and covariates can be introduced in the model to explain the unexplained variance in the data (as it can also be done in an analysis of covariance, i.e. ANCOVA). Random effects, in turn, are factors which are not primary to the research, but it is those factors that provide LMMs with an advantage over more traditional statistical techniques. Random effects have the potential to explain more variation in the data, which increases the statistical power of the results. These could be, for instance, different participants in a study or, as is the case here, different subtitles.

Using the statistical software IBM SPSS version 27, two linear mixed models were created. The first model looked at both live and semi-live subtitles and included two broadcasters: TVP and Polsat (TVN was excluded as the station did not broadcast semi-live subtitles). To be able to examine the data from TVN, another model was then created that included all the three broadcasters and looked at live subtitling only (semi-live subtitling was excluded). Both models excluded subtitles shorter than 500ms (the reasons for excluding these are discussed in detail in Section 6.5.3).

There are different approaches to creating or *fitting* linear mixed models. Here, the maximal-to-minimal-that-improves-fit approach was used. That is, the model was first run with all the relevant random and fixed effects. Then the variables which turned out to be redundant or had very low estimates were eliminated until the statistical software was able to successfully compute an error-free model. This is known as a confirmatory approach, and it is recommended whenever clear hypotheses are being tested. The model was then further modified by removing random effects that explain little or no variance and do not improve the fit. The quality of fit was assessed here by comparing Akaike's information criterion (AIC), with lower score meaning a better fit (Meteyard & Davies, 2020). The aim of this was to arrive at the so-called parsimonious model (Bates et al., 2015), that is a model that balances, on the one hand, including all the significant effects and, on the other hand, achieving maximum statistical power by excluding less important parameters. The final models reported here are the models which had the lowest AIC and did not return any error. We will now look at both final versions of these two models one by one, starting with a description of how each model was created and what insights it provides. This procedure will then be repeated when analysing subtitle speed.

The goal of creating Model 1 was to answer the following research questions:

(1) Does latency differ between live subtitling and semi-live subtitling?
(2) Does latency increase or decrease over time as broadcasters gain more experience at providing live subtitles?

The expectation is that semi-live subtitling should allow for little or no latency, whereas for live subtitles the latency will be higher. And the latency should either be constant across time or, hopefully, it should be decreasing as broadcasters and their live subtitlers become more experienced at providing live subtitles.

The initial dataset had 13,620 rows of data. After excluding the subtitles of a duration shorter than 500 miliseconds as well as all the subtitles from TVN, the dataset was reduced to 9,559 rows of data. The dependent variable was latency. Regarding fixed effects, both factors and covariates were included in the model. The following three factors were added: TV station, Live vs. semi-live and Quarter. The interactions between Quarter*TV station and TV station*Live vs.

semi-live were also included as fixed effects. The former interaction allows the model to consider the possibility that latency varies to different extents across time (as suggested by descriptive statistics). In an effort to control for potential confounding variables, Subtitle speed, Subtitle length (measured in the number of characters) and the Gap between consecutive subtitles were included in the model as covariates (grand-mean centred). In order to account for the possible influence of individual characteristics of each show as well as each sample (e.g. different topics, different guests with an individual style of speaking), the model also included the following random effects: TV show and Sample (sample being understood as a set of subtitles from a specific TV show on a specific day). These were expected to explain extra variance in latency.

Of all the fixed effects, TV station, Live vs. semi-live, Quarter and the interactions Quarter*TV station and TV station*Live vs. semi-live were considered essential to respond to the main research questions; hence, they were not removed from the final model irrespective of statistical significance and model fit.

Quarters were introduced as a linear variable (coded as 0, 1 and 2) and as a quadratic variable (coded as 0, 2 and 4) in order to account for a possible non-linear relationship between time points. As the two variables were highly correlated, both variables were coded orthogonally as well. The linear variable was coded as -1, 0, 1 and the quadratic variable was coded as -2, -1 and 1. The quadratic variable turned out not to be significant, which means that the growth was linear. Consequently, Quarter as a quadratic variable was removed from the final model. Subtitle length turned out to be insignificant as a predictor of latency and was also removed from the model. Table 16 presents the results of the final version of this model that reached the lowest AIC value (182203).

Table 16: *Fixed and random effects estimates for latency for TVP and Polsat*

Fixed effects			
	Estimate (Std. error)	*95% CI*	*p*
Intercept	10160.13 (1735.85)	[5352.55, 14967.70]	.004
TV station (TVP vs. Polsat)	3909.45 (2631.89)	[-2806.20, 10625.10]	.196
Gap	.15 (.02)	[.10, .19]	<.001
Subtitle Length	12.31 (4.67)	[2.87, 21.75]	.012
Subtitle Speed	109.06 (15.77)	[77.48, 140.64]	<.001
Live vs. semi-live	-8194.99 (1496.10)	[-11193.53, -5196.45]	<.001
Quarter	1738.91 (523.78)	[670.36, 2807.47]	.002

(*Continued*)

Table 16: Continued

Fixed effects			
TV station*Live vs. semi-live	-882.99 (2311.79)	[-5538.06, 3772.08]	.704
TV station*Quarter	-1112.15 (784.90)	[-2685.07, 460.76]	.162

Random effects			
	Variance (Std. error)	*95% CI*	*p*
Residual	11185593.72 (163901.77)	[10868921.21, 11511492.68]	.000
Sample (Intercept)	6088015.85 (1210728.61)	[4122841.50, 8989901.02]	<.001
Subtitle length | Sample slope	851.29 (290.06)	[436.56, 1659.98]	.003
Subtitle speed | Sample slope	11051.90 (2895.33)	[6613.67, 18468.47]	<.001
Show intercept	6845198.79 (6365644.90)	[1106157.90, 42359907.78]	.282

Note. Number of data points = 9559. The reference category is Polsat, which means that there is no estimate for this TV station as it was used as the reference point for TVP.

Starting with fixed effects, the analysis showed that when taking all the quarters together, there is no statistically significant difference in latency of live subtitles between TVP and Polsat (p = .196). Also, there is no statistically significant difference in latency of semi-live subtitles between the stations (p = .704). The model does show a highly significant difference in latency between live and semi-live subtitles for both stations (p <.001). The difference is estimated to be lower by 8.2 seconds in the case of semi-live subtitling when all the other effects are held constant. Interestingly, the model shows that the gap between consecutive subtitles and the subtitle speed are statistically significant as predictors of latency. Longer gaps between subtitles and faster subtitle speed predict slightly higher latency.

Quarter turned out to be significant as a linear variable (p = .002). An increase in quarter led to an increase in latency. Thus, the model confirmed that the trend of increasing latency is statistically significant. For Polsat, the increase is larger than for TVP as the model estimates an increase by 1.7 seconds from one quarter to another. For TVP the estimated increase is 0.63 seconds. (Please note this is an average effect both for live and semi-live subtitles.) The model shows no statistically significant difference between the stations when it comes to latency in live subtitles in the second quarter. However, there is a statistically significant difference for Polsat but just between Q2 2021 (first quarter analysed in the study) and Q1 2023 (third quarter analysed). The model estimates that the latency of live subtitles increased by 6 seconds between these quarters.

Model 1 answered the two research questions formulated above. Latency does differ significantly between live and semi-live subtitling. And, contrary to expectations, latency is increasing over time. This is true for both live and semi-live subtitles as well as both broadcasters (TVP and Polsat).

To examine live subtitles for all the three broadcasters, Model 2 was created. The aim of this model was to answer the following research questions:

(1) Does the latency of live subtitles differ between the three broadcasters?
(2) Does latency increase or decrease over time as broadcasters gain more experience at providing live subtitles?

The same structure of the dataset was used as for the previous model. Departing from the initial dataset that had 13,620 rows of data, all subtitles of a duration shorter than 500 miliseconds were excluded. All the semi-live subtitles were excluded as well. This way the dataset was reduced to 8,022 rows of data.

As with the previous model, Latency was the dependent variable. Regarding fixed effects, both factors and covariates were included in the model. The following factors were added: TV station and Quarter. The interaction Quarter*TV station was also included as a fixed effect. Subtitle speed, Subtitle Length and Gap between consecutive subtitles were included in the model as covariates. TV show and Sample were included as random effects. The final version of the model (see Table 17 below) achieved the AIC score of 155766.

Table 17: *Fixed and random effects estimates for latency of live subtitles for all three broadcasters*

Fixed effects			
	Estimate (Std. error)	*95% CI*	*p*
Intercept	18,065.71 (1590.40)	[14646.44, 21484.98]	<.001
TV station (TVP vs. TVN)	-2,780.46 (2814.20)	[-9010.32, 3449.40]	.345
TV station (Polsat vs. TVN)	-9,287.07 (2578.30)	[-14831.27, -3742.87]	.003
Gap	0.24 (0.03)	[0.19, 0.29]	<.001
Subtitle length	40.78 (5.70)	[29.37, 52.19]	<.001
Subtitle speed	137.78 (20.88)	[95.34, 180.22]	<.001

(Continued)

Table 17:   Continued

Fixed effects			
Quarter	436.95 (847.29)	[-1259.71, 2133.62]	.608
TVP*Quarter	799.46 (1467.67)	[-2140.46, 3739.37]	.588
Polsat*Quarter	2,864.96 (1418.12)	[23.95, 5705.97]	.048
Random effects			
	Variance (Std. error)	*95% CI*	*p*
Residual	28,294,648.93 (458950.29)	[27409271.14, 29208626.30]	<.001
Samples (Intercept)	15,023,275.07 (2955252.90)	[10216999.62, 22090516.02]	<.001
Subtitle length | Sample slope	562.08 (338.13)	[172.88, 1827.47]	.096
Subtitle speed | Sample slope	5,589.15 (4161.85)	[1298.72, 24053.41]	.179
Show intercept	5,368,633.92 (4,531,633.08)	[1026524.82, 28077480.12]	.236

Note. Number of data points = 8022. In the case of broadcasters, TVP and Polsat were compared with TVN as the reference point.

The model estimates that the latency is lower by 2.8 seconds on TVP as compared with TVN for the first quarter. This result is not statistically significant ($p = .345$). However, the model does show a statistically significant difference between Polsat and TVN in terms of latency ($p = .003$). The model estimates that Polsat has 9.3 seconds less latency than TVN when all other predictors are held constant. (Please note that this result is only true for the first analysed quarter, Q2 2021).

When analysing together the subtitles of all the broadcasters, there is no statistically significant difference between quarters ($p = .608$). Over time, in the case of TVP (as compared to TVN) there is a slight increase in latency (by 0.8 in the second quarter and twice that in the third quarter), which is not statistically significant ($p = .588$). In the case of Polsat, there is a much higher increase (by 2.9 s in the second quarter and twice that in the third quarter), which is significant.

Thus, the model estimates the difference in latency between Polsat and TVN as -9.3 seconds in the first quarter, -6.4 seconds in the second quarter and -3.5 seconds in the third quarter. (The interaction with the quarter is not statistically significant for Polsat, meaning that the difference in latency remains significant over time.) The model confirms the findings from the descriptive statistics. Most importantly, it confirms the statistical significance of the difference in latency between Polsat and TVN as well as the trend of latency increasing on Polsat. The model also shows that subtitle speed, subtitle length and the gap between consecutive subtitles all have significant effect on latency (even though the effect is small).

Summing up the results on latency, live subtitling on Polish news TV has very high latency (16.75 seconds), which is higher than what was found in other studies in the UK, USA and France. The statistical models answered the research questions on (1) whether latency differs between live and semi-live subtitling and (2) whether the latency of live subtitles differs between the three broadcasters and (3) whether it increases or decreases over time. In line with the expectations, the analysis found that semi-live and live subtitling differ significantly in terms of latency. Contrary to the expectations, there are no signs of improvement over time. Indeed, the statistical analysis confirms the trend of latency increasing over time. The biggest increase was found on Polsat where the latency of live subtitles increased steeply by 9.9 seconds (from 9.5 seconds in Q2 2021 to 19.4 seconds in Q1 2022). Even after controlling for fixed effects and random effects, the model still estimated a significant increase in latency for this broadcaster (by 6 seconds).

Regarding differences between broadcasters, both statistical models found significant differences between the three TV stations in the latency of subtitles, both live and semi-live. The statistical model estimated that even when all other predictors were held constant, there was still a huge difference of 9.3 seconds between the broadcaster that had the lowest latency (Polsat) and the one with the highest latency (TVN) in Q2 2021. The result shows that some broadcasters achieve much better results than others, potentially because differences in live subtitling workflows.

The fact that overall latency is higher on Polish news channels than in the case of UK and USA could be explained in various ways: (1) Polish broadcasters having less experience with live subtitling; (2) the use of different workflows as some US broadcasters use stenocaptioning which can produce lower latency than respeaking with self-correction, while some Polish broadcasters might be using respeaking with live parallel correction which tends to produce even higher latency than respeaking with self-correction; (3) the use of antenna delay. However, broadcasters in English-speaking countries are traditionally resistant to the use of antenna delay to minimize latency in live subtitling (Fresno, 2019; Romero Fresco, 2011). Consequently, the third explanation can be rejected.

The increase in latency among all the Polish broadcasters over time is a sign of a worrying trend. It could be explained by changes in their workflows, not using or no longer using antenna delay, high staff rotation and employing less experienced subtitlers in the following quarters or, in general, less care towards quality.

Regarding the changes in the subtitling workflows, one option would be a change in the method of creating live subtitles; for instance, from respeaking with parallel correction to automatic speech recognition with human correction. For both Polsat and TVP such a change could explain the results on accuracy (a decrease in accuracy across the three quarters). However, the use of automatic speech recognition (ASR) rather than respeaking should lead to a decrease in latency rather than an increase that we are observing in the data. The use of ASR should also lead to the decrease in reduction rate as ASR produces verbatim text. We will re-visit the hypothesis of a change in the method of producing live subtitles once we have analysed the results on the reduction rate in Section 6.5.4.

For now, a more likely explanation seems to be that broadcasters do not pay enough attention to improving or at least sustaining the quality of live subtitling. In this context, it should be pointed out that since Polish news broadcasters introduced live subtitling in 2020, up until now, there has been no research on the quality of live subtitling and the Polish regulator did not issue any guidelines or recommendations on the topic (despite publishing various such documents in the past on SDH in general, sign language interpreting or audio description). Thus, it is possible that broadcasters might be disregarding quality in an attempt to minimize costs or due to the challenges involved in recruiting, training and retaining live subtitlers. Due to lax regulatory approach adopted by the media regulator, the broadcasters might think they can get away with low quality subtitling. Also, as discussed in Chapter 4, broadcasters do not actively seek viewers feedback and, in the case of Polsat and TVN, there is actually no apparent way for viewers to reach out to the station. If users of subtitling want to complain about its quality, the only option seems to be filing a complaint with the National Broadcasting Council, a cumbersome formal process that many viewers might be unaware of. In any case, such a complaint can be rejected on the grounds that the Council did not establish any quality criteria on live subtitling.

With the average latency in the third analysed quarter found to be 18.77 seconds, it is likely that watching a show with live subtitles is not very comfortable. After a journalist asks a question, viewers have to wait for almost 19 seconds to see this question in the subtitles. As the news shows are accompanied by on-screen text, graphics and images, it is possible that once the viewers are reading the subtitle, the other on-screen information is already referring to another topic. If there are three or more speakers and they are not clearly identified in the subtitles, distinguishing between the speakers with such large latency is likely impossible.

On this bleak backdrop of increasing latency, there is one optimistic finding. If one of the broadcasters (Polsat) was able to achieve latency of 9.5 seconds in Q2 2021 (which is higher than the threshold proposed by American or British guidelines, but still lower than the maximum latency of 10 seconds recommended by the French Conseil Supérieur de l'Audiovisuel), surely it is technically and organizationally feasible for other Polish broadcasters to achieve noticeable improvements and at least lower their latency to that level.

6.5.3. Gaps between consecutive subtitles

Apart from latency, another aspect of synchronicity is related to gaps between consecutive subtitles. The assumption is that in the case of continuous speech in a TV show (in other words, when there are no pauses or longer periods of silence), subtitles should also appear continuously, one after another, respecting the minimum technical gap between the subtitles. This way the broadcaster avoids a situation when viewers see people talking in a TV show and yet do not see any subtitle, which might be confusing for viewers. Indeed, on TVP and Polsat whenever there is continuous speech, subtitles tend to be displayed one after another with only short breaks of a few frames between the subtitles. However, in the case of TVN there are longer gaps between subtitles even if the speech is continuous.

To explore that further, the gaps between consecutive subtitles were measured in milliseconds. The measurement was done by comparing the out-time of one subtitle with the in-time of the following subtitle. The last subtitle in each sample (with sample understood as an excerpt of a subtitled TV show) was excluded from this analysis as it was not possible to measure the gap (there was no following subtitle that could be used for reference).

The results show (see Table 18 below) that indeed TVN tends to have long gaps between subtitles (with an average duration of almost 2 seconds). This seems a bad practise as those longer gaps could be eliminated if the subtitles are displayed a bit longer, which would also give viewers more time to read each subtitle. An ANOVA ran with Gap as the dependent variable and TV stations as the independent variable showed a significant effect of TV station ($p <.001$), confirming that the differences between the stations are statistically significant.

Table 18: *Average gap (measured in milliseconds) between consecutive subtitles in the study*

TV station	Type of subtitles	Mean (ms)	N	SD	Minimum	Maximum
TVP	Live	371.66	2187	2,162.23	0	75800
	Semi-live	359.96	2357	2,136.54	0	50584
	Total	365.59	4544	2,148.72	0	75800
Polsat	Live	728.07	1912	1,362.01	33	20040
	Semi-live	589.83	3163	809.32	33	16067
	Total	641.91	5075	1,054.20	33	20040
TVN	Live	1,965.84	3882	2,911.51	0	30440
	Total	1,965.84	3882	2,911.51	0	30440
Total	Live	1232.46	7981	2,524.54	0	75800
	Semi-live	491.68	5520	1,528.68	0	50584
	Total	929.59	13501	2,203.48	0	75800

So far, we have analysed the results on accuracy and synchronicity of subtitles. However, even if live subtitles are very accurate and have low latency, they might still offer little value to the viewers unless the subtitles are displayed long enough for viewers to be able to read them. Thus, we will now look at subtitle speed.

6.5.4. Subtitle speed

Subtitle speed has to do with how long a subtitle is displayed on screen and how much time viewers have to read the subtitle relative to the text within this subtitle (see Section 5.5.3 for a detailed discussion on subtitle speed). In the research presented here, it was measured in characters per second (cps).

When analysing the data, 7 outliers were found with extremely high subtitle speeds (between 40 and 70 cps). A closer look revealed that all these subtitles also had very short duration and some had more than three lines (one even had 12 lines of text). In other words, these were subtitles which were displayed by accident and quickly removed. A subtitler would realize he or she sent the subtitle by mistake and would undo this action. (For instance, a live editor would be editing a number of lines of text and instead of sending just two lines of text, would send all the text available.) The effect for the viewer would be a subtitle that is only displayed for a fraction of a second.

Calculating subtitle speed for ultrashort subtitles seems pointless as viewers do not actually read such subtitles and might not even have enough time to notice them. And including such subtitles in subtitle speed analysis would distort the results. Therefore, all the subtitles that had a duration of 500ms or less were excluded from the dataset (in effect, excluding the 7 outliers mentioned above). For comparison, Polish guidelines on subtitling stipulate a minimum duration of 1 second (Künstler & Butkiewicz, 2019), whereas Netflix guidelines establish the minimum duration of five-sixths of a second (which translates to 813ms)[59]. While 500ms is an arbitrary threshold, it was chosen based on the assumption that viewers can notice and read subtitles which are slightly shorter than a second. Also, while all the subtitles in the study with a duration of 500ms or shorter had subtitle speeds above 40 cps (which are extremely high), the subtitles with a duration longer than 500ms had more typical speeds (between 7.14 cps and 25.88 cps). Summing up, the subtitles with a duration of 500ms or shorter were excluded from all the analysis in this research.

The final dataset shows an average subtitle speed of 15.01 cps for all news programming that was analysed (see Table 19 below). If only live subtitles are concerned, the average subtitle speed is 13.79 cps, whereas for semi-live subtitles it goes up to 16.81 cps.

Table 19: *Average subtitle speed for live and semi-live subtitles in the study*

Type of subtitles	Mean (cps)	N	SD	Minimum	Maximum
Live	13.79	8022	5.07	.69	33.41
Semi-live	16.81	5449	4.95	1.21	38.33
Total	15.01	13471	5.24	.69	38.33

The average subtitle speed for live subtitles is lower than the result obtained by Fresno (2019) for live subtitles in the US (14.45 cps) but higher than what was reported by Romero Fresco (2016) for news programmes in the UK (152 words per minute, which translates to 12.67 cps).

The average subtitle speed is higher than 12 cps recommended by the Polish National Broadcasting Council for pre-recorded SDH and the data shows that semi-live subtitling tends to be even faster than live subtitling. That is because when live subtitling is created through respeaking, respeakers will tend to condense the text and omit redundant words. Also, if a speaker has a very high speech rate, respeakers might not be able to follow that pace as they also have to add punctuation and other commands. In the case of respeaking with parallel

---

59   Netflix Timed Text Style Guide: General Requirements, https://partnerhelp.netflix studios.com/hc/en-us/articles/215758617-Timed-Text-Style-Guide-General-Requi rements (Accessed on February 29, 2024).

correction, live editors occasionally delete some words or entire sentences if these include serious errors and editors decide that trying to fix such errors will take too much time and increase the latency excessively. Summing up, there is a limitation on how much text respeakers can dictate and live editors can correct. However, when semi-live subtitling is created, the text is available in the news system and tends to be verbatim. Condensing this text requires extra effort and time. As some of the text might become available quite late before the show starts, the subtitlers might have little time to edit this text, which makes condensation challenging. Also, while respeakers have a sense of how fast a speaker is speaking and can adapt to that (for instance, by condensing more the utterance of fast speakers and less the utterances of slow speakers), when preparing semi-live subtitles, the subtitlers might not know how fast the speech is going to be (as they have access to the text in the news system but not necessarily to the recording).

For comparison, the average speech rate in the TV shows analysed in the study was 131.26 words per minute and it was almost the same for shows with live and semi-live subtitles (see Table 20 below). However, it should be pointed out that the range of values was much wider in the case of shows with live subtitles (between 94.01 wpm and 170.14 wpm). This is not surprising as news bulletins (which are subtitled semi-live) tend to have a more constant speech rate, whereas in the case of chat shows, the speed will depend on the speaker as some guests will speak faster than others and it is also possible to have overlapping speech by two or more speakers. The average speech rate in Polish news TV shows was lower than 175 wpm found for news programmes in the UK (Romero Fresco, 2016). Again, this result is not surprising as English has shorter words than Polish, and it is typical to find faster speech rates in English.

Table 20: *Average speech rate for TV shows with live and semi-live subtitles in the study*

Type of subtitles	Mean (wpm)	N	SD	Minimum	Maximum
Live	131.23	66	14.51	94.01	170.14
Semi-live	131.33	30	6.27	119.64	148.42
Total	131.26	96	12.49	94.01	170.14

Let us now look in more detail at the results for each broadcaster to see if subtitle speed is similar across all the stations (see Table 21). Again, we find that the results differ between stations with the lowest subtitle speed for live subtitles found on TVP (11.85 cps), slightly faster speed on TVN (13.3 cps), and the highest subtitle speed for live subtitles found on Polsat (17.01 cps). In the case of semi-live subtitles, again, the highest speed was found on Polsat (18.10 cps) and the lowest on TVP (15.11 cps).

Table 21: *Average subtitle speed for live and semi-live subtitles on TVP, Polsat and TVN*

TV station	Live vs. semi-live	Mean (cps)	N	SD	Minimum	Maximum
TVP	Live	11.85	2199	5.78	.69	33.41
	Semi-live	15.11	2354	4.28	1.42	38.33
	Total	13.54	4553	5.32	.69	38.33
Polsat	Live	17.01	1911	6.52	1.47	32.63
	Semi-live	18.10	3095	5.02	1.20	38.33
	Total	17.69	5006	5.67	1.21	38.33
TVN	Live	13.30	3912	2.40	1.29	24.02
	Total	13.30	3912	2.40	1.29	24.02
Total	Live	13.79	8022	5.07	.69	33.41
	Semi-live	16.81	5449	4.95	1.21	38.33
	Total	15.01	13471	5.24	.69	38.33

Even though research shows that some viewers can keep up with subtitle speeds as high as 20 cps (Szarkowska & Gerber-Morón, 2018), the speeds found on Polsat are certainly very high, higher that the threshold of 12 cps mandated by the Polish National Broadcasting Council for SDH in general as well as the threshold of 15 cps put forward by the Spanish norm on live subtitles. Ofcom also cautions against speeds above the threshold of 200 wpm (approx. 17 cps), which can be challenging for many viewers (Romero Fresco, 2016). Let us now examine the results for live subtitles across the three quarters to see if subtitle speed changes over time (see Table 22 below).

Table 22: *Average subtitle speed for live subtitles by quarter and broadcaster*

Quarter	TV station	Mean (cps)	N	SD	Minimum	Maximum
Q2 2021	TVP	12.24	747	5.50	1.42	33.07
	Polsat	13.01	950	5.37	1.46	28.81
	TVN	14.77	1330	1.22	4.61	24.02
	Total	13.59	3027	4.28	1.42	33.07

(Continued)

Table 22: Continued

Quarter	TV station	Mean (cps)	N	SD	Minimum	Maximum
Q3 2021	TVP	11.66	670	6.41	1.21	33.41
	Polsat	17.26	131	5.75	3.01	29.98
	TVN	12.10	1335	2.69	1.29	18.37
	Total	12.28	2136	4.59	1.21	33.41
Q1 2022	TVP	11.65	782	5.46	.69	28.82
	Polsat	21.55	830	4.57	3.62	32.63
	TVN	13.01	1247	2.20	1.70	20.00
	Total	15.12	2859	5.79	.69	32.63
Total	TVP	11.85	2199	5.78	.69	33.41
	Polsat	17.01	1911	6.52	1.46	32.63
	TVN	13.30	3912	2.41	1.29	24.02
	Total	13.79	8022	5.07	.69	33.41

On TVP, the average subtitle speed decreases slightly across quarters (from 12.24 cps to 11.65 cps). The decrease might be a positive thing if it is achieved through conscious and careful condensation, but it could also be a sign of more omission. We already know that accuracy decreased on TVP across quarters, which might suggest that there is more omission. Subtitle speed also decreases on TVN from 14.77 cps to 13.01 cps, which probably is due to more omission as well. The analysis of text reduction should provide more clarity on how this decrease was achieved.

Similarly to the results for latency, the biggest changes over time are observed in the case of Polsat. This broadcaster goes from a relatively low speed of 13 cps in Q2 2021 to a rather high average speed of 17.3 cps in Q3 2021. In 2022, subtitle speed increases even further to 21.5 cps. This shows a worrying trend for this broadcaster with subtitle speed being unacceptably high and on the increase. This might be explained by changes in live subtitling workflows, possibly a switch to using automatic speech recognition with human editing as opposed to respeaking with parallel correction. Again, the analysis of text reduction should provide more clarity on whether that could be the case.

The results for semi-live subtitling (see Table 23 below) show that subtitle speed fluctuates across quarters for TVP (with values around 15 cps) and increases for Polsat from 17.13 cps to 18.99 cps. Again, Polsat has the highest average subtitle speed, which might make it hard for viewers to follow news programmes with subtitles.

Table 23: *Average subtitle speed for semi-live subtitles on TVP and Polsat*

Quarter	TV station	Mean (cps)	N	SD	Minimum	Maximum
Q2 2021	TVP	15.22	779	2.92	6.23	26.93
	Polsat	17.13	1149	4.46	4.54	38.33
	Total	16.36	1928	4.02	4.54	38.33
Q3 2021	TVP	14.58	783	5.74	1.42	33.92
	Polsat	18.38	1000	5.34	2.21	33.18
	Total	16.72	1783	5.83	1.43	33.92
Q1 2022	TVP	15.52	792	3.64	2.58	38.33
	Polsat	18.99	946	5.12	1.21	33.42
	Total	17.41	1738	4.82	1.21	38.33
Total	TVP	15.11	2354	4.28	1.43	38.33
	Polsat	18.10	3095	5.02	1.21	38.33
	Total	16.81	5449	4.94	1.21	38.33

So far, we have looked at average subtitle speeds. However, looking at just the average speed can be misleading. There is usually a wide range of values of subtitle speed with some subtitles achieving very low speeds and others reaching very high speeds. This is true for the research presented here as subtitle speed values range from 0.69 cps to 38.33 cps. The average speed alone "might not always reflect how challenging a set of subtitles really is" (Fresno & Sepielak, 2020, p. 11). Therefore, the percentage of subtitles delivered at fast and very fast speeds is also reported (see Table 24).

Table 24: *Percentage of subtitles delivered above 15, 18 and 25 cps*

Type of subtitles	> 15 cps	> 18 cps	> 25 cps
Live	34.7%	15.8%	3.8%
Semi-live	63.4%	36.9%	5.2%

The results show that very high subtitle speeds are particularly a problem in the case of semi-live subtitles. As many as 63.4% of all the semi-live subtitles in the study are above 15 cps (the maximum subtitle speed as per the Spanish norm). And 36.9% are above 18 cps. While the results for live subtitles are far from ideal (with 15.8% of live subtitles displayed at speeds faster than 18cps), they are better than for semi-live subtitles (see Figs. 37 and 38) and lower that what was found by Fresno (2019) in the US where as many as 57% live subtitles had speeds higher than 15 cps, 43% went above 18 cps and as many as 21% were faster than 25 cps. Still, quite a lot of subtitles on Polish news channels are presented at speeds that are likely to be uncomfortable for most viewers.

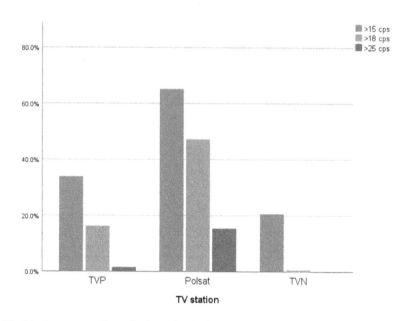

Fig. 37: *Percentage of live subtitles with subtitle speed higher than 15 cps, 18 cps and 25 cps*

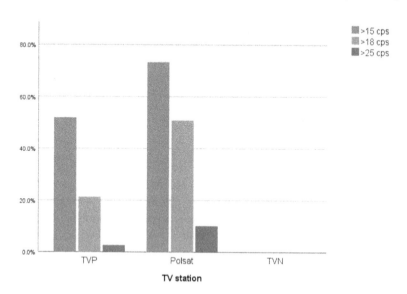

Fig. 38: *Percentage of semi-live subtitles with subtitle speed higher than 15 cps, 18 cps and 25 cps*

So far, we have looked at descriptive statistics regarding subtitle speed. As previously with latency, we will now examine the data with the use of linear mixed models to check if the trends we have identified up until now are statistically significant. The same approach and steps were used here as described in the previous section for latency. Again, it was necessary to create two separate statistical models. Model 3 includes both live and semi-live subtitles for TVP and Polsat (but excludes TVN). And Model 4 includes all the three broadcasters but excludes semi-live subtitles.

The aim of Model 3 was to answer the following research questions:

(1) Does subtitle speed differ between live subtitling and semi-live subtitling?
(2) Does subtitle speed increase or decrease over time?

The same dataset was used as for Model 1 with 9,559 rows of data. (As previously, the subtitles of a duration shorter than 500ms as well as all subtitles from TVN were excluded.) The dependent variable was Subtitle speed. Regarding fixed effects, both factors and covariates were included in the model. The following three factors were added: TV station, Live vs. semi-live, Quarter. The interactions between Quarter*TV station and TV station*Live vs. semi-live were also included as fixed effects. The former interaction allows the model to consider the possibility that subtitle speed varies to different extents across time (as suggested by descriptive statistics for Polsat). In an effort to control for potential confounding variables, Subtitle length (measured in the number of characters) and Gap between consecutive subtitles were included in the model as covariates. In order to account for the possible influence of individual characteristics of each show as well as each sample (e.g. different topics, different guests with an individual style of speaking), the model also included TV show and Sample as random effects. These were expected to explain extra variance in Subtitle speed.

As in the previous analysis of latency, of all the fixed effects, TV station, Live vs. semi-live, Quarter and the interactions Quarter*TV station and TV station*Live vs. semi-live were considered essential to respond to the main research questions; hence, they were not removed from the final model irrespective of statistical significance and model fit.

Quarters were introduced as a linear variable (with values 0, 1 and 2) and as a quad variable (with values 0, 2 and 4). This was done to check if the growth is linear or not. As the two variables were highly correlated, it was then also coded as an orthogonal variable (with values -1, 0, 1). Again, as with the previous models on latency, the quad variable and the orthogonal variable were not significant and were removed from this model. Table 25 presents the results of the final version of this model that reached the lowest AIC value (55134).

Table 25: *Fixed and random effects estimates for subtitle speed for TVP and Polsat*

Fixed effects			
	Estimate (Std. error)	*95% CI*	*p*
Intercept	14.80 (.92)	[12.15, 17.45]	<.001
TVP	-.82 (1.39)	[-4.48, 2.85]	.585
Gap	-.01 (2.73)	[-.01, -5.32]	<.001
Subtitle length	.15 (.01)	[.13, .17]	<.001
Quarter	1.19 (.25)	[.69, 1.69]	<.001
Live vs. semi-live	1.06 (.84)	[-.62, 2.76]	<.001
TVP*Live vs. semi-live	-1.75 (1.28)	[-1.68, -.21]	.181
TVP*Quarter	-.94 (.37)	[-4.34, .85]	.013
Random effects			
	Variance (Std. error)	*95% CI*	*p*
Residual	18.88 (.28)	[18.35, 19.43]	.000
Sample (Intercept)	1.15 (.26)	[.74, 1.79]	<.001
Subtitle length | Sample slope	.01 (.01)	[.01, .01]	<.001
Show intercept	1.94 (1.87)	[.29, 12.76]	.298

Note. Number of data points = 9,559. There is no estimate for Polsat because this TV station was used here as the reference point for TVP.

The model found a significant difference in subtitle speed between live and semi-live subtitles (*p* = <.001) when all the other predictors are held constant (e.g. when controlling for Subtitle length or Gap between consecutive subtitles, etc.). Interestingly, both Subtitle Length and Gap between consecutive subtitles were found to be significant predictors of Subtitle Speed.

The model showed no statistically significant difference in subtitle speed between the two broadcasters (TVP and Polsat) in the first quarter for live subtitles (*p* = .585) when all the other predictors are held constant. However, the difference in subtitle speed between TVP and Polsat becomes statistically significant across quarters (*p* <.001). The model estimates that the average subtitle speed on Polsat is 2.72 cps faster in the third analysed quarter (Q1 2022) as compared to the first analysed quarter (Q2 2021). The interaction between TV station and quarter for TVP is not statistically significant (*p* = .181). In the second quarter, the speed increases on Polsat in live subtitling by 1.75 cps (the model shows that the difference between Polsat and TVP decreases by 1.60 cps but we know already that this is because of an increase on Polsat). So in the second quarter the difference in speed for live is -3.13 cps and in the third quarter -4.17 cps.

Thus, the model confirms that there is a statistically significant difference in subtitle speed between live and semi-live subtitles. Also, there is a significant increase of subtitle speed over time on Polsat. In the case of TVP, the increase is not statistically significant.

As previously, another model was created to analyse the data on live subtitles for all the three broadcasters. The aim of Model 4 was to answer the following research questions:

(1) Does subtitle speed of live subtitles differ between the three broadcasters?
(2) Does subtitle speed of live subtitles increase or decrease over time?

The same structure of the dataset was used as for the previous model. Departing from the initial dataset that had 13,620 rows of data, all subtitles of a duration shorter than 500ms were excluded. All the semi-live subtitles were excluded as well. This way the dataset was reduced to 8,022 rows of data.

As with the previous model, Subtitle speed is the dependent variable. Regarding fixed effects, both factors and covariates were included in the model. The following factors were added: TV station and Quarter. The interaction Quarter*TV station was also included as a fixed effect. Subtitle length and Gap between subtitles were included in the model as covariates. TV show and Sample were included as random effects. In the previous models, Quarter as quadratic variable turned out not to be significant (as the change found over quarters was linear) and was removed from the models. However, the variable was significant in this model and was not removed. The final version of the model achieved AIC of 42713.

The results for Model 4 (see Table 26 below) show that Quarter was statistically significant here as a predictor of subtitle speed. The model shows that the decrease in Subtitle speed over the three quarters is not linear (it is a quadratic decrease that flattens over time). Please note this is only true for the reference category (TVN).

Table 26: *Fixed and random effects estimates for latency of live subtitles for all three broadcasters*

Fixed effects			
	Estimate (Std. error)	*95% CI*	*p*
Intercept	13.77 (.49)	[12.71, 14.82]	<.001
TVP	.19 (.76)	[-1.45, 1.85]	.799
Polsat	3.20 (.78)	[1.47, 4.93]	.002
Gap	-.01 (1.64)	[-.01, -7.02]	<.001

(*Continued*)

Table 26: Continued

Fixed effects			
Subtitle length	.12 (.01)	[.10, .14]	<.001
Quarter (orthogonal)	-1.17 (.24)	[-1.63, -.69]	<.001
Quarter (quadratic)	.36 (.12)	[.12, .60]	.003
TVP*Quarter	1.04 (.27)	[.50, 1.57]	<.001
Polsat*Quarter	2.10 (.29)	[1.52, 2.68]	<.001
Random effects			
	Variance (Std. error)	**95% CI**	*p*
Residual	14.87 (.18)	[14.52, 15.23]	.000
Samples (Intercept)	.78 (.15)	[.54, 1.13]	<.001
Character numer | Sample slope	.01 (.01)	[.01, .01]	<.001
Show intercept	.97 (.52)	[.34, 2.76]	.060

Note. Number of data points = 8022. In the case of broadcasters, TVP and Polsat were compared with TVN as the reference point. As the estimates are based on the geometric means, they vary from the descriptive statistics which are based on the arithmetic means.

The model shows no statistically significant difference between TVP and TVN in terms of subtitle speed in the first quarter (*p* = .799). The difference between the broadcasters did become statistically significant in the second analysed quarter, where TVP has a higher speed than TVN by 1.24 cps (*p* <.001). Polsat had higher subtitle speed than TVN in the first quarter (3.2 cps; *p* = .002) and then the difference increased in the second quarter (5.3 cps) and the third quarter (7.4 cps; *p* <.001). For TVN, the speed decreases over time but the change slows down (this is shown by Quarter as an orthogonal variable). So for the first quarter the decrease is -1.17cps (less than .001), and for the second quarter it is -0.8 cps (.003).

Thus, the model answers the two research questions: there are statistically significant differences in subtitle speed between the three broadcasters and there are significant changes in subtitle speed over time. While TVN slightly reduced the speed over time, TVP did not change it much and Polsat increased it. The model indicates a very noticeable increase in subtitle speed on Polsat. It estimated that the subtitle speed of live subtitles increased between Q2 2021 and Q1 2022 by 7.4 cps for this broadcaster when all other predictors are held constant.

Summing up the results on subtitle speed, we have seen that both live and semi-live subtitles on Polish news TV achieve averages speeds that are above the recommended maximum speeds for SDH in Poland and above the maximum speeds recommended for live subtitling in Spain, the UK or Canada. The situation is particularly concerning in the case of semi-live subtitling, where more than one third (36.9 %) of all semi-live subtitles in the study were displayed at speeds above 18 cps that are likely to be uncomfortable for most viewers. On top of that, there is a worrying trend of subtitle speed going up, especially on Polsat where the average subtitle speed increased from 13 cps to 21.5 cps across the three analysed quarters. Such increases in subtitle speed should be related to changes in the reduction rates of subtitles, which we will examine now.

6.5.5. Reduction rate

Reduction rate was used as a measure of completeness of subtitles. As discussed in Section 5.1., the US media regulator, FCC, identifies completeness as one of four key quality parameters of subtitling. Completeness is understood as subtitles being provided for the entire programme. From this perspective, all the samples were fully subtitled in a sense that subtitles ran from the beginning to the end of each sample. While there were cases of missing subtitles and longer gaps in between subtitles with the longest gap of 75.8 seconds, there were no cases of subtitles stopping altogether or starting in the middle of a TV show.

However, it should be pointed out that some of the recordings made for the study had to be rejected as they did not include subtitles at all. It is possible than some shows, despite the fact that they were graphically identified by the broadcasters as subtitled (see Fig. 39 for an example), did not actually include subtitles. It is difficult to find out whether the subtitles were missing because they were not broadcast by the television station (for instance, due to technical or organizational issues) or the lack of subtitles was due to a technical issue on the part of the company handling the signal such as a cable TV provider. Finally, the lack of subtitles could be attributed to the decoder's malfunction.

Fig. 39: *The on-screen text identifying the show as subtitled*

Note. The broadcasts which are subtitled are identified graphically by an on-screen text (as depicted on the image above, on the right) that reads "PROGRAM Z NAPISAMI" ("SUBTITLED PROGRAMME"), the text is accompanied by the icon with the letter "N" (which stands for "napisy", i.e. "subtitles").

Another way to analyse completeness is to calculate the reduction rate, which is a percentage. It shows how much less or more text there is in the subtitles as compared to the verbatim transcript. The reduction rate can be measured by comparing the number of words or the number of characters. In the study, both calculations were carried out and these measures were found to be highly correlated (a Pearson correlation was computed; $r = .927$, $N = 96$, $p < .001$). The reduction rate is reported here as calculated based on the number of characters (on the assumption that it is more precise than the number of words).

While theoretically it is possible for the reduction rate to be negative (as subtitles can include speaker identifiers and sound descriptions), in practice subtitles tend to include less text than the verbatim transcript. Reduction rate might be an indicator of the fact that the subtitlers, in an effort to lower subtitle speed, make conscious decisions to rephrase the text so as to omit redundant or less important information or condense the text so as to express the same information with fewer words. However, high reduction rate might also mean that respeakers were not able to follow the pace of the speaker or that the text produced through respeaking or ASR included numerous errors that were deleted by the live corrector. Thus, it is difficult to determine a threshold of acceptable or unacceptable reduction rate (as is possible in the case of accuracy or subtitle speed). Both low and high reduction rates can be problematic. For instance, a low reduction rate can lead to excessive subtitle speed, and a high reduction rate can be a result of omitting important information, which will translate into low accuracy. Consequently, the results on the reduction rate should not be interpreted in isolation.

The average reduction rate found in the study (see Table 27) was 36.47% for live subtitles and 9.57% for semi-live subtitles, which shows that, in general, semi-live subtitles tend to have less text reduction (i.e. they are more verbatim). This is in line with the results on subtitle speed (with higher speeds for semi-live subtitles as compared to live ones) and accuracy (with higher accuracy found for semi-live subtitles). In other words, low reduction rate for semi-live subtitles translates into high accuracy. However, this is achieved at the cost of high subtitle speeds.

Table 27: *Average reduction rate (%) for live and semi-live subtitles in the study*

Type of subtitles	Mean (%)	N	SD	Minimum	Maximum
Live	36.47	66	.14	-5%	65%
Semi-live	9.57	30	.05	4%	31%
Total	28.06	96	.17	-5%	65%

The range of results is quite wide as the lowest reduction rate was -5% (that is the subtitles had more text than the verbatim transcript) and was found in a sample of a live discussion during the news show *Wydarzenia 21.50* (Polsat). The highest reduction rate was 65% and was found in a sample of a political chat show *Kropka nad i* (TVN).

The average reduction rate for live subtitles (36.47%) on Polish news TV is much higher than the one found by Fresno (2009) in the US ($\approx$6%) and a bit higher than was found for live subtitles in the UK study on chat shows (32%). However, the average reduction rate for semi-live news shows (9.57%) on Polish TV is lower than 13% found on British TV channels (Romero Fresco, 2016).

Let us know look at the results for each broadcaster (see Table 28 below). In the case of live subtitles, TVN has the highest text reduction (43%) followed by TVP (41%). Polsat has much less text reduction (20%). Both TVP and Polsat have lower reduction in case of semi-live subtitles.

Table 28: *Average reduction rate (%) for semi-live and live subtitles for all stations*

TV station	Live vs. semi-live	Mean (%)	N	SD		Minimum	Maximum
TVP	Live	41	16	.08	19		56
	Semi-live	11	15	.06	5		31
	Total	27	31	.17	5		56
Polsat	Live	20	18	.13	-5		43
	Semi-live	08	15	.03	4		15
	Total	14	33	.11	-5		43
TVN	Live	43	32	.09	19		65
	Total	43	32	.09	19		65
Total	Live	36	66	.14	-5		65
	Semi-live	09	30	.05	4		31
	Total	28	96	.17	-5		65

Higher reduction rate might suggest that the subtitles had undergone more extensive editing (which was found to be true in the study by Fresno), but a closer look reveals that in the Polish corpus reduction rate can be either linked to successful condensation (as is often the case on TVP) or to arbitrary omission (on TVN). Let us now examine the results quarter by quarter (see Table 29) to check if the text reduction increases or decreases over time as the broadcasters are becoming more experienced with providing live subtitling.

Table 29: *Average reduction rate (%) by quarter, broadcaster and type of subtitling*

Quarter	TV station	Live vs. semi-live	Mean (%)	N	SD	Minimum	Maximum
Q2 2021	TVP	Live	36	5	.09	19	44
		Semi-live	6.87	5	.01	5	08
		Total	21.43	10	.16	5	44
	Polsat	Live	34.14	6	.05	29	43
		Semi-live	5.86	5	.01	4	08
		Total	21.28	11	.15	4	43
	TVN	Live	38.46	11	.10	19	57
		Total	38.46	11	.10	19	57
	Total	Live	36.72	22	.08	19	57
		Semi-live	6.36	10	.01	4	08
		Total	27.23	32	.16	4	57

Table 29: Continued

Quarter	TV station	Live vs. semi-live	Mean (%)	N	SD	Minimum	Maximum
Q3 2021	TVP	Live	45.74	6	.07	34	56
		Semi-live	15.43	5	.09	7	31
		Total	31.97	11	.17	7	56
	Polsat	Live	14.38	6	.12	-5	26
		Semi-live	9.54	5	.01	7	12
		Total	12.18	11	.09	-5	26
	TVN	Live	46.45	10	.04	39	56
		Total	46.45	10	.04	39	56
	Total	Live	37.51	22	.16	-5	56
		Semi-live	12.49	10	.07	7	31
		Total	29.69	32	.18	-5	56
Q1 2022	TVP	Live	41.57	5	.05	35	50
		Semi-live	10.63	5	.03	8	15
		Total	26.10	10	.16	8	50
	Polsat	Live	11.10	6	.04	5	16
		Semi-live	09.05	5	.03	6	15
		Total	10.17	11	.03	5	16
	TVN	Live	45.44	11	.10	30	65
		Total	45.44	11	.10	30	65
	Total	Live	35.19	22	.17	5	65
		Semi-live	09.84	10	.03	6	15
		Total	27.27	32	.18	5	65
Total	TVP	Live	41.39	16	.08	19	56
		Semi-live	10.98	15	.06	5	31
		Total	26.68	31	.17	5	56
	Polsat	Live	19.87	18	.12	-5	43
		Semi-live	08.15	15	.02	4	15
		Total	14.54	33	.11	-5	43
	TVN	Live	43.35	32	.09	19	65
		Total	43.35	32	.09	19	65
	Total	Live	36.47	66	.14	-5	65
		Semi-live	09.57	30	.05	4	31
		Total	28.06	96	.17	-5	65

The results over the three quarters show a slight increase in the reduction rate for live subtitles on TVN (from 38.46% to 45%) and on TVP (from 36% to 41.57%). On Polsat, in turn, there is a very noticeable trend (see Fig. 40 below) of reduction rate decreasing from 34.14% to 11.10%, which might suggest a change in the method of creating live subtitles. In Q2 2021 (the first analysed quarter), Polsat provided live subtitles that were far from verbatim (similarly to the other two broadcasters), whereas in Q1 2022 (the third analysed quarter) the live subtitles on Polsat were near-verbatim.

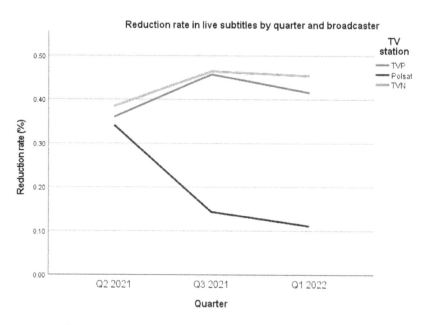

Fig. 40: *Reduction rate in live subtitles for TVP, Polsat and TVN across the three analysed quarters*

In the case of semi-live subtitles, there is a slight trend of reduction rate increasing but the subtitles are still near-verbatim in the third analysed quarter (see Fig. 41).

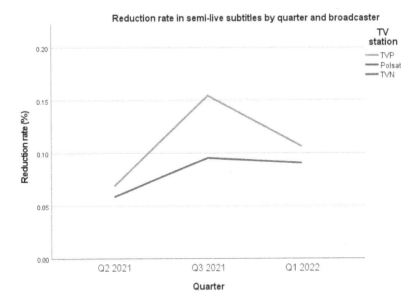

Fig. 41: *Reduction rate in semi-live subtitles for TVP and Polsat across the three analysed quarters*

To check if these results are statistically significant, a 2x2 analysis of covariance (ANCOVA) was carried out with Reduction rate score as dependent variable. The two independent variables were TV station (Polsat, TVP) and Type of subtitles (live vs. semi-live). Speech rate was added as a covariate. For the needs of this analysis, subtitles from TVN had to be excluded (to be able to compare live and semi-live subtitles). Altogether, 63 TV broadcasts were analysed.

The resulting data failed the assumption of normality and the assumption of the homogeneity of variance. Log transformation and square root transformation were used on the data in an attempt to improve it. Log transformation succeeded in normalizing the data. Therefore, the log-transformed data was used for analysis. To improve the power of the analysis further, bootstrapping was performed, which confirmed the results. Bootstrapping solved the problem with homogeneity of variance, confirming that the results are reliable.

The analysis showed a strong, statistically significant main effect of TV station on the reduction rate, $F(1, 57) = 18.80$, $p = <.001$, $eta^2 = .248$. There is also a strong and significant main effect of Subtitle type on the reduction rate, $F(1, 57) = 79.65$, $p = <.001$, $eta^2 = .583$. Also, a significant interaction was found between the two independent variables: the TV stations and Type of subtitles

(p = 0.23), although the effect size is rather weak (eta^2 = .087). The interaction is due to the fact that reduction rate changes dramatically on Polsat for live subtitles but not for semi-live subtitles. The analysis found no effect of Speech rate on Reduction rate (p = .626). In other words, the shows where speakers talked faster did not have a higher reduction rate when both live and semi-live subtitles where considered.

The estimated marginal means (see Fig. 42) are reported for the average speech rate of 134.06 words per minute. Please note that the analysis was done with log-transformed data and, consequently, the estimated means cannot be compared directly with the descriptive statistics reported previously. However, the estimates show a similar difference between the types of subtitles and the two TV broadcasters as the in the case of the descriptive averages analysed earlier.

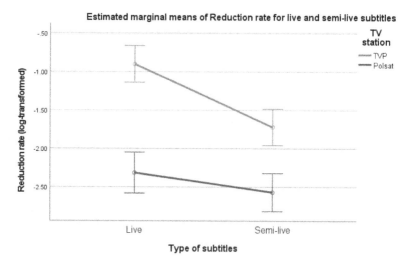

Fig. 42: *Estimated marginal means of Reduction rate for live and semi-live subtitles for TVP and Polsat (based on log-transformed data)*

To compare live subtitles between all the three broadcasters, a one-way analysis of variance (ANOVA) was carried out with Reduction rate as dependent variable. The independent variable was TV station. For the needs of this analysis, semi-live subtitles were excluded. Altogether, 66 TV broadcasts were analysed.

The resulting data failed the assumption of normality but passed the assumption of homogeneity of variance. Log transformation and square root transformation were used on the data in an attempt to improve it, but these techniques did not normalize the data. Therefore, the non-transformed data was used for analysis. It should be noted that the data failed the assumption of normality only by a narrow margin and it did pass the Shapiro-Wilk test, which can also be used to test normality. The issue with the data was due to one outlier (as discussed already in the case of accuracy in Section 6.5.1). As the dataset had an unequal number of samples per broadcaster (TVN had more samples of live subtitles than other broadcasters as it only provided live subtitles), the post-hoc test used was Hochberg's GT2 (Genizi & Hochberg, 1978). Due to the use of the post-hoc test, it was not possible to include Speech rate as a covariate in this analysis.

The analysis found a very strong effect of TV station (p <.001, eta2 = .505). The GT2 test showed that there is a significant difference between TVP and Polsat (p <.001) as TVP has a higher reduction. There is no significant difference between TVP and TVN (p = .899) but there is a significant difference between Polsat and TVN (p <.001).

To be able to check whether Speech rate predicts Reduction rate, a one-way ANCOVA was carried out with Reduction rate as the dependent variable, TV station as the independent variable and Speech rate as the covariate. This ANCOVA confirmed the differences between the stations as identified in the previous tests and found that Speech rate significantly predicts Reduction rate for live subtitles (p = .046). In other words, when speakers talk very fast, the respeakers omit or condense part of the text either because they cannot follow the pace of the original speaker, or they attempt to condense the text because they want to avoid excessive subtitle speeds. The estimated marginal means (see Fig. 43) are reported for the average speech rate of 131.23 words per minute and the estimated means are in line with the descriptive statistics reported previously.

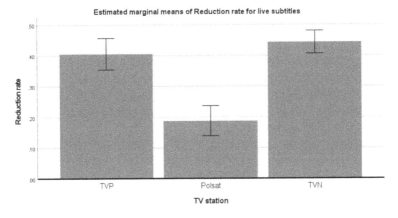

Fig. 43: *Estimated marginal means of Reduction rate for live subtitles for TVP, Polsat and TVN (based on – transformed data)*

As the previous two-way ANOVA that included both live and semi-live subtitles found that Speech rate did not significantly predict Reduction rate, and the current analysis found that it does predict Reduction rate for live subtitles, another one-way ANCOVA was carried out with the only difference that this time live subtitles were excluded and the data for only semi-live subtitles was tested. The analysis confirmed that Speech rate does not predict Reduction rate for semi-live subtitles ($p = .159$). This ANCOVA also found a significant difference between TVP and Polsat in the Reduction rate for semi-live subtitles ($p = 0.43$).

To further investigate the link between the speech rate in TV shows and the reduction rate in live subtitles, a Person correlation was computed with Speech rate and Reduction rate as variables. Live subtitles for all broadcasters were included and semi-live subtitles were excluded. Contrary to the expectations, the analysis found no significant correlation between the Speech rate and the Reduction rate, $r = -.023$, N = 66, $p = .858$. The analysis was then repeated separately for each broadcaster and found no significant correlation in the case of TVP and Polsat. Interestingly, there is a significant correlation for TVN, $r = .489$, N = 32, $p = .005$. Consequently, higher speech rates do mean higher reduction rates but only in the case of live subtitles on TVN.

If higher speech rates do not correlate with higher reduction rates on TVP and Polsat, then one could expect that whenever speakers talk faster, the subtitle speed will increase. Surprisingly, however, there is no significant correlation between Speech rate and Subtitle speed in live subtitles, $r = .021$, N = 66, $p = .865$. A similar analysis computed separately for each broadcaster found no correlation in the case of TVP and Polsat. Again, the correlation was found for TVN only ($r = -.609$, N = 32, $p < .001$). Semi-live subtitles were also analysed separately. Interestingly, a highly significant correlation exists between Speech rate and Subtitle speed in semi-live subtitles, $r = .564$, N = 30, $p < .001$. Summing up, when speech rate increases, the subtitle speed also increases for semi-live subtitles in the case of both broadcasters using this type of subtitles (TVP and Polsat). When live subtitles are concerned, when speech rate increases, the subtitle speed does increase but only on TVN (there is no link between the speech rate and the subtitle speed on TVP and Polsat).

When discussing the reduction rate it is important to note that lower reduction rate does not necessarily mean better quality and higher reduction does not necessarily mean worse quality unless we believe that subtitles have to be verbatim. If we accept that subtitles can be edited and the meaning can be condensed, then a higher reduction rate can mean two things. Either it means that the reduction is due to omitting information, in which case it will mean lower accuracy and should correspond to a lower NER score. Or it could mean that the subtitles have been successfully condensed, expressing the same ideas with fewer words. This would not affect quality inversely. In fact, condensation can improve quality if it is done to avoid excessive subtitle speeds.

To further look into this, a Pearson correlation was computed with Subtitle speed and Reduction rate as the variables. Live subtitles for all the three broadcasters were included and semi-live subtitles were excluded. As expected, the analysis found a highly significant negative correlation, $r = -.522$, $N = 66$, $p < .001$. This means that, in general, a higher reduction rate leads to lower subtitle speed. Pearson correlation was also computed for semi-live subtitles and found no correlation there, $r = -.143$, $N = 30$, $p = .450$.

6.5.6. Placement and display mode

All the three stations use fixed subtitle placement that was never modified in the samples analysed. Individual subtitles were never raised or lowered in reaction to graphics or texts appearing on screen. However, each station uses a different placement (see Fig. 44): on TVP Info subtitles are at the bottom of the screen, on TVN24 they are at the top of the screen and on Polsat News they are slightly raised.

Fig. 44: *Examples of subtitle positioning on Polsat (left), TVP (right) and TVN (bottom)*

Out of these three options, TVP Info uses the least successful solution as subtitles often cover other on-screen text such as graphics with the names of speakers or news headlines. Moving subtitles to the top (the case of TVN24) has the advantage of not covering on-screen text or graphics but occasionally subtitles cover speakers' eyes. The solution used by Polsat News is a compromise as the subtitles are moved a bit higher so that they do not cover on-screen text or graphics presented in the lower third of the screen. The disadvantage is that they occasionally cover a bit of lower part of the graphics presented in the centre of the screen.

Regarding the display mode all the subtitles were presented as block subtitles. No scrolling or roll-up subtitles were found in the samples, which is in line with the recommendation that scrolling subtitles should not be used (Saerens et al., 2020).

6.5.7. Text segmentation

As discussed in Section 5.5.5, the text in subtitling needs to be divided between subtitles and lines (in the case of two-line or three-line subtitles), which raises a need for deciding where a new line or a new subtitle should start. When words or phrases are strongly linked syntactically, separating them between lines or (even more importantly) between subtitles is considered an error. In previous studies on the quality of live subtitling, text segmentation have received far less attention than other quality dimensions such as latency, accuracy or reduction rate. That is in part because of the use of scrolling or word-by-word display mode for live subtitling in some territories, most notably in the US. When the text appears word by word, segmentation is no longer an issue. Another reason for paying less attention to segmentation in live subtitling is that up until now there has been no metric to measure the quality of text segmentation.

The research presented here found that all the three broadcasters display subtitles as blocks of text with Polsat and TVN using only one-line and two-line subtitles, whereas TVP also uses three-liners. Occasionally, subtitles with more lines of text appeared on TVP and Polsat but these had a very short duration, indicating that such multiple-line subtitles were displayed by mistake and quickly cleared from the screen.

In this research I developed and tested a new metric to evaluate text segmentation (as put forward in Section 5.3.3) with three types of errors which were assigned weights, depending on the perceived severity of each error. The final score was calculated by multiplying each error by its weight and summing up the values of all the errors in the sample. Thus, the segmentation score allows one to compare the quality of text segmentation between samples and broadcasters. The lower the score, the fewer segmentation errors there were in each sample and the higher the quality of text segmentation.

The results of this analysis show that live subtitles have more segmentation errors than semi-live subtitles (see Table 30). This is not surprising; the time pressure involved in creating live subtitles means that it is more difficult to ensure proper text segmentation.

Table 30: *Mean segmentation values for TV shows with live and semi-live subtitles*

Type of subtitles	Mean	N	SD	Minimum	Maximum
Live	20.64	66	24.67	.00	115.50
Semi-live	4.82	30	6.15	.00	24.75
Total	15.70	96	21.96	.00	115.50

Note. Higher values indicate more text segmentation errors.

Let us now examine the results for each broadcaster (see Table 31). TVP achieves the lowest segmentation value (0.45 for live subtitles), corresponding to almost no errors in text segmentation. Interestingly, for this broadcaster, semi-live subtitles have slightly more errors than live subtitles (1.58). TVN achieves a far worse result (24.46) and Polsat achieves an even higher segmentation value for live subtitles (31.76), which reflects numerous text segmentation errors. This broadcaster achieves a much better text segmentation in semi-live subtitles (8.05). It should be pointed out that there is a wide range of results as some TV shows had no segmentation errors at all (.00), while one of the shows on Polsat reached the value of 115.50 (indicative of the fact that most subtitles in the sample included one or more segmentation errors).

Table 31: *Mean text segmentation value for live and semi-live subtitles on TVP, Polsat and TVN*

TV station	Live vs. semi-live	Mean	N	SD	Minimum	Maximum
TVP	Live	0.48	16	0.77	.00	3.00
	Semi-live	1.58	15	1.85	.00	5.50
	Total	1.01	31	1.49	.00	5.50

(Continued)

Table 31: Continued

TV station	Live vs. semi-live	Mean	N	SD	Minimum	Maximum
Polsat	Live	31.76	18	40.58	.00	115.50
	Semi-live	8.05	15	7.24	.00	24.75
	Total	20.98	33	32.27	.00	115.50
TVN	Live	24.46	32	8.70	1.00	46.50
	Total	24.46	32	8.70	1.00	46.50
Total	Live	20.64	66	24.66	.00	115.50
	Semi-live	4.81	30	6.14	.00	24.75
	Total	15.69	96	21.95	.00	115.50

Note. Higher values indicate more text segmentation errors.

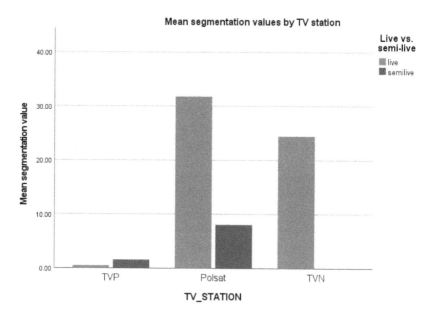

Fig. 45: *Mean segmentation values by TV station (higher values are indicative of more segmentation errors and lower quality)*

The comparison between stations (see Fig. 45 for the visualization) shows a stark contrast between TVP and the other two broadcasters. It is clear from the results that TVP puts a lot of care in ensuring proper text segmentation and achieves impressive results (despite the time pressure involved in live subtitling). Polsat has only occasional segmentation errors in semi-live subtitles but seems to struggle with ensuring proper segmentation in live subtitling. The text segmentation is far from perfect on TVN, but this broadcaster still achieves a slightly better result than Polsat. Let us now examine the situation quarter by quarter to see if the broadcasters improve text segmentation over time (see Table 32 below).

Table 32: *Mean text segmentation values by quarter for live and semi-live subtitles on TVP, Polsat and TVN*

Quarter	TV station	Live vs. semi-live	Mean	N	SD	Minimum	Maximum
Q2 2021	TVP	Live	.30	5	.44	.00	1.00
		Semi-live	1.9	5	2.52	.00	5.50
		Total	1.12	10	1.91	.00	5.50
	Polsat	Live	1.58	6	1.49	.00	3.75
		Semi-live	.35	5	.22	.00	.50
		Total	1.02	11	1.24	.00	3.75
	TVN	Live	25.07	11	11.12	1.00	46.50
		Total	25.07	11	11.12	1.00	46.50
	Total	Live	13.0	22	14.54	.00	46.50
		Semi-live	1.15	10	1.89	.00	5.50
		Total	9.32	32	13.25	.00	46.50
Q3 2021	TVP	Live	.33	6	.54	.00	1.25
		Semi-live	.70	5	.54	.25	1.50
		Total	.50	11	.54	.00	1.50
	Polsat	Live	14.20	6	3.57	7.75	18.00
		Semi-live	12.45	5	3.80	8.25	18.25
		Total	13.41	11	3.61	7.75	18.25
	TVN	Live	23.50	10	6.66	16.75	38.50
		Total	23.50	10	6.66	16.75	38.50
	Total	Live	14.65	22	10.86	.00	38.50
		Semi-live	6.57	10	6.70	.25	18.25
		Total	12.12	32	10.36	.00	38.50

(Continued)

Table 32:   Continued

Quarter	TV station	Live vs. semi-live	Mean	N	SD	Minimum	Maximum
Q1 2022	TVP	Live	.85	5	1.21	.25	3.00
		Semi-live	2.10	5	1.99	.00	5.25
		Total	1.47	10	1.68	.00	5.25
	Polsat	Live	79.50	6	37.24	13.25	115.50
		Semi-live	11.35	5	7.55	6.50	24.75
		Total	48.52	11	44.53	6.50	115.50
	TVN	Live	24.75	11	8.35	13.25	38.00
		Total	24.75	11	8.35	13.25	38.00
	Total	Live	34.25	22	35.52	.25	115.50
		Semi-live	6.72	10	7.13	.00	24.75
		Total	25.65	32	32.21	.00	115.50
Total	TVP	Live	.48	16	.78	.00	3.00
		Semi-live	1.58	15	1.86	.00	5.50
		Total	1.02	31	1.49	.00	5.50
	Polsat	Live	31.76	18	40.58	.00	115.50
		Semi-live	8.05	15	7.24	.00	24.75
		Total	20.98	33	32.27	.00	115.50
	TVN	Live	24.47	32	8.70	1.00	46.50
		Total	24.47	32	8.70	1.00	46.50
	Total	Live	20.64	66	24.67	.00	115.50
		Semi-live	4.82	30	6.15	.00	24.75
		Total	15.70	96	21.96	.00	115.50

The results over the three quarters do not indicate improvements in text segmentation neither for live nor for semi-live subtitles. In fact, there is a noticeable increase in text segmentation errors for Polsat. In the case of semi-live subtitles, the average text segmentation value for Polsat increases from an excellent result of .35 in Q2 2021 to 11.35 in Q1 2022 (see Fig. 46 for the visualization). There is an even more steep increase in text segmentation errors for live subtitles, where Polsat goes from 1.58 to 79.50 (see Fig. 47).

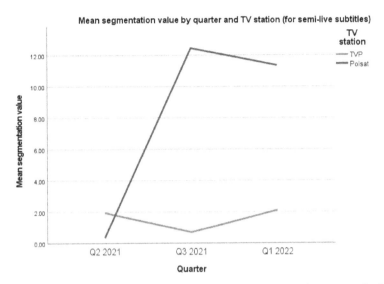

Fig. 46: *Mean segmentation value for semi-live subtitles by quarter and TV station (higher value indicates more segmentation errors)*

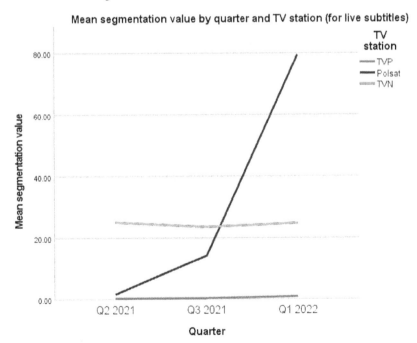

Fig. 47: *Mean segmentation value for live subtitles by quarter and TV station (higher value indicates more segmentation errors)*

The analysis shows that TVP is quite consistent in its good text segmentation standards and TVN is consistent in its bad text segmentation standards. Polsat, in turn, moves from having very few segmentation errors to having lots of them. The change is even more noticeable in the case of live subtitles where the results show quite a dramatic increase in the number of errors. Summing up the results, the data shows that subtitlers at TVP take very good care of text segmentation in both live and semi-live subtitles. On TVN, there seems to be some attempt at controlling the text segmentation, while still many errors make it to the screen.

On Polsat, in the case of semi-live subtitles, the standards of segmentation go down over time. In the case of live subtitles, Polsat has impressive results in the first analysed quarter with almost no segmentation errors. By the third analysed quarter, however, most live subtitles on Polsat have segmentation errors as there seems to be no attempt at controlling text segmentation. This might indicate a change of the method of creating live subtitling, perhaps to a more automated method where segmentation is no longer controlled in any way by subtitlers.

To check if these results are statistically significant, a 2x3 analysis of variance was carried out with Segmentation score as dependent variable. There were two independent variables: TV station (Polsat, TVP) and Type of subtitles (live vs. semi-live)[60]. For the needs of this analysis, subtitles from TVN had to be excluded (to be able to compare live and semi-live subtitles). Altogether, 64 TV broadcasts were analysed. The analysis found a strong and statistically significant main effect of TV station on Segmentation score, $F(1, 60)=11.81, p <.001, eta^2 = .164$. Type of subtitles also had an effect on Segmentation score, albeit less strong, $F(1, 60)=4.24, p <.001, eta^2 = .066$. The interaction between the two independent variables was significant ($p = 0.28$), as the differences in segmentation between live and semi-live subtitles were observed on Polsat but not on TVP.

To compare live subtitles between all the three broadcasters, a one-way analysis of covariance (ANCOVA) was carried out with Segmentation score as dependent variable. The independent variable was TV station. Speech rate was included as a covariate to see if higher speech rates mean that subtitlers pay less attention to segmentation as they prioritize accuracy or latency. For the needs of this analysis, semi-live subtitles were excluded. Altogether, 66 TV broadcasts were analysed. As expected, the analysis found a strong and statistically significant main effect of TV station on Segmentation score of live subtitles, $F(2, 62)= 11.54, p <.001, eta^2 = .271$. Interestingly, Speech rate was found to be a significant

---

60   Terms such as Type of subtitles, Speech rate, Latency or Subtitle speed are capitalized
     whenever used as names of variables when discussing statistical analysis.

predictor of Segmentation score, F (1, 62)=6.14, p - .016, eta^2 = .090. To follow up on this result, another similar ANCOVA was run with Latency as a covariate, and it showed that Latency is also a significant predictor of Segmentation score, F (1, 62)=9.79, p = .003, eta^2 = .136. This seems to suggest that as Speech rate or Latency increase, live subtitlers tend to pay less attention to text segmentation as they prioritize other quality dimensions.

6.5.8. Putting it all together: The interaction of quality dimensions

So far, we have examined various quality dimensions of semi-live and live subtitling separately. However, the results of some of the metrics such as reduction rate cannot be interpreted in isolation. Indeed, it is likely that all the quality dimensions interact with each other and should be taken into account together. In this section, we will put all the results together to see the big picture of the quality of subtitles analysed in the study.

All the results discussed previously showed again and again that when viewers watch Polish news channels and turn on subtitles, there are two strong predictors of the quality of subtitles that viewers will encounter. First, if the subtitles are live or semi-live. Second, which broadcaster produced these subtitles (see Table 33 below for an attempt at summarising the differences between the three broadcasters as found in the study; due to a radical change in quality across time, Polsat is described once for the first analysed quarter and then again for the third analysed quarter).

Table 33: *Summary of main differences in live subtitling between TVP, TVN and Polsat*

	TVP Info	Polsat Q2/2021	Polsat Q1/2022	TVN24
Latency	17.27s	9.51s	19.41s	17.87s
Reduction level	medium	medium	low	high
Approach to text reduction	condensation (through rephrasing and omitting redundant content)	condensation (through rephrasing and omitting redundant content)	verbatim (almost no reduction)	truncation (omitting whole idea units)
Accuracy	high (few errors, mostly minor)	high (few errors, mostly minor)	low (lots of errors; text is difficult to understand)	medium (some errors but many errors seem to have been avoided by omitting whole idea units)

Table 33:   Continued

	TVP Info	Polsat Q2/2021	Polsat Q1/2022	TVN24
Subtitle speed	11.85 cps (low)	13.01 cps (low)	21.55 cps (very high)	13.30 (low)
Segmentation	very good	good	very poor	poor
Consistency (subtitling conventions)	high	high	low	average

In the case of live subtitles, the results of the study show that each broadcaster has adopted a very different approach to creating them. TVN24 has a very high text reduction, which results in many independent idea units being lost. The subtitles are at best a summary of some of the points of what is being said (see Fig. 48 below for an example). And the choice of which idea units are included and which are omitted seems accidental at times. The content is oversimplified and many important points as well as details are lost.

Fig. 48: *Typical example of text reduction on TVN24 (the subtitles offer a very short summary)*

VERBATIM TRANSCRIPT: LIVE SUBTITLES:

Minister Szijjarto – ja uważam, że   Kowal: Polski rząd chwalił ostatnio
powinno się go cały czas cytować w   interwencję rosyjską w Kazachstanie.
Polsce. Żeby polski rząd codziennie

wiedział, co ten gość opowiada. On chwalił ostatnio interwencję rosyjską w Kazachstanie.

Proszę to sobie wyobrazić, facet, który pochodzi z partii Orbána. Orbán wypłynął na uczczeniu ofiar interwencji sowieckiej w Budapeszcie w 1956 roku. A teraz ten gość wychodzi, po prostu mówi, że super, że świetnie. Przyjmuje ordery na Kremlu.

Przyjmują ordery na Kremlu.

(English translation)

KOWAL: Minister Szijjarto… I think he should be quoted all the time [by the media] in Poland. So that every day the Polish government knows what this guy is talking about. Recently, he praised Russian intervention in Kazakhstan.

Can you imagine? It's a guy who comes from Orbán's party. Orbán became famous after honouring the victims of the Soviet intervention in Budapest in 1956. And now this guy appears and says it's great, it's all okay. And he shows up to receive medals at the Kremlin.

(English translation)

Kowal: The Polish government recently praised Russian intervention in Kazakhstan.

They receive medals at the Kremlin.

Note. In this case, the subtitles are also inaccurate with a serious error that changes the meaning. "He" (referring to Szijarto, a minister in the Hungarian government) is changed to "Polish government" and then again to "they". "Kowal" is a speaker identifier (the surname of the guest).

Such low accuracy as the one achieved by TVN is usually associated with the use of automatic speech recognition with no human correction. However, ASR produces verbatim subtitles and tends to have low latency, whereas live subtitles on TVN have very high latency and very high reduction rates. In fact, when comparing the subtitles to the verbatim transcript, almost half of the words are omitted. A closer look at the NER analysis confirms that as most errors are related to omission rather than misrecognition. The results suggest that TVN creates subtitles through respeaking with parallel correction or with respeaking with self-correction.[61] However, the workflow used by this broadcaster is clearly not effective in terms of producing good quality. Possible reasons might include respeakers and live correctors not getting the right training and not having enough time to properly prepare for each broadcast. There might also be issues with speech recognition system not producing good output or not being regularly trained with the current terminology and proper names that appear in the news broadcasts. Very high reduction rate might mean that live subtitlers struggle with respeaking and have to omit a lot of content to cope with performing the task. Such high reduction rate coupled with long gaps between some consecutive subtitles could also be indicative of the use of respeaking with self-correction as respeakers would have to pause respeaking to be able to correct misrecognitions themselves. If recognition errors are frequent, that would explain why respeakers omit so much information (as they have to pause respeaking again and again).

The subtitles offered by TVP have the best quality among the broadcasters analysed in the study, taking into account both semi-live and live subtitling across all the three quarters. In the case of live subtitles, while TVP has high reduction rates, it also achieves very good accuracy with high NER scores. As opposed to TVN where text reduction is mostly a result of omission, in the case of TVP text reduction mostly is due to successful condensation. Consequently, high reduction rates in live subtitles do not seem to be an issue. In fact, they can be seen as a positive result insofar as they make it possible to achieve lower subtitle speeds. Indeed, the subtitle speed is quite acceptable for live subtitles on TVP. This broadcaster also achieves a very good text segmentation. All these results show that TVP, which produces subtitles through respeaking with live parallel correction, uses this method quite effectively.

The only major concern in the case of live subtitles on TVP is latency, which is too high. The results for Polsat in the first analysed quarter (Q2 2021) show that it is feasible to achieve lower latency without compromising other quality dimensions. In part, the difference in latency might have been due to Polsat reducing latency by introducing an antenna delay of 5 seconds. Assuming that TVP is not

---

61   One could argue that given high reduction rate live subtitles on TVN could be produced by one or two subtitlers typing on keyboards. However, the NER analysis did not find any misspellings (which are typical when typing) and did find numerous misrecognitions (which are typical for SR-based methods). Also, it seems unlikely that typing would not create such high latency.

currently using antenna delay, starting to do so, perhaps combined with some improvements in live subtitling workflow, would be a way to lower latency.

Interpreting the results for Polsat is quite tricky as this broadcaster showed most noticeable variation in results across time. The analysis of various quality metrics again and again suggested radical changes in live subtitling workflow. The results for Polsat in the first analysed quarter (Q2 2021) are very good and indicate that the broadcaster was quite successful in using respeaking with parallel correction to create live subtitles. The reduction rate was quite high but lower than for other broadcasters and seemed to be due to successful condensation as the accuracy was high. The values of the metrics on text segmentation and subtitle speed are also acceptable. Latency, while still concerning, was lowest among the three broadcasters.

In the second analysed quarter (Q3 2021), Polsat introduced changes in its programming and no longer subtitled chat shows, limiting live subtitling to unscripted parts of news bulletins. In the third analysed quarter (Q1 2022), however, Polsat reinstates live subtitling for chat shows. This time the metrics paint a very different picture of the quality of these subtitles. The reduction rate goes down dramatically as the subtitles become near-verbatim, which would indicate a switch from respeaking with parallel correction to automatic speech recognition with some human postediting. There is a steep decrease in accuracy, which shows that viewers get more words but not necessarily more reliable information. In fact, low NER scores indicate that the text is hard to understand and there are numerous serious errors that correspond to the subtitles including false information.

While automatic speech recognition can produce such bad results at its worst, it should at least have the advantage of lowering latency. However, there is no evidence of that; the latency increases. That could be explained in part by the broadcaster no longer using antenna delay (which could not be confirmed) but it still suggests either the use of high-latency speech recognition system that is not a good fit for television broadcasting or inefficient postediting or both. Whatever changes the broadcaster introduced in its live subtitling workflow between the first and the third analysed quarter, they did not translate into better quality for the viewers. They did translate into more words, but this did not improve accuracy, quite the opposite, and it came at the cost of a steep increase in subtitle speed. While the subtitles could be called near-verbatim in a sense that the reduction rate is very low, such a description would be confusing because due to many misrecognitions the subtitles include a similar number of words, but these are not necessarily the same words as included in the verbatim transcript and they do not necessarily express the same ideas.

When discussing various quality dimensions of live subtitling, it is important to observe that while certain values of latency, subtitle speed or accuracy might seem acceptable when analysed in isolation, their interaction can have an important impact on the experience of the users of subtitling. Let us now explore some ways in which the combination of various quality issues such as high latency, inaccurate text and sloppy text segmentation can make it impossible for a viewer to follow a TV show and understand the content.

For instance, poor segmentation might affect the readability of subtitles, but it becomes an even more serious issue when subtitles are not displayed one by one and instead there are longer gaps between them (even when the subtitles represent continuous speech of one speaker). This is most problematic when words that are strongly linked syntactically are separated between two subtitles (see Fig. 49 for an example). If there is a longer gap between the two subtitles, viewers can forget what was the previous word and, thus, the following text can lose its meaning or be misunderstood.

Fig. 49: *An example of poor segmentation*

Note. One subtitle (left) ends with "nie" ("not") and the other subtitle (right) starts with the verb. Thus the negation ("not") and the verb it refers to are divided between two subtitles with a long gap in between these two subtitles.

In the case of samples of live subtitling from Polsat News from the third analysed quarter, there is an interaction between various quality issues. The difficulty of understanding the text (which is due to low accuracy as words are frequently misrecognized) is amplified by poor segmentation, lack of punctuation or incorrect punctuation and lack of or incorrect speaker identification. As a result, when reading the subtitles, it is often difficult to work out when one sentence ends and another begins or when a new speaker starts speaking.

Conclusions

The research presented here has shown that it is possible to evaluate the quality of live subtitling objectively, taking into account different dimensions of quality such as accuracy, synchronicity (including latency and gaps between consecutive subtitles), subtitle speed, reduction rate, text segmentation, placement and display mode. The NER score used as a measure of accuracy was found to be reliable even when assessing subtitles that differ greatly in reduction rates. The proposed method of measuring the quality of text segmentation turned out to be successful as an indicator of differences between broadcasters and types of subtitling.

The study confirmed that semi-live subtitling tends to produce better quality results than live subtitling and, thus, live subtitling should not be attempted for scripted shows where it is possible to use semi-live subtitling. Both TVP Info and Polsat News use the semi-live method quite successfully and usually achieve very good accuracy, low latency and good text segmentation. However, it should be pointed out that semi-live subtitles achieved rather high subtitle speeds. While the average subtitle speed was 16.81 cps, as many as 36.9% of all the semi-live subtitles reached speeds higher than 18 cps, indicating a need for more condensation. Still, it is surprising that one of the analysed broadcasters (TVN24) did not use semi-live subtitling. Viewers of TVN24 would be much better served were this broadcaster to provide semi-live subtitling for some of its news shows.

The results also show that respeaking with parallel correction is an effective method of creating live subtitles even in such highly inflected lnaguages as Polish and it can be used in the broadcasting settings to obtain quality results that are acceptable and comparable to the results obtained in English by broadcasters in the UK or the US (with the exception of latency, which tends to be higher with this method but it can be remedied through the use of antenna delay). At the same time, no other method was identified that could produce better results for live subtitling in Polish.

The corpus of subtitles analysed in the study shows that the quality of subtitling for live content on Polish news channels is quite diverse. In view of all the quality dimensions analysed, the news shows had subtitles that can be considered excellent, very good, good, substandard or extremely bad depending on the broadcaster, the type of subtitles and the quarter. The statistical significance of the results has been confirmed through the use of analysis of variance as well as linear mixed models.

The analysis of subtitles on TV shows across three quarters, from Q2 2021, through Q3 2021 till Q1 2022, indicates that subtitling quality is decreasing in the case of all three broadcasters. As of the beginning of 2022, while the quality of semi-live subtitles was still usually acceptable, the analysis shows that the quality of live subtitling currently offered by Polish news channels is far from satisfactory. For instance, on the 10-point scale, the average accuracy drops from 5/10 (acceptable) to 2/10 (substandard) for both TVP Info and Polsat News, while it is 0/10 in the case of TVN24. Thus, for some of the TV shows analysed in the study, live subtitles had unacceptably low accuracy and high latency, with values that are believed to indicate "virtually unreadable subtitles" (Romero Fresco, 2021, p. 744).

The analysis of accuracy, latency, subtitle speed, reduction rate and text segmentation all showed a strong statistically significant effect of TV station. This suggests that subtitling workflows differ greatly between the stations. Workflows used by some of the broadcasters seem inadequate and do not produce satisfactory results. As some broadcasters are doing better than others, there is clearly room for improvement. For instance, while the average latency was 16.8 seconds, the statistical model estimated that even when all other predictors were held constant, there was still a huge difference of 9.3 seconds between the broadcaster which had the lowest latency (Polsat News) and the one with the highest latency (TVN24) in Q2 2021.

Both TVP Info and TVN24 had very high reduction rates (with the average rate of 41% and 43% respectively) and while in the case of TVP Info a lot of text reduction was achieved through successful condensation, the statistical analysis indicated negative correlation between the reduction rate and NER scores for TVP Info and TVN24, showing that at least some of the text reduction is due to omitting information and has a negative impact on accuracy. Interestingly, the analysis found no significant effect of speech rate on reduction rate or accuracy, which is surprising and contrary to the current assumption in respeaking training that fast speech rates are a major challenge for respeakers. More research is needed to explain this paradox. However, a correlation was found between speech rate and segmentation score. This suggests that when speakers talk slowly, live subtitlers are able to focus on ensuring proper text segmentation. At the same time, subtitlers seem to view segmentation as less important than accuracy or latency. When speech rate increases, subtitlers disregard text segmentation and prioritize other dimensions of quality, which might explain why accuracy is not affected when speech rate increases.

As per the results of the study, the most important quality issues that need to be addressed by Polish broadcasters are subtitle speed (in the case of semi-live subtitling) as well as accuracy and latency (in the case of live subtitling). It should be stressed that one of the main findings is a statistically significant and deeply worrying trend of lowering quality (most notably, decreasing accuracy combined with increasing latency) across all the broadcasters and types of subtitling. Thus, the results of the study show that while the current regulatory framework was successful in providing viewers with more subtitling for live TV content (which is an important step forward and a regulatory success that should be appreciated), the lax regulatory approach failed at ensuring the adequate quality of live subtitling that is available to Polish viewers. As of 2022, while the live subtitles on Polish news channels technically serve to fulfil the legal obligation of providing subtitling, at least some of these subtitles do not fulfil the needs of the users. Low accuracy and high latency mean that many of the live TV shows have subtitles which either express inaccurate or downright false information or are very difficult to understand. In the worst case scenario, low quality subtitles offer no added value to the users (as compared with having no subtitling at all) and do not provide access to TV content for the Deaf and the hard of hearing.

The results show a need to improve the quality of live subtitling available for Polish viewers, which will require various stakeholders to collaborate and take action. The research community needs to continue monitoring the quality as well as creating new metrics and perfecting existing one. Audience research is needed to learn more about the impact of various quality dimensions of live subtitling on the experience of the users of subtitling so that we can confirm or adjust the thresholds which are now used to determine if the quality is acceptable or not.

The media regulator needs to adopt a more active role, the so-called hard approach (Romero Fresco, 2021) which has proven effective in the UK or Canada but requires investing resources to conduct research and monitor the quality of accessibility services. The broadcasters as well as the subtitling companies should be required to submit to external reviews and should be willing to modify their workflows and procedures if necessary (see the following section for a set of more detailed recommendations for broadcasters as well as the media regulator). Users also have a role to play to make their voices heard by the broadcasters and the regulator as well as be open to participating in reception research.

The task of improving the quality of live subtitles will require effort on the part of all the stakeholders as they have to overcome various challenges but "there should be no excuse not to try it", given that to do nothing "should not be an option at all" (Romero Fresco, 2021, p. 749).

Recommendations for Broadcasters and Media Regulators

Following an analysis of live subtitling practices among specific broadcasters, a set of generalized recommendations has been developed for television broadcasters at large as well as media regulators.

Broadcasters

- Use accuracy metrics such as NER to evaluate samples of live subtitling internally in order to monitor and uphold the accuracy of live subtitles.
- Reduce latency in live subtitling through technical adjustments, such as introducing an antenna delay of approximately 5–10 seconds, to allow subtitlers more time to prepare accurate subtitles.
- Regulate subtitle speeds in semi-live subtitling by enforcing guidelines for condensation, ensuring subtitles are readable but not overly condensed.
- Adopt semi-live subtitling for programs where live subtitling may not offer the required accuracy, such as news bulletins.
- Enhance live subtitler training to boost accuracy and ensure consistent quality. This could involve standardizing training programs and implementing ongoing professional development.

Media regulators

- Play a more active role by issuing guidelines on live subtitling, setting standards and monitoring quality.
- In particular, issue guidelines on live subtitling, including standards for accuracy, speed, and latency, to guide broadcasters in providing high-quality subtitles.
- Set clear benchmarks for maximum latency (e.g. 10 seconds or less) and minimum accuracy (e.g. a NER score of 98% or more) to standardize live subtitling practices.
- Monitor and enforce quality standards through regular reviews and audits of live subtitling services, offering feedback and requiring improvements where necessary.
- Encourage broadcasters to use semi-live subtitling whenever possible.

While it is surely in the society's interest to increase quality of live captioning as a means of guaranteeing effective access to the information and the media in general for the Deaf and the Hard of Hearing citizens, it is important to note that not all the media regulators might have the legal mandate or the means to actively monitor subtitling quality or enforce quality standards. However, even in such cases there is a number of actions that regulators can take, examples of which include publishing statements, issuing non-binding guidelines, fostering self-regulation among broadcaster, ensuring that viewers have effective ways of making complaints to the broadcasters or partnering with academic institution to encourage more research into the quality of live captioning.

Within the scope of the study presented in this book, tailored recommendations were formulated for each broadcaster under review, reflecting the challenges identified within their workflows. The detailed recommendations[62] have been communicated to the respective broadcasters and are summarised below (Dutka et al., 2023):

TVP

- Improve the training of live subtitlers to increase accuracy in live subtitling and guarantee more reliable quality across different days.
- Avoid excessive subtitle speeds in semi-live subtitling by applying more condensation when preparing semi-live subtiltes.
- Lower the latency in live subtitling by adding an antenna delay of 10 seconds and/or making other changes in the live subtitling workflow.

Polsat

- Return to the previous live subtitling workflow as the current one produces very high latency and very low accuracy.
- Avoid excessive subtitle speeds in semi-live subtitling by applying more condensation when preparing semi-live subtitles.

TVN

- Start providing semi-live subtitling for news bulletins.
- Improve live subtitling by increasing accuracy.

---

62 The full report, including the detailed recommendations, was published by the Media Accessibility Observatory at the University of Warsaw, and is available online (in Polish): https://bit.ly/3wJSIt9

- Lower the latency in live subtitling by adding an antenna delay of 10–15 seconds.
- Modify live subtitling software settings to keep subtitles displayed for longer and avoid longer gaps between consecutive subtitles.

Disclosure

In the years 2012–2013, the author worked as a live subtitler for TVP (legal name: TVP SA; one of the broadcasters included in the study) and was responsible for semi-live and live subtitling of the news show *Wiadomości* (one of the news shows included in the study). However, when the study was being conducted, the author did not work for TVP in any capacity and does not currently have any links with this broadcaster.

The author is a member of the Management Board of Dostępni.eu (legal name: Intro PR Sp. z o.o.), an accessibility services provider that set up and managed a live subtitling unit for Polsat (legal name: Telewizja Polsat Sp. z o.o.) in the years 2020–2021. The author was personally involved in creating the live subtitling unit for Polsat as well as training live subtitlers for this broadcaster. However, the author was not involved in creating any of the subtitles analysed in the study. The author does not currently have any links with Polsat and was not working for the station in any way when the study was being conducted. Neither Dostępni.eu nor Polsat had any influence on the design of the study or the interpretation of the results.

The Polish National Broadcasting Council (KRRiT) was consulted when designing this research and participated in preparing some of the recordings used for the analysis. KRRiT did not have any influence on the interpretation of the results.

In the years 2022–2023, the author was a member of the Board of Directors of the Global Alliance for Speech-to-Text Captioning, a non-profit organization registered in Washington, USA, which aims to champion quality standards in live subtitling. The Global Alliance did not have any influence on the design of the research presented here or the interpretation of the results.

References

Apone, T., Brooks, M., & O'Connell, T. (2010). Caption accuracy metrics project. *Caption viewer survey: Error ranking of real-time captions in live television news programs*. Boston.

Armstrong, M., Brown, A., Crabb, M., Hughes, C. J., Jones, R., & Sandford, J. (2015). *Understanding the Diverse Needs of Subtitle Users in a Rapidly Evolving Media Landscape*. BBC. http://downloads.bbc.co.uk/rd/pubs/whp/whp-pdf-files/WHP307.pdf

Arumí Ribas, M., & Romero Fresco, P. (2008). A practical proposal for the training of respeakers (10), 106–127.

Baevski, A., Zhou, H., Mohamed, A., & Auli, M. (2020). wav2vec 2.0: A framework for self-supervised learning of speech representations. *arXiv preprint*, arXiv:2006.11477.

Bates, D., Kliegl, R., Vasishth, S., & Baayen, H. (2015). Parsimonious mixed models. *ArXiv Preprint*, ArXiv:1506.04967.

Benzeghiba, M., Mori, R. de, Deroo, O., Dupont, S., Erbes, T., Jouvet, D., Fissore, L., Laface, P., Mertins, A., & Ris, C. (2007). Automatic speech recognition and speech variability: A review. *Speech Communication, 49*(10–11), 763–786.

Besacier, L., Barnard, E., Karpov, A., & Schultz, T. (2014). Automatic speech recognition for under-resourced languages: A survey. *Speech Communication, 56*, 85–100. https://doi.org/10.1016/j.specom.2013.07.008

Bogucki, Ł. (2010). Audiovisual translation in Poland in the 21st century. *Meaning in Translation, 19*, 415–424.

Bogucki, Ł. (2020). *A relevance-theoretic approach to decision-making in subtitling* (1st ed.). Springer International Publishing.

Bogucki, Ł., & Díaz-Cintas, J. (2020). An excursus on audiovisual translation. In Ł. Bogucki & M. Deckert (Eds.), *The Palgrave handbook of audiovisual translation and media accessibility*. Springer International Publishing.

Brocki, Ł., Marasek, K., & Koržinek, D. (2012). Multiple model text normalization for the Polish language. In L. Chen (Ed.), *LNCS sublibrary. SL 7, Artificial intelligence: Vol. 7661. Foundations of intelligent systems: 20th International Symposium, ISMIS 2012, Macau, China, December 4–7, 2012: proceedings*. Springer.

Canadian Association of the Deaf. (2018). *Understanding User Responses to Live Closed Captioning in Canada*. https://crtc.gc.ca/eng/archive/2019/2019-9.htm

Catford, J. C. (1978). *A linguistic theory of translation: An essay in applied linguistics*. Van Schaik.

Chaume, F. (2018). An overview of audiovisual translation: Four methodological turns in a mature discipline. *Journal of Audiovisual Translation, 1*(1), 40–63. https://doi.org/10.47476/jat.v1i1.43

Chesterman, A. (2016). *Memes of translation: The spread of ideas in translation theory* (Revised edition). *Benjamins Translation Library: Vol. 123*. John Benjamins Publishing Company.

Chmiel, A., Lijewska, A., Szarkowska, A., & Dutka, Ł. (2018). Paraphrasing in respeaking – Comparing linguistic competence of interpreters, translators and bilinguals. *Perspectives, 26*(5), 725–744. https://doi.org/10.1080/0907676X.2017.1394331

Chmiel, A., Szarkowska, A., Koržinek, D., Lijewska, A., Dutka, Ł., Brocki, Ł., & Marasek, K. (2017). Ear–voice span and pauses in intra-and interlingual respeaking: An exploratory study into temporal aspects of the respeaking process. *Applied Psycholinguistics, 38*(5), 1201–1227.

Cravo, A., & Neves, J. (2007). Action research in translation studies. The Journal of Specialised Translation, 7, 92–107. http://jostrans.org/issue07/art_cravo.pdf

CRTC. (2019). *Broadcasting Notice of Consultation CRTC 2019-9*. Ottawa. Retrieved from https://crtc.gc.ca/eng/archive/2019/2019-9.htm

de Korte, T. (2006). Live inter-lingual subtitling in the Netherlands. *InTRAlinea. Online Translation Journal …SsueinTRAlinea. Online Translation Journal … Ssue: Respeaking.*

Delabastita, D. (1989). Translation and mass-communication. *Babel. Revue Internationale De La Traduction / International Journal of Translation, 35*(4), 193–218. https://doi.org/10.1075/babel.35.4.02del

Di Giovanni, E. (2020). Reception studies and audiovisual translation. In Ł. Bogucki & M. Deckert (Eds.), *The Palgrave handbook of audiovisual translation and media accessibility* (pp. 397–414). Springer International Publishing.

Di Giovanni, E., & Gambier, Y. (Eds.). (2018). *Benjamins Translation Library. Reception studies and audiovisual translation*. John Benjamins Publishing Company. https://doi.org/10.1075/btl

Díaz Cintas, J. (2004). In search of a theoretical framework for the study of audiovisual translation. In P. Orero (Ed.), *Benjamins Translation Library: v. 56. Topics in audiovisual translation* (pp. 21–40). John Benjamins Pub.

Díaz Cintas, J. (2005). Audiovisual Translation Today–A question of accessibility for all. Translating Today,(4)(3–5).

Díaz Cintas, J., Orero, P., & Remael, A. (Eds.). (2007). Approaches to Translation Studies: v.30. Media for All: Subtitling for the Deaf, Audio Description, and Sign Language. BRILL. https://ebookcentral.proquest.com/lib/gbv/detail.act ion?docID=5598365

Cintas, J. D. (Ed.). (2009). New trends in audiovisual translation (Vol. 36). Multilingual Matters.Díaz Cintas, J., Gerber-Morón, O., & Szarkowska, A. (2021). Quality is in the eye of the stakeholders: What do professional subtitlers and viewers think about subtitling? *Universal Access in the Information Society*, *20*(4), 661–675.

Díaz Cintas, J., & Remael, A. (2007). *Audiovisual translation: Subtitling*. St. Jerome Publishing.

Domagała-Zyśk, E. (2017). Zapisywanie symultaniczne-adekwatna forma wspierania edukacji, pracy oraz udziału w życiu społecznym i kulturalnym osób niesłyszących i słabosłyszących. *Lubelski Rocznik Pedagogiczny*, *36*(2), 105–114.

Downey, G. J. (2008). *Closed Captioning: Subtitling, Stenography, and the Digital Convergence of Text With Television (Johns Hopkins studies in the history of technology): Subtitling, stenography, and the digital convergence of text with television. Johns Hopkins studies in the history of technology.* Johns Hopkins University Press.

Dumouchel, P., Boulianne, G., & Brousseau, J. (2012). Measures for quality of closed captioning. In A. Serban, A. Matamala, & J.-M. Lavaur (Eds.), *Audiovisual translation in close-up: Practical and theoretical approaches* (2nd ed., pp. 161–172). Peter Lang AG, Internationaler Verlag der Wissenschaften.

Dutka, Ł., Szczygielska, M., Szarkowska, A., Szeląg, K., Dobrowolska, A., Senda, T., Urban, A., & Grabska, A. (2023). Raport o jakości napisów na żywo w polskich stacjach telewizyjnych. Obserwatorium Dostępności Mediów Uniwersytetu Warszawskiego, Warszawa. https://avt.ils.uw.edu.pl/media-accessibility-observatory/

Eugeni, C. (2008). Respeaking the TV for the Deaf: For a real special needs-oriented subtitling. Studies in English Language and Literature, 21, 37–47.

Eugeni, C. (2012). Measuring Audiovisual Translation. A model for the analysis of intralingual live subtitles. US-China Foreign Language, 10(6), 1276–1286.

Eugeni, C., & Marchionne, F. (2014). Beyond Computer Whispering: Intralingual and French into Italian TV Respeaking Compared. In M. Petillo (Ed.), *Reflecting on Audiovisual Translation in the Third Millennium*. Editura Institutul European: Bucarest.

Even-Zohar, I. (2012). The position of translated literature within the literary polysystem. In L. Venuti (Ed.), *The translation studies reader* (3rd ed.). Routledge.

FCC. (2014). *The 2014 closed captioning declaratory ruling, order, and notice of proposed rulemaking*. Federal Communications Commission.

Fresno, N. (2019). Of bad hombres and nasty women; the quality of the live closed captioning in the 2016 US final presidential debate. *Perspectives, 27*(3), 350–366. https://doi.org/10.1080/0907676X.2018.1526960

Fresno, N., & Sepielak, K. (2020). Subtitling speed in media accessibility research: Some methodological considerations. *Perspectives*, 1–17. https://doi.org/10.1080/0907676X.2020.1761841

Gambier, Y. (2012). The position of audiovisual translation studies. In *The Routledge handbook of translation studies* (pp. 45–59). Routledge. https://doi.org/10.4324/9780203102893.ch3

Gambier, Y. (2018). Translation studies, audiovisual translation and reception. In E. Di Giovanni & Y. Gambier (Eds.), *Benjamins Translation Library. Reception studies and audiovisual translation* (pp. 43–66). John Benjamins Publishing Company.

Genizi, A., & Hochberg, Y. (1978). On improved extensions of the T-method of multiple comparisons for unbalanced designs. *Journal of the American Statistical Association, 73*(364), 879–884.

Gerber-Morón, O., & Szarkowska, A. (2018). Line breaks in subtitling: An eye tracking study on viewer preferences. *Journal of Eye Movement Research, 11*(3).

Gottlieb, H. (1994). Subtitling: Diagonal translation. *Perspectives*(1), 101–121.

Gottlieb, H. (1997). *Subtitles, translation & idioms*. Center for Translation, University of Copenhagen.

Gottlieb, H. (1998). Subtitling. In M. Baker (Ed.), *Routledge encyclopedia of translation* (pp. 244–248). Routledge.

Graham, J. (2016). Checking, revision and editing. In C. Picken (Ed.), The translator's handbook (pp. 59–70). Aslib.

Greco, G. M. (2018). The nature of accessibility studies. *Journal of Audiovisual Translation, 1*, 205–232. https://www.jatjournal.org/index.php/jat/article/view/51

Greco, G. M. (2019). Accessibility studies: Abuses, misuses and the method of poietic design. In C. Stephanidis (Ed.), *Lecture Notes in Computer Science. HCI International 2019 – Late Breaking Papers* (Vol. 11786, pp. 15–27). Springer International Publishing. https://doi.org/10.1007/978-3-030-30033-3_2

Greco, G. M., & Jankowska, A. (2019). Framing Media Accessibility Quality. *Journal of Audiovisual Translation, 2*(2), 1–10.

Greco, G. M., & Jankowska, A. (2020). Media accessibility within and beyond audiovisual translation. In Ł. Bogucki & M. Deckert (Eds.), *The Palgrave* handbook of audiovisual translation and media accessibility (pp. 57–81). Springer International Publishing.

GUS. (2021). Health status of population in Poland in 2019. GUS. https://stat. gov.pl/en/topics/health/health/health-status-of-population-in-poland-in-2019,4,2.html

Gutt, E.-A. (2000). Translation and relevance: Cognition and context. St. Jerome Publishing.

Holmqvist, K., Nystrom, M., Andersson, R., Dewhurst, R., Jarodzka, H., & van Weijer, J. de. (2015). Eye tracking: A comprehensive guide to methods and measures (First published in paperback). Oxford University Press.

Huang, X., Baker, J., & Reddy, R. (2014). A historical perspective of speech recognition. Communications of the ACM, 57(1), 94–103.

In-Seok Kim (2006). Automatic speech recognition: Reliability and pedagogical implications for teaching pronunciation. Journal of Educational Technology & Society, 9(1), 322–334. http://www.jstor.org/stable/jeductechsoci.9.1.322

ITU. (2011). Making TV accessible. International Telecommunication Union. https://www.itu.int/en/ITU-D/Digital-Inclusion/Persons-with-Disabilities/ Documents/Making_TV_Accessible-English.pdf

Ivarsson, J., & Carroll, M. (1998). Code of good subtitling practice. Language Today, April, 14, 39.

Jakobson, R. (1959). On linguistics aspects of translation. In R. A. Brower (Ed.), Harvard studies in comparative literature: Vol. 23. On translation (pp. 232–239). Harvard University Press.

Jankowska, A. (2020). Audiovisual media accessibility. In E. Angelone, M. Ehrensberger-Dow, & G. Massey (Eds.), Bloomsbury companions: 2020: 1. The Bloomsbury companion to language industry studies. Bloomsbury Academic.

Jurafsky, D., & Martin, J. (2009). Speech and language processing: An introduction to natural language processing, computational linguistics, and speech recognition (2nd ed.). Prentice Hall series in artificial intelligence. Pearson Education, Inc.

Jurafsky, D., & Martin, J. (2023). Speech and Language Processing: An Introduction to Natural Language Processing, Computational Linguistics, and Speech Recognition. https://web.stanford.edu/~jurafsky/slp3/ed3book.pdf

Karamitroglou, F. (1998). A proposed set of subtitling standards in Europe. Translation Journal, 2(2), 1–15.

Koenecke, A., Mei, K., Schellmann, H., Sloane, M., & Choi, A. S. G. (2024). Careless whisper: speech-to-text hallucination harms. arXiv preprint, arXiv:2402.08021.

Kothari, B., & Takeda, J. (2000). Same language subtitling for literacy: Small change for colossal gains. Information and communication technology in development, 176–186.

KRRiT. (2016). *Stanowisko w sprawie jakości i sposobu realizacji napisów dla niesłyszących w utworach audiowizualnych.* http://www.archiwum.krrit.gov. pl/krrit/aktualnosci/news,2213,stanowisko-w-sprawie-jakosci-i-sposobu-rea lizacji--napisow-dla-nieslyszacych-w-utworach.html#_ftn2

KRRiT. (2018). Sprawozdanie Krajowej Rady Radiofonii i Telewizji z działalności w 2017 roku. http://www.archiwum.krrit.gov.pl/Data/Files/_public/ Portals/0/sprawozdania/spr-i-inf-2017/sprawozdanie_26_03.pdf

KRRiT. (2019). Sprawozdanie Krajowej Rady Radiofonii i Telewizji z działalności w 2018 roku. http://www.archiwum.krrit.gov.pl/Data/Files/_public/Portals/ 0/sprawozdania/spr-2018/sprawozdanie-2018---projekt-z-28.05_iii_kore kta.pdf

Kruger, J. L., Szarkowska, A., & Krejtz, I. (2015). Subtitles on the moving image: An overview of eye tracking studies. *Refractory: A Journal of Entertainment Media, 25*, 1–14.

Kruger, J.-L., Wisniewska, N., & Liao, S. (2022). Why subtitle speed matters: Evidence from word skipping and rereading. *Applied Psycholinguistics, 43*(1), 211–236. https://doi.org/10.1017/s0142716421000503

Künstler, I. (2008). Napisy dla niesłyszących – problemy i wyzwania. *Przekładaniec, 2008*(Numer 20 – O przekładzie audiowizualnym), 115–124. http://www.ejournals.eu/Przekladaniec/2008/Numer-20/art/3050/

Künstler, I., & Butkiewicz, U. (2019). *Napisy dla osób niesłyszących i słabosłyszących – zasady tworzenia.* Fundacja Kultury bez Barier. https://kulturabezbar ier.org/wp-content/uploads/2019/12/Napisy-dla-nieslyszacych_zasady-two rzenia_2019.pdf

Ladd, P. (2003). Understanding Deaf culture. In P. Ladd (Ed.), *Understanding deaf culture.* Multilingual Matters.

Lambourne, A. (2006). Subtitle respeaking. A new skill for a new age. *InTRAlinea. Online Translation Journal. Special Issue: Respeaking > Subtitle Respeaking.*

Lambourne, A., Hewitt, J., Lyon, C., & Warren, S. (2004). Speech-based real-time subtitling services. *International Journal of Speech Technology, 7*(4), 269–279.

Liao, S., Yu, L., Reichle, E. D., & Kruger, J. L. (2021). Using eye movements to study the reading of subtitles in video. *Scientific Studies of Reading,* 1–19. https://doi.org/10.1080/10888438.2020.1823986

Linde, Z. de, & Kay, N. (1999). Processing subtitles and film images: Hearing vs Deaf viewers. *The Translator, 5*(1), 45–60.

Loof, J., Gollan, C., & Ney, H. (2009). Cross-Language Bootstrapping for Unsupervised Acoustic Model Training: Rapid Development of a Polish Speech Recognition System. Lehrstuhl Fur Informatik(6).

Meteyard, L., & Davies, R. A. I. (2020). Best practice guidance for linear mixed-effects models in psychological science. *Journal of Memory and Language, 112*, 104092.

Miłkowski, M. (2012). *The Polish Language in the Digital Age. White Paper Series.* Springer, Berlin/Heidelberg; Imprint; Springer. http://site.ebrary. com/lib/alltitles/docDetail.action?docID=10650596 https://doi.org/10.1007/ 978-3-642-30811-6

Mliczak, R. (2019). *A diachronic study of subtitling for the deaf and the hard of hearing in Poland* [PhD]. University College London.

Munday, J. (2016). *Introducing translation studies: Theories and applications.* Routledge. https://doi.org/10.4324/9780203121252

Neves, J. (2005). *Audiovisual translation: Subtitling for the Deaf and Hard of hearing* [PhD]. Roehampton University, London. http://citeseerx.ist.psu.edu/view doc/download?doi=10.1.1.129.1405&rep=rep1&type=pdf

Neves, J. (2008). 10 fallacies about Subtitling for the d/Deaf and the hard of hearing. *The Journal of Specialised Translation, 10*, 128–143.

Nida, E. A. (2003). Principles of correspondence. In *Toward a science of translating* (pp. 156–192). BRILL.

Ofcom. (2005). *Subtitling – An Issue of Speed?* Ofcom. https://www.ofcom.org. uk/__data/assets/pdf_file/0018/16119/subt.pdf

Ofcom. (2006). *Television Acces Services. Review of the Code and Guidance.* Ofcom. https://www.ofcom.org.uk/__data/assets/pdf_file/0016/42442/acc ess.pdf

Ofcom. (2015). Measuring live subtitling quality: results from the Measuring live subtitling quality: results from the fourth sampling exercise. https://es.scribd. com/document/552210915/REPORT-2015-Measuring-Live-Subtitling-Qual ity-OFCOM

Ofcom. (2017). Ofcom's code on television access services. https://www.ofcom. org.uk/__data/assets/pdf_file/0020/97040/Access-service-code-Jan-2017.pdf

Oncins, E., Eugeni, C., & Bernabé, R. (2019). The Future of Mediators for Live Events: LTA Project-Academic and Vocational Training. Cultus: The Intercultural Journal of Mediation and Communication, 12, 129–153.

Orero, P. (2004). Introduction: Audiovisual translation: A new dynamic umbrella. In P. Orero (Ed.), Benjamins Translation Library: v. 56. Topics in audiovisual translation (pp. vii–xiii). John Benjamins Pub.

Orero, P., Kruger, J.-L., Matamala, A., Pedersen, J., Perego, E., Romero Fresco, P., Rovira-Esteva, S., Soler-Vilageliu Olga, & Szarkowska, A. (2018). Conducting experimental research in audiovisual translation (AVT): A position paper. *The Journal of Specialised Translation, 30,* 105–126.

Peacocke, R. D., & Graf, D. H. (1990). An introduction to speech and speaker recognition. *IEEE Computer, 23,* 26–33.

Pedersen, J. (2011). *Subtitling norms for television: An exploration focussing on extralinguistic cultural references. Benjamins Translation Library: v. 98.* John Benjamins Pub. Co.

Pedersen, J. (2017). The FAR model: Assessing quality in interlingual subtitling. *Journal of Specialised Translation, 28,* 210–229.

Perego, E. (2008). What would we read best? Hypotheses and suggestions for the location of line breaks in film subtitles. *The Sign Language Translator and Interpreter, 2*(1), 35–63.

Pérez González, L. (2014). *Audiovisual translation: Theories, methods and issues.* Routledge.

Pérez-González, L. (2009). Audiovisual translation. In M. Baker & G. Saldanha (Eds.), *Routledge encyclopedia of translation studies* (2nd ed., pp. 13–20). Routledge.

Pérez-González, L., Cornu, J.-F., & O'Sulliva, C. (Eds.). (2019). *The Routledge handbook of audiovisual translation* (First published.). Routledge Taylor and Francis Group. https://doi.org/10.4324/9781315717166

Pomianos, G., Neti, C., Gravier, G., Garg, A., & Senior, A. W. (2003). Recent advances in the automatic recognition of audiovisual speech. *Proceedings of the IEEE, 91*(9), 1306–1326. https://doi.org/10.1109/JPROC.2003.817150

Pöchhacker, F [Franz], & Remael, A. (2018). New efforts? A competence-oriented task analysis of interlingual live subtitling. *Linguistica Antverpiensia New Series-Themes in Translation Studies, 18.*

Preiser, W. F. E., & Smith, K. H. (2011). *Universal design handbook* (2nd ed.). McGraw-Hill.

Pym, A. (2017). Exploring translation theories (2nd Edition). Routledge.

Radford, A., Kim, J. W., Xu, T., Brockman, G., McLeavey, C., & Sutskever, I. (2022). Robust speech recognition via large-scale weak supervision. *arXiv preprint,* arXiv:2212.04356.

Rajendran, D. J., Duchowski, A. T., Orero, P., Martínez, J., & Romero-Fresco, P [Pablo] (2013). Effects of text chunking on subtitling: A quantitative and qualitative examination. *Perspectives, 21*(1), 5–21. https://doi.org/10.1080/09076 76X.2012.722651

Ramondelli, F. (2006). La sottotitolazione in diretta con la stenotipia. *New Technologies in Real Time Intralingual Subtitling. Intralinea. Special Issue.*

Reiss, K. (1989). Text types, translation types and translation assessment. In A. Chesterman (Ed.), *Readings in translation theory* (pp. 105–115). Finn Lectura.

Remael, A. (2007). Sampling subtitling for the deaf and the hard of hearing in Europe. In *Media for all* (pp. 23–52). Brill Rodopi.

Remael, A. (2010). Audiovisual translation. In Y. Gambier & L. van Doorslaer (Eds.), *Handbook of translation studies* (Vol. 1, pp. 12–17). John Benjamins Publishing Company. https://doi.org/10.1075/hts.1.aud1

Robert, I [Isabelle], & Remael, A. (2016). Quality control in the subtitling industry: An exploratory survey study. *Meta: Journal Des Traducteurs, 61*(3), 578. https://doi.org/10.7202/1039220AR

Robert, I [Isabelle], & Remael, A. (2017). Assessing quality in live interlingual subtitling: A new challenge. *Linguistica Antverpiensia, New Series – Themes in Translation Studies, 16*(0), 168–195. https://lans-tts.uantwerpen.be/index.php/LANS-TTS/article/download/454/393

Robert, I., Iris, S., & Ella, D. (2019). Trainers' and Employers' Perceptions of Training in Intralingual and Interlingual Live Subtitling. Journal of Audiovisual Translation, 2(1), 1–25. https://doi.org/10.47476/jat.v2i1.61

Robson, G. D. (2004). *The closed captioning handbook.* Gulf Professional Publishing.

Romero Fresco, P. (2011). *Subtitling through speech recognition: Respeaking* (First issued in hardback). *Translation practices explained: Vol. 13.* Routledge/Taylor & Francis Group.

Romero Fresco, P. (Ed.). (2015). *The reception of subtitles for the deaf and hard of hearing in Europe.* Peter Lang.

Romero Fresco, P. (2016). Accessing communication: The quality of live subtitles in the UK. *Language & Communication, 49,* 56–69.

Romero Fresco, P. (2018a). In support of a wide notion of media accessibility: Access to content and access to creation. *Journal of Audiovisual Translation, 1*(1), 187–204. https://doi.org/10.47476/jat.v1i1.53

Romero Fresco, P. (2018b). Respeaking. In L. Pérez-González (Ed.), *The Routledge handbook of audiovisual translation* (pp. 96–113). Routledge. https://doi.org/10.4324/9781315717166-7

Romero Fresco, P. (2019). Accessible filmmaking. Translation and accessibility from production. In L. Pérez-González, J.-F. Cornu, & C. O'Sulliva (Eds.), The Routledge handbook of Audiovisual Translation (First published.). Routledge Taylor and Francis Group.

Romero Fresco, P. (2021). Negotiating quality assessment in media accessibility: The case of live subtitling. *Universal Access in the Information Society*, *20*(4), 741–751. https://doi.org/10.1007/s10209-020-00735-6

Romero Fresco, P., & Martínez Pérez, J. (2015). Accuracy rate in live subtitling: The NER model. In R. Baños Piñero & J. D. Cintas (Eds.), *Palgrave studies in translating and interpreting. Audiovisual translation in a global context: Mapping an ever-changing landscape* (Vol. 3, pp. 28–50). Palgrave Macmillan. https://doi.org/10.1057/9781137552891_3

Romero Fresco, P., & Pöchhacker, F [Franz] (2018). Quality assessment in interlingual live subtitling: The NTR Model. *Linguistica Antverpiensia, New Series – Themes in Translation Studies*, *16*(0). https://lans-tts.uantwerpen.be/index.php/LANS-TTS/article/download/438/402

Romero Fresco, P., & Eugeni, C. (2020). Live Subtitling Through Respeaking. In Ł. Bogucki & M. Deckert (Eds.), The Palgrave Handbook of Audiovisual Translation and Media Accessibility (pp. 269–295). Springer International Publishing.

Saerens, G., Tampir, M., Dutka, Ł [Ł.], Szczygielska, M., Szarkowska, A., Romero-Fresco, P [P.], Pöchhacker, F [F.], Figiel, W., Schrijver, I., Haverhals, V., & Robert, I [I.]. (2020). *How to implement live subtitling in TV settings: Guidelines on making television broadcasts accessible to hard of hearing and Deaf people as well as foreigners.* The ILSA Project. http://ka2-ilsa.webs.uvigo.es/guidelines/

Sacha, A., & Kasperkowiak, M. (2012). Napisy dla osób głuchych oraz słabosłyszących i tłumaczenia w języku migowym w telewizji – standardy, dobre praktyki, stan obecny. http://www.archiwum.krrit.gov.pl/Data/Files/_public/Portals/0/konsultacje/2012/niepelnosprawni/doc/19.niepelnosprawni_fdc_zalacznik-2.doc

Sak, H., Saraclar, M., & Gungor, T. (2010). Morphology-based and sub-word language modeling for Turkish speech recognition. In S. C. Douglas (Ed.), IEEE International Conference on Acoustics, Speech and Signal Processing (ICASSP), 2010: 14–19 March 2010, Sheraton Dallas Hotel, Dallas, Texas, USA ; proceedings (pp. 5402–5405). IEEE. https://doi.org/10.1109/ICASSP.2010.5494927

Silva, B. B., Orrego-Carmona, D., & Szarkowska, A. (2022). Using linear mixed models to analyze data from eye-tracking research on subtitling. *Translation Spaces*, *11*(1), 60–88.

Snell-Hornby, M., Pöchhacker, F [Franz], & Kaindl, K. (1994). *Translation studies: An interdiscipline. Benjamins Translation Library: v. 2.* J. Benjamins. http://search.ebscohost.com/login.aspx?direct=true&scope=site&db=nlebk&db=nlabk&AN=360367

Szarkowska, A. (2008). Przekład audiowizualny w Polsce–perspektywy i wyzwania. *Przekładaniec, 20*, 8–25.

Szarkowska, A. (2009). The audiovisual landscape in Poland at the dawn of the 21st century. *Foreign Language Movies–Dubbing Vs. Subtitling*, 185–201.

Szarkowska, A. (2010). Accessibility to the media by hearing impaired audiences in Poland: Problems, paradoxes, perspectives. In *New Insights into Audiovisual Translation and Media Accessibility* (pp. 137–158). BRILL.

Szarkowska, A. (2016). Report on the results of an online survey on subtitle presentation times and line breaks in interlingual subtitling. Available from https://dev-avt.ckc.uw.edu.pl/wp-content/uploads/sites/170/2016/10/SURE_Report_Survey1.pdf

Szarkowska, A., Barreto Silva, B., & Orrego-Carmona, D. (2021). Effect of subtitle speed on proportional reading time: Re-analysing subtitle reading data with mixed effects models. *Translation, Cognition & Behavior*. Advance online publication. https://doi.org/10.1075/tcb.00057.sza

Szarkowska, A., & Gerber-Morón, O. (2018). Viewers can keep up with fast subtitles: Evidence from eye movements. *PloS One, 13*(6), e0199331. https://doi.org/10.1371/journal.pone.0199331.

Szarkowska, A., & Gerber-Morón, O. (2019). Two or three lines: A mixed-methods study on subtitle processing and preferences. *Perspectives, 27*(1), 144–164.

Szarkowska, A., Krejtz, K., Dutka, Ł., & Pilipczuk, O. (2018). Are interpreters better respeakers? *The Interpreter and Translator Trainer, 12*(2), 207–226. https://doi.org/10.1080/1750399X.2018.1465679

Szarkowska, A., Silva, B., & Orrego-Carmona, D. (2021). Effects of subtitle speed on viewers' gaze: Re-analysing proportional reading time with linear mixed-effects models. *Translation, Cognition & Behavior, 4*(2), 305–330.

Szczygielska, M. (2019). Napisy dla niesłyszących w Polsce. Historia, problemy, wyzwania. *Półrocznik Językoznawczy Tertium, 4*(193–210). https://doi.org/10.7592/Tertium2019.4.1.Szczygielska

Szczygielska, M., & Dutka, Ł [Ł.ukasz]. (2016, November 3). *Live subtitling through automatic speech recognition vs. respeaking: Between technical possibilities and users' satisfaction*. Languages and the Media, Berlin.

Szczygielska, M., & Dutka, Ł. S. (2019). Historia napisów na żywo tworzonych metodą respeakingu w Polsce. In *Imago Mundi. Tłumaczenie wczoraj, dziś i jutro* (pp. 129–164). Instytut Lingwistyki Stosowanej UW.

Titford, C. (1982). Subtitling-constrained translation. *Lebende Sprachen, 27*(3), 113–116.

Tomaszkiewcz, T. (2006). *Przekład audiowizualny*. Wydawnictwo Naukowe PWN.

Toury, G. (1978/2012). *Descriptive translation studies – And beyond* (Rev. ed.). *Benjamins Translation Library: v. 100*. John Benjamins Pub. Co.

Vanderplank, R. (2016). Captioned media in foreign language learning and teaching: Subtitles for the deaf and hard-of-hearing as tools for language learning. Springer.

van Noorden, L. P. A. S. (1988). A provisional evaluation of a new chord keyboard, the Velotype. In G. C. Veer & G. Mulder (Eds.), *Human-computer interaction: Psychonomic aspects* (pp. 318–333). Springer, Berlin/Heidelberg. https://doi.org/10.1007/978-3-642-73402-1_20

Waes, L., Leijten, M., & Remael, A. (2013). Live subtitling with speech recognition. Causes and consequences of text reduction. *Across Languages and Cultures, 14*(1), 15–46. https://doi.org/10.1556/Acr.14.2013.1.2

World Health Organization. (2021). World report on hearing. https://www.who.int/publications/i/item/world-report-on-hearing

Yves Gambier. (2003). Introduction. *The Translator, 9*(2), 171–189. https://doi.org/10.1080/13556509.2003.10799152

Zarate, S. (2021). *Captioning and subtitling for d/Deaf and hard of hearing audiences*. UCL Press. https://doi.org/10.14324/111.9781787357105

Ziółko, B., & Ziółko, M. (2011). *Przetwarzanie mowy*. Wydawnictwa AGH.

Żelasko, P., Ziółko, B., Jadczyk, T., & Skurzok, D. (2016). AGH corpus of Polish speech. *Language Resources and Evaluation, 50*(3), 585–601. https://doi.org/10.1007/s10579-015-9302-y

Index of Notions

ŁÓDŹ STUDIES IN LANGUAGE
Edited by
Barbara Lewandowska-Tomaszczyk and Łukasz Bogucki

www.peterlang.com

www.ingramcontent.com/pod-product-compliance
Lightning Source LLC
LaVergne TN
LVHW092009050326
832904LV00002B/26